T0285219

FEARLESS

Wilma Soss
and America's Forgotten
Investor Movement

FEARLESS

Wilma Soss
and America's Forgotten
Investor Movement

JANICE M. TRAFLET   ROBERT E. WRIGHT

All Seasons Press

2881 E. Oakland Park Blvd. Suite 456
Fort Lauderdale, FL 33306

Interior design by Kim Hall

FIRST EDITION: AUGUST 2022

Library of Congress Cataloging-in-Publication Data has been applied for.

ISBNs: 978-1-958682-30-2 (hardcover), 978-1-958682-31-9 (ebook)

Printed in the USA

9   10   7   8   5   6   3   4   1   2

To American Heritage Center archivist Gene M. Gressley, who saved Wilma Soss from historical obscurity because he understood her importance and the enduring relevance of her pro-free speech, pro-economic growth, pro-stable dollar, pro-equal opportunity views.

And to all those who believe in the power of the investor—whoever they are, and no matter how small.

PR whiz and shareholder activist Wilma Soss, circa 1950s (left), and fellow corporate gadfly Evelyn Y. Davis, 1962 (right). Soss photo by Blackstone studios, Inc. 20 West 57th Street, New York City. Wilma Soss Papers, AHC collection: #10249, Photo Folder – accretion number 81-12-21. American Heritage Center, University of Wyoming. Davis photo courtesy of James Patterson.

"Conflict is the gadfly of thought. It stirs us to observation and memory. It instigates to invention. It shocks us out of sheeplike passivity and sets us at noting and contriving."

– John Dewey

ACKNOWLEDGEMENTS

Profound thanks are extended to the authors' families, without whom this book would not be possible. Also, the authors thank the staff of the American Heritage Center at the University of Wyoming in Laramie for key access to the Wilma Soss Papers; our agent, Marilyn Allen at Allen Literary Agency, for placing this book so well and putting up with us during the Great Covid Pandemic, and Kristin Aguilera, editor of *Financial History* magazine, for publishing an early take on the Queen of the Corporate Gadflies.

We also thank several scholars who read parts of the manuscript or offered advice on corporate governance matters or financial feminism, especially Christy Ford Chapin, Larry Cunningham, Harwell Wells, Nell Minow, Simon Constable, Sarah Haan, Amy Froide, George Robb, Andie Tucher, James McRitchie, and Sonali Garg. In addition, James Patterson, Gerald Armstrong, Rephah Berg, and Myron Kandel helped bring this book alive by sharing their recollections of Wilma Soss and/or Evelyn Davis. Likewise, by granting access to the Graduate School of Journalism Records, the staff at the Rare Book and Manuscript Library at Columbia University enabled us to garner insights into Wilma Soss's years as a journalism student. Appreciation also is extended to William R. Gruver, Kenneth Langone, Charles Mitchell, Lynne Doti, Suki Connor, as well as Sue and Skip McGoun. Responsibility for any shortcomings, of course, remains with the authors.

The support of our institutions, including sabbatical and grants, as well as that of the Economic Business History Society, was valuable in the long journey of researching and writing this book. Boldly challenging the corporate status quo, Wilma Soss and her cadre fearlessly critiqued the biggest boards and top CEOs. At the same time, they believed ardently in the power of share ownership, the potential of the stock market as a wealth generator, the sanctity of free speech, and the virtues of capitalism. Thanks, therefore, to all who facilitated the authors resuscitating the contributions of Wilma Soss, Evelyn Y. Davis, and the long-forgotten Federation of Women Shareholders in American Business.

FOREWORD

I share something in common with Wilma Soss, the pioneering "gadfly" whose life is sketched in this well-researched and important book.

It centers around Evelyn Y. Davis, or EYD as she liked being called. She, too, was a figure corporate boards loved to hate, joining the gadfly cause just as *Wilma Soss* became a household name. Only a handful of people truly listened to Evelyn, though she was memorably vocal. Soss listened in the 1950s and '60s. I listened from the 1980s until the end of her life in 2018.

When the 1953 Broadway play *The Solid Gold Cadillac*, loosely based on Soss's life as a corporate gadfly, began its run, EYD, in another sense, began her run to become "Queen of the Corporate Jungle." She sought out the much older Soss for career advice. She longed for a dignified business career that at the time seemed beyond the reach of a young Dutch woman with a hearing disability, fear of public speaking, no family support, and lingering trauma from her time in concentration camps during World War II.

The connection proved fateful for Evelyn, who gained the dignity and courage she needed to become more than a gadfly. She became a formidable force in corporate America and wrote the book on marketing her personal brand when few others knew the value. But in truth, she was running away—from her Holocaust experience, two failed college attempts, her Jewish heritage, a failed marriage, and her "wicked" stepmother in Maryland. She ended up in the arms of motherly Wilma Soss who, as much as anyone could, understood her.

For a few years, the two women were inseparable. Soss saw Evelyn as an "intelligent, business-minded woman." Soss mentored her and became, in her words, "the mother I never had." She loved Soss for giving her a career and later told me that Soss was the first person who ever took an interest in her. Evelyn was a difficult person, to put it mildly. She was almost totally deaf. She spoke loudly. Most people avoided her because she had a superiority complex that is difficult to explain and was impossible for most people to tolerate. Evelyn needed the wisdom of an older woman throughout her life. Soss provided as much wisdom as Evelyn could accept.

As for me, my life with EYD—and eventual marriage to her in 2005—was exciting and exhausting. I arrived in D.C. in 1984 and learned of her reputation as a "bomb thrower" during a conversation with an attorney. Corporate executives, politicians, celebrities, bureaucrats—your position didn't matter. If you got on the wrong side of Evelyn Davis, you'd hear about it.

"If you need a 'bomb thrower,' send Davis anonymous tips in the mail," the attorney advised. I'd be lying if I told you I wasn't intrigued.

After a chance meeting with EYD at George Washington University's Gelman Library, I sent her a card thanking her for her philanthropy to the institution. She called me soon after and suggested we meet for coffee. The conversation was highly unusual, centering largely around her passion for business.

We departed after the end of her lecture and I figured I'd never hear from her again. But to my surprise, she called the next day and invited me to her Watergate office. It was a former closet she had converted to an editorial office for her publication, *Highlights and Lowlights*. Unable to fit more than three people standing shoulder-to-shoulder, she endearingly called it a "slice of pizza." We spent hours in the office discussing corporate issues, business letters she was drafting, content for her annual publication, business books, her travel, politics, U.S. foreign trade, and "the world according to EYD." What a world!

Highlights and Lowlights was ahead of its time in its use of photographs. She had cover photos with a prominent businessman or political figure. She also featured a Facebook-like page of six photographs of her meetings with corporate executives, politicians, and university presidents during the business year. The photos showed her subscribers she had access to, and friendships with, powerful men and women. In her photos with powerful men, EYD directed them to look at her as she smiled at the camera. "Men can't take their eyes off me," she told reporters. That was Evelyn.

Her insults, too, were national treasures. I carried a notebook solely to jot down her outbursts at CEOs, corporate security guards, waiters, fundraisers, taxi drivers, and "flunkies" of all sorts. She had eccentricities, as did most businessmen from Joseph Kennedy to William Randolph Hearst to Howard Hughes to Donald Trump.

Wilma Soss and James Patterson listened to a person who lived a troubled life. I don't think Soss ever considered EYD crazy, as corporate boards would often lament. I certainly didn't, and we remained friends after we divorced in 2006. She was a trailblazer, and what that meant was she had to break a couple of rules along the way. Her mentor did the same.

EYD was the star of her life—and Wilma Soss the star of hers. History almost lost track of their stories but, as you'll see, they're worth remembering. Not just for the costumes, the progress, the antics, or the laughs but for the reminder that with a little wit and a lot of drive, even the most unconventional dreams can be within your reach.

James E. Patterson, former U.S. diplomat

TABLE OF CONTENTS

I

HERE TO STAY

Business Women Are Here to Stay

—Wilma Soss, 1945[1]

Briskly walking the crowded midtown Manhattan street, trimly attired as always, public relations whiz Wilma Soss couldn't help but notice how much the city still bustled with a wartime vibe. In New York, as elsewhere in the country three months past Japan's August 14th surrender, demobilization was far from complete. Many apartment residents had not yet taken down their heavy black-out window shades, and many windows still displayed service flags, some emblazoned with a gold star, signaling a family member who had made the ultimate sacrifice.

Middle-aged and married but childless, Soss had not lost a loved one during the war, but she felt a keen sense of empathy towards those families that had, and she looked forward to a lasting peace and a smooth transition to a prosperous peacetime economy.

Still, as an astute observer of the business scene and its impact on consumers' pocketbooks, Soss knew that transition would take time. For one thing, rationing wouldn't go away overnight, not as long as shortages remained; so those ubiquitous coupon booklets would remain essential for shoppers at grocery stores, gasoline stations, and elsewhere. Too, there was an acute shortage of housing for returning veterans.

Hardly least was the possibility that rampant inflation would engulf the economy once the Office of Price Administration began to wind down wartime price controls. Older Americans in particular feared a repeat of the deep recession that had blanketed the United States after the First World War, and it could not be ruled out that the sudden withdrawal of the war spending stimulus could even jolt the economy back into depression.

With all this in mind, the War Department was dutifully publishing pamphlets to help prepare GIs for the transition home, many returning to towns and cities transformed by war, and wondering if they would come back home to good jobs—or, at least, their old jobs.

Beyond the bread and butter issues loomed emerging and contentious geopolitical questions: how to achieve an enduring peace with ally-turned-foe Russia; how much should America aid in rebuilding the countries in devastated, war-torn Europe; how (and whether) to hunt down not only the chief perpetrators of the Holocaust, but also their many culpable underlings?

Wilma Soss was one of those rare individuals who pondered deeply both the grand questions and the pragmatic ones. Yet for all the looming uncertainty, she sensed good times ahead. Optimistic by nature, she was not easily scared, not even by the inflation bogeyman.

Besides, on this chilly, late autumn afternoon, returning from the offices of Forbes Magazine, its forthcoming issue in her white gloved hand, her focus was on another matter of enormous economic import—one to which few others, including the nation's leading economists, had scarcely given a passing thought: the future of women in the American workplace.

In the momentous conflict just past, women had played a crucial role in securing victory, with more than five million replacing men in factories across the country; even now, Rosie the Riveter remains one of the iconic images of the age. Still, it was widely assumed—by both sexes—that with peace, the domestic sphere would return to pre-war norms. After all, many women who'd replaced men in the wartime workforce thought of themselves of as having had "jobs"— likely temporary ones—rather than "careers."

But Wilma Soss had been transformed by her own wartime experience and had a very different perspective. She envisaged a time when women would not only be welcome in every field of endeavor, but also have every opportunity to rise to the top.

For her, this was a matter of logic as well as fairness. The result would be of incalculable benefit not just to individual women but to capitalist America itself, at last able to use the skills of *all* its citizens.

Nor, in her case, were such calculations a matter of abstract theory. Hadn't she herself forged a hugely successful career in a professional realm overwhelmingly dominated by men? Hadn't she done so solely by virtue of her own mind and determination, without benefit of privilege or connections? And all the while, hadn't she also managed to sustain a rich and fulfilling marriage?

Soss's career had indeed been a remarkable one. From a chaotic childhood passed between relations in Brooklyn and San Francisco—later some would laughingly surmise her famous love affair with trains came from bouncing between the coasts as a child—she emerged a young woman with the self-possession to attend Columbia University's new but already prestigious School of Journalism. She would find herself a newspaper job and in short order transition into the developing field of public relations, where under the guidance of Harry Reichenbach, (still legendary for the outrageous stunts he'd concoct to draw notice to his clients), she emerged as a major creative force in her own right. Moving from promoting plays and films to high fashion, her fees from Saks Fifth Avenue, Shoecraft, and The Tailored Woman during the depths of the Great Depression brought in the equivalent of well over half a million dollars today, even as she shaped the career of the rising mezzo-soprano star Gladys Swarthout on the side.

While such a life trajectory was highly unusual for a woman in that era, it was not unprecedented. The high-flying career woman, portrayed by the likes of Katherine Hepburn or Jean Arthur in all those classics of the Thirties, was by then something of a cultural prototype. Blessed with classic good looks and ready charm, Soss featured the mix of velvet-gloved strength and feminine flair with which it was associated. When it suited her purposes, she could play up her femininity to the hilt. As public relations director of the International Silk Guild, she appeared in public only in the finest silk. And, cognizant of the biases against married women in the workplace, she assiduously avoided introducing herself as "Mrs. Soss."

For all her success, Soss had been more or less typecast, having to center her work overwhelmingly on products and services aimed at women. But that changed in 1941. With war already raging abroad, and the likelihood of America getting drawn in growing by the day, she was recruited by Evans Products, a Michigan-based manufacturer of wood products ranging from railroad ties to broom sticks. It started to manufacture a new product line that suddenly seemed to hold promise—plywood gliders.

The concept was not new—the potential use of gliders to land troops and supplies near battlefields had been debated for years in U.S. Army strategic planning circles. Cheap to build, lightweight, silent, and able to land in tight spaces, their advantages in combat were obvious. But gliders also had drawbacks, starting with their extreme vulnerability. In her new role, Soss took the company's lead in the effort to persuade General Henry 'Hap' Arnold, chief of the Army Air Corps, to develop a military glider program.

Though Evans would not be chosen to supply military gliders, Soss still found triumph in the endeavor. She was now regularly interacting not just with America's top brass, but with the many women working in Evans' plants, and finding herself deeply impressed by their remarkable degree of dedication and skill.

But she also knew that in most cases, it was the only job they would ever have—or seek. Once the war was over, they would marry, have children and, except in rare cases, their skills would be lost to the American workforce.

Wilma Soss had never been afraid of change, professionally or otherwise; to the contrary, easily bored and always up for a challenge, she embraced it. So, it was not coincidence, given her wide circle of contacts, that with the war winding down and seeking new opportunities, she found herself in the office of B.C. Forbes, publisher of the eponymous magazine he'd founded in 1917. Or that she was about to be presented the opportunity of her lifetime.

$ $ $

In recent years, *Forbes* had been losing ground to its chief competitors in the business field, *Business Week* and *Fortune*, both in terms of declining circulation and, equally worrisome, diminishing relevance. For decades, the magazine had thrived with its unique format—heavy on the business-man-as-hero stories, moralistic writing, and abundant praise of capitalism. But in changing times, the formula had grown stale.

Yet for B.C., that formula had always been less a gimmick than a life philosophy. He was the ultimate self-made man. An immigrant from Scotland, Forbes was the son of a tailor, who early discovered he possessed a strong aptitude for writing, and quickly progressed from cub reporter at a small-town paper, to financial editor for William Randolph Hearst's *New York American* before setting out on his own. The year after his magazine's founding, he encapsulated its credo in a book entitled *Keys to Success:* "Your success depends upon you. Your happiness depends upon you. You have to steer your own course. You have to shape your own fortune. You have to educate yourself. You have to do your own thinking." Most importantly, people had to assume large risks if they were to reap large rewards: "The men who have done big things are those who were not afraid to attempt big things, who were not afraid to risk failure to gain success."[2]

B.C. was in his late sixties by now, and ready to relinquish at least some control of the magazine to his sons, especially Malcolm, just back from the war with a Bronze Star, Purple Heart, and desire to rebrand his father's creation.

B.C. Forbes and Wilma Soss were a natural fit. Both were unapologetic boosters of capitalism, competition, and private enterprise, and like the media mogul, the PR whiz saw her own life story as testimony to the power of hard work and initiative.

Though B.C. isn't remembered for being a strong advocate for women, maybe he should be. Long before others, he'd shown interest in covering women in the workplace. Indeed, *Forbes'* very first issue in September 1917 had featured a cover line reading: "Unique Department: Women in Business."[3]

He was especially interested in women as investors. Believing that equity investors were the true owners of American corporations and the profits they produced, he made a point of using the term shareowner in lieu of the elitist-sounding stockholder or shareholder. Aware that communist propagandists liked to project the cartoon image of bloated stockholders getting rich at ordinary people's expense, he wanted to promote the image of average people investing in and being uplifted by the stock market. As his magazine instructed: "Sharing, from Biblical times, has been advocated, lauded. The greatest sharers of today are our corporate enterprises and institutions . . . If popularizing the use of the term 'share owner' does even a little to better the atmosphere, to inspire individuals and families to invest their savings in shares, it will be very much worthwhile."[4]

B.C. believed that at its best, America encouraged ordinary people to take calculated business risks, and this was good not just for those who profited from their ventures, but for everyone. A rising tide lifted all boats, particularly when a dominant form of business organization in the country remained the publicly traded corporation, in which individuals from all walks of life could buy shares. Deeply invested in the battle to preserve capitalism from the collectivist menaces of fascism and communism, he had been preaching well before the outbreak of the Cold War that maintaining a strong America was the best defense against the allure of totalitarian ideologies; and giving ordinary citizens a tangible stake in American business was the best way to make it happen, providing countless millions with a personal incentive to protect America, its institutions, and property rights.

At the same time, B.C. well remembered the scams in earlier decades that had robbed amateur investors of their hard-earned savings. And though the establishment of the Securities and Exchange Commission (SEC) in 1934 had somewhat addressed that, B.C. felt more was needed to ensure a level playing field. His conclusion was that investors needed to band together and wield immeasurably greater power in markets and policy circles to look after their own interests.[5]

Not that this was a wholly original concept. There already existed, for example, the American Federation of Investors, established by former Illinois Senator Hugh Magill. But it remained small and ineffectual. Like other such investor organizations, it had floundered because of investor passivity since few were prepared to bear the costs and consequences of organizing and decisively acting.

Back in 1942, during a round of golf at Pinehurst in North Carolina with a stockbroker friend, B.C. had decided to give it a go. He had been successful at so many other things, so why not this? Surely the nation would be better off with a vibrant, well run investors' association.

Following up in a *Forbes* column shortly thereafter, B.C. found that readers loved the idea, and soon formed the Investors Fairplay League, eventually shortened to the Investors League. When former President Herbert Hoover and his 1928 Democratic rival Alfred E. Smith both declined to lead the organization, B.C. himself took the reins as president, and held the post for the next seven years.

In 1945, when Soss walked into his office, wondering if they might find a way to work together, B.C. was two years into his Investors League experiment and still highly optimistic about the organization's potential. Impressed by his visitor's evident self-assurance, not to mention her economic acumen and journalism background, the venerable publisher had a thought. How about a piece on the degree to which women were represented in the nation's share ownership ranks? It was a coup for a woman at the time to land such an assignment. Like other media outlets, *Forbes* generally used women writers, when at all, for softer stuff.

Soss went after it with characteristic zeal. She would later maintain that she did not yet see herself as a crusader for women in business, and that her aim was to report, not proselytize. But, in fact, the story would have consequences far beyond what even the visionary B.C. could have imagined. And for Wilma Soss, it would make the economic liberation of women and all small investors the animating force of her life.

Three months after that meeting in B.C.'s office, holding the fresh-off-the press December 15th issue of *Forbes*, she knew the story—blandly titled "Business Women are Here to Stay"—would be an eye opener.

The research had been intense. The New York Stock Exchange did not track female stockholdings at the time; indeed, they had no idea how many total shareowners of any sort existed. Nor did the government have any such record. So she'd gone to some of the largest listed companies on the New York Stock Exchange one by one—among them, General Motors (GM), American Telephone and Telegraph (AT&T), U.S. Steel, and Continental Can—and asked for a hand count of their listed female stockholders.[6] Though the result would not be definitive, the numbers would paint a reasonably accurate picture of female share ownership in the country as a whole.

Both Wilma Soss and NYSE President Keith Funston (depicted above) shared a passion for enlarging the country's retail shareowner base. Photo by Unknown, Wilma Soss Papers, AHC collection: #10249, Photo Folder – accretion number 81-12-21. American Heritage Center, University of Wyoming.

Moreover, in her characterization, women shareholders were indeed businesswomen, if not in the usual sense of the term, and it was time corporations, and the women themselves, started thinking of them that way.

But the real shocker was that women shareholders equaled or outnumbered men in most of the large corporations she researched. They constituted 45 percent of General Electric's shareholders, slightly outnumbering male shareowners at 43 percent. (The remaining 12 percent were institutions, not individuals, a very low proportion compared to today). They likewise dominated at General Motors, where 51.7 percent of all individual shareholders were women. At DuPont, the percent of women common stockholders was 42.2 percent, compared to 39.7 percent men. AT&T boasted 55.5 percent women shareholders to 27.4 percent men, with 11.7 percent holding joint accounts. American Home Products had 49 percent women shareholders, compared to 35 percent men.

In all, the numbers turned conventional thinking on its head.

While the piece didn't explore the reasons why so many women owned shares in America's largest corporations, several factors seemed clear. AT&T, for example, had a strong employee stock ownership program (ESOP) that included its telephone operators, many of whom were women. Moreover, because women tended to live longer than men, some inherited stocks from their husbands, brothers, and fathers.[7]

The piece emphasized for *Forbes* readers, largely business executives, the need to understand the implications of widespread female stockownership. "Though you may not have a product which sells directly to women," Soss explained, "the chances are that your customers, your label, or your stockholders include many women." "Break down the ownership list of your company's stock," she continued, and "you'll find that women are not only heavily represented but, probably, are your majority stockholders." Bluntly, she added, "indications are that the control of the nation's invested capital is falling into women's hands—and is going to remain there."[8]

She did note that a handful of companies had appointed women to prominent positions, singling out IBM and General Foods for each making a woman vice president for the first time. A very few women had even managed to become presidents, like "Miss Mary Dillon" at Brooklyn Gas Company and "Mrs. Vera V. Seymour" at the American Gas and Power Company. Women, she emphasized, "are slowly infiltrating the executive ranks of industry" and the "trend is growing." It was true even in journalism and publishing, she slyly noted, where "More and more of the 'men' who write about business to-day turn out to be women—notably the senior editors of *Time* and *Fortune*."

She argued that more corporations had to be proactive in treating women equally in every capacity, whether as shareowners, workers, customers, or employees. More companies needed to make sure all the rungs of the corporate ladder were open for women to ascend, not just for the sake of the women involved but for the ultimate good of the corporation. "The sooner management welcomes women beyond the clerical and machine stages into the councils of the inner circle and trains them to understand and share executive responsibility as they come up through the ranks," she wrote, "the more it will profit in its ultimate labor and consumer relations." And by the same token, companies that stubbornly ignored the trend were fighting a losing battle, as in the postwar world the female share of total employment was bound to grow, with women likely to constitute fully a quarter of the workforce by 1950.

"Since even the Pope [Pius XII] recently broadcast 'equals rights for women,' urged women to go into public life, and proclaimed 'for the same work output a woman is entitled to the same wages as a man,'" she intoned, "corporate business must begin to face the fact that women in the post-war world will not long remain owners of stock in name only—if they are so today." Indeed, she predicted women shareowners soon would abandon passivity and would come to demand more from the corporations they owned.[9]

It was only logical to assume that in time women should be running them too.

In making her argument, there were inconvenient truths Soss conveniently ignored. Although individual women shareowners indeed outnumbered male shareholders in many public corporations, small groups of men typically owned a greater number of outstanding shares, which made corporate elections more plutocratic than democratic.

Nonetheless, the article concluded with a dire warning. If businesses continued to avoid employing women in an executive capacity and to ignore female shareowners, women's approval of the free enterprise system itself could so decline that they would "find a siren song in 'Statism' and the propaganda which has set out to undermine the private ownership of American business."[10]

In short, the piece had thrown down the gauntlet to American corporations. They needed to reform themselves before women did it for them in the political arena.

Having set out on the assignment as a reporter, by the time she'd sat down to write the actual article, Soss had become an advocate. Her goal—which would become a crusade—was full equality for women in the upper echelons of American business, including on corporate boards.

In the years to follow, Wilma Soss would rock the corporate world. As the leader of the Federation of Women Shareholders in American Business (FOWSAB), host of a radio show with millions of listeners, and even the inspiration for a popular play and movie, she would pick up a range of colorful sobriquets: the Joan of Arc of Industry, the Greta Garbo of Gadflies, the Corporate Conscience, the Guardian Angel of Shareholders, the Most Talked About Woman on Wall Street, the Woman of a Million Words.

But the one she considered most apt was "economic suffragette." For through it all, she never wavered in her mission—securing vital reforms in corporate governance for the benefit of small investors. Indeed, using their combined voting power as her cudgel, her fight was ultimately on behalf of those of both sexes.

Soss's efforts would succeed to a remarkable degree. For as the heat of the Second World War gave way to the frigidity of the Cold War, enhanced corporate democracy and greater opportunities for women served to greatly strengthen the argument for capitalism itself in the pitched battle for hearts and minds. Wilma Soss's transformation from reporting the news to making the news may have started with that little piece in *Forbes,* but it would continue with a not-so-little company called U.S. Steel.[11]

2

WOMAN OF STEEL

Why isn't there a woman on the Board of Directors?
Women are not represented in a company which is
financed by their capital and which does business in an
economy in which women have a plurality of the vote.

—Wilma Soss to the U.S. Steel Board,
Hoboken, N.J., 1947[12]

Although Soss's *Forbes* headline in 1945 declared women in the workforce were "Here to Stay," corporate execs had other plans. Employers fired roughly 675,000 women workers within a month of the war's end. As returning GIs took back Rosie's positions, the number of women in the U.S. labor force fell by some 750,000 by 1946. Some women were happy to return to domestic life after answering the country's call and content to leave the paid workforce.

But roughly 75 percent of women employed during the war wanted to retain their wartime positions. The figure was even higher for women over the age of 45, few of whom needed to care for young children. Women wanted, and often needed, to work, and many had become accustomed to doing so.[13]

In the backdrop of these changes, the economy started to grow quickly. Servicemen returned to their old jobs. Technological advances made in the war effort, like jet engines and early computers, entered civilian life and spurred productivity. New families formed and brought with them a "baby boom" of new mouths to feed. American consumers, well-aware of the costs of their newfound peace, had a new motivation to spend and invest—giving their children the comforts war had made elusive. Soss sensed, as did many families, that they might be able to achieve these goals more easily if the mother worked for wages or a salary, if only part-time or for a portion of the family cycle. Many employers also came to realize the benefits of a broader workforce, and the trend toward employing more women (including married women) remained strong in the long-term.

The short-term, however, was a bit more combative. When a manufacturing company in Connecticut laid off wartime hires, labeling the work as "too physically demanding" for the women who filled in during the war effort, twenty-four women picketed in protest. In Detroit, many who had served as bus drivers during the war were dismissed in the summer of 1946. The job's new requirement, "for men only," caused roughly 300 newly laid-off employees to protest the street railway company's action at City Hall. That same year, at a General Motors plant in Pontiac, Michigan, executives fired several of their female workers for being a "distracting influence." Six of them, all members of United Auto Workers Local 653, successfully filed a grievance against GM and won their jobs back.[14]

A similar case would unfold at the NYSE, but with less desirous an outcome. During the war, dozens of women had been hired to work as pages on the floor, running orders between the posts where specialist broker-dealers plied their crafts. Historically, NYSE membership was, in-practice, only for men. Women were not allowed on the floor, unless accompanied by a man. The page "girls" were pioneers, and by all accounts performed their jobs well.[15] By 1947, some of these women pages had worked the floor for years and were ripe for promotion to floor broker positions—something previously unachievable for women in the industry. The NYSE, when given the opportunity to break this barrier, would send the pages back to their original back-office clerical jobs instead.

Highly dissatisfied with the monotony, especially after the excitement of the exchange floor, several of the reassigned turned to their union for help. Lengthy arbitration hearings ensued, but the women ultimately failed in their bid to remain on the floor. As one NYSE official later recalled, "We used girl pages on the exchange floor during World War II, but we replaced them with men again the moment we could."[16]

As stories like this played out across the country, Wilma Soss strove to induce companies to elevate more women into top executive positions and directorships. Thinking ahead, she believed that placing more *qualified* women in corporate leadership positions would be the means to open up greater opportunities in the workplace. Women, she reasoned, would help other women. Of course, she had other motives too for the advocacy. No one said the job of "economic suffragette" should be thankless.

$ $ $

In her *Forbes* article, Soss surprised many readers with her claim that more females owned shares in many leading U.S. public corporations than males. Though the distribution of share ownership was ignored, her claims were true and her presentation of the facts was compelling. Business executives reading Soss's story, some of whom were in the process of deciding the fate of their women wartime employees, contemplated whether they should start cultivating women as investors and customers as well as employees, given that all three categories often overlapped. For Soss and others looking to solidify women's place in the corporate world, a plethora of women shareholders was a feel-good story, one that suggested women could exert greater influence in corporate America with their ownership stakes.

But most women were not shareowners. Neither were most men. Relative to the American population, owners of common shares, male or female, were uncommon. AT&T had by the far the largest number, but even its rolls contained only about 668,000 names. U.S. Steel had 225,414 shareowners, about the same number as General Electric, which reported a record number of investors in 1945. Moreover, investors in one company often showed up on the rolls of other companies, so the number of investors in corporations totaled well below the sum of each individual company's tally. Neither Soss nor the NYSE completely understood the full share ownership picture and the NYSE wouldn't commission a comprehensive shareholder census until 1952. At that time, the Brookings Institute concluded that less than 4.5 percent of the U.S. population (roughly 6.5 million Americans) owned even one share of any stock in any company, even indirectly. Share ownership remained concentrated, a problem for those espousing the rising notions of democratic capitalism.[17]

In fact, in 1945, while writing about the state of share ownership in America, Soss herself owned no common stock. Like many citizens, she vividly remembered the 1929 Crash, and the sickening, almost 90 percent plunge of the Dow Jones Industrial Average (DJIA) from its peak in September 1929 to its nadir in the summer of 1932. She remembered, too, the hearings, led by Ferdinand Pecora, into unsavory Wall Street practices that dominated headlines during the Depression, convincing many that the "little fellows" in the market were bound to get fleeced, as insiders had stacked the deck against them.[18]

As a young woman, Soss had inherited some money from her grandparents placed in the care of a trustee, who proceeded to lose it all in the swooning market. Stung by the losses, she vowed to steer clear of stocks, viewing equity investing as too risky for her taste, and more akin to speculation than genuine investment. She recalled, "I swore when I grew up that I would never own another share of stock."[19]

Swearing off the market during the 1930s was fairly common. Plus, few Americans during the Great Depression, a time of terrible unemployment, had enough disposable income to buy stock anyway. Soss, of course, was unusual in that she weathered the Depression quite well due to her rapidly rising career. She had money, and could have invested in the market had she desired. But memories of the Crash deterred her.

Even during the war years, the DJIA did not fully return to its pre-Crash highs and neither did Wall Street's reputation. World War II spurred growth of what President Dwight D. Eisenhower would later term the military-industrial complex, but high wartime taxes muted corporate profits, and dampened their stock prices.

Americans, fearful of another crash, or at least an immediate postwar recession, remained wary of stocks.

After writing the *Forbes* piece, and likely due to her research for it, Soss changed her takeaway from the Crash—it was a bad idea to give her savings to some "fiduciary" with dubious incentives. What would be a good idea, instead, was trusting herself. In their book *Security Analysis* (1934), Columbia University professors Benjamin Graham and David Dodd argued that disciplined investors who were willing to do their homework on companies could protect themselves from the danger of extreme loss if they estimated the intrinsic value of each company and only bought shares that were undervalued in the market.[20]

Some of the promotional campaigns the New York Stock Exchange (NYSE) ran after the war, advertisements that stressed the importance of buying stock for both personal and patriotic reasons, may also have influenced Soss's thinking. Buying a share of stock was buying a share in America, so said the NYSE. Seeing what the country accomplished during wartime, who would bet against the United States?

But perhaps the biggest reason she reentered the market was the fact that owning even one share of a company allowed her to attend its annual meetings. With her background in journalism, she knew the value of getting the story first-hand, and buying one share seemed a relatively cheap way to gain access.

Soss bought a single share of U.S. Steel, a position she gradually increased to a grand total of five. The investment was a paltry sum for someone whose PR business had thrived for a decade and a half. But that one share set her down the path of shareholder activism, turning her into a "professional investor," or a "corporate gadfly" as corporate apologists preferred.

Brandishing her shares in Steel, she eventually became a major irritant to its management, most especially its venerable Chairman, Irving Olds. She would go on to buy more stock in more companies, and a host of Fortune 500 executives would come to rue what they called the "Wilma problem."

$ $ $

In May 1946, Soss decided to attend U.S. Steel's annual stockholder meeting, her first ever. Like most Americans, she also paid attention to events unfolding on the world stage, as tensions ratcheted up between an expanding Soviet Union and its former allies, particularly the United States. Early that month, former British Prime Minister Winston Churchill, visiting Westminster College in Fulton, Missouri, warned Americans that "From Stettin in the Baltic to Trieste in the Adriatic, an iron curtain has descended across the continent." On stage with him sat Missouri native Harry Truman, who had succeeded Franklin D. Roosevelt as President thirteen months earlier. Truman had to contend with the growing Soviet threat and meet Churchill's challenge to the United States—to face up to its position as "the pinnacle of world power" and curtail the Soviet Union's expansionist tendencies.[21]

The immediate reaction to Churchill's "Iron Curtain" speech was sharply negative. Americans had just emerged from a long war and prayed for a prosperous, peaceful future. Soss and others feared getting dragged into another conflict but also dreaded the spread of communism worldwide and sought to render the free enterprise system resilient.

She may have attended the U.S. Steel meeting as a distraction, as a means of determining if she should buy additional shares, or as a ploy to drum up business for her PR consultancy. At the time, few investors bothered to attend stockholder meetings, which were often short affairs held in small venues in out-of-the-way places. At Standard Oil's meeting in 1934, only three shareholders attended. Same for a General Motors meeting held "in the little Du Pont Law Library in Wilmington, Delaware." Only 25 of 60,000 shareholders showed up at a Republic Steel meeting in 1952. And the few share-holders who appeared rarely spoke up. Investors tended to be passive if only because they realized they were nearly powerless anyway. As late as 1950, gurus like Jackson Martindell argued that corporations were not democracies and that powerless stockholders could only "accept management on faith."[22]

Moreover, selling shares was far cheaper than fighting manage-ment on its own turf. Most individual investors, and even large insti-tutions, followed the so-called "Wall Street Rule" and sold their shares when they suspected malfeasance or mismanagement. To agitate for reform resembled running into a fire instead of away. Economists call this the "free rider" or "collective action" problem. Why should A bear the costs of helping B, C, D, and, in the largest corporations, tens of thousands of others? Soss, however, held that "there is no more cynical philosophy than to sell a stock because you do not like some managerial practice."[23]

Annual meetings were also lightly attended because corporations typically did the legal minimum to publicize their meetings. Man-agement at U.S. Steel employed the standard playbook: indirectly discourage investors from attending the annual meeting, get through it as fast as possible, and limit any rogue comments.

Despite struggling during the Depression, U.S. Steel did rather well during and immediately after the war. Irving S. Olds, a product of Yale University and Harvard Law School, had taken the helm of

U.S. Steel in 1940, and shepherded Steel through the challenge of the war economy. By the late 1940s, U.S. Steel's annual sales exceeded two billion dollars and in 1948 it achieved a record profit of almost $130 million. The rebound obviously pleased shareholders, but Steel was far from perfect, suffering from labor issues and other problems.[24]

Brandishing his delightfully Dickensian name, Chairman Olds called the sparsely attended meeting to order. Despite her gregarious nature, Soss sat and listened to Olds and other top managers briefly overview the year just past. A few bold shareowners occasionally dared to interrupt with tough questions about Steel's labor relations. She inwardly stewed at how rudely and sarcastically Olds treated her fellow shareholders. "I saw a lot of things I didn't like," she later recalled, including the time a labor representative received the "brush-off." As she saw it, management somehow abrogated the authority of the company's rightful owners and controlled them, instead of the other way around.[25]

Soss left the meeting rather disillusioned, having just witnessed in person a problem that law professor Adolph Berle and economist Gardiner Means had described in their 1932 book, *The Modern Corporation and Private Property*. Stockholders, they showed, did not wield much power despite technically owning the corporate enterprise. Berle and Means noted that ownership became separated from control in part because stockholders were so dispersed and scattered that they lacked the unity to impact the direction of the enterprise. "The property owner who invests in a modern corporation so far surrenders his wealth to those in control of the corporation," the duo explained, "that he has exchanged the position of independent owner for one in which he may become merely recipient of the wages of capital. [Such owners] have surrendered the right that the corporation should be operated in their sole interest." Berle and Means found this a problem in need of remedy and suggested various reforms that Soss later would embrace, such as improved voting rights for shareholders and increased corporate transparency.[26]

She didn't have much time to dwell on the problem of passive investors and arrogant managers. Management's behavior at the U.S. Steel meeting in 1946 clearly irked her, but she had a public relations consultancy to run, and it continued to demand considerable attention. It would not, however, be her last shareholder meeting with the board of U.S. Steel and the incomparable Chairman Olds.

$ $ $

Always working to acquire new business for her public relations consultancy, Soss routinely wrote to executives. In particular, she tried to convince executives that she could help them to come to friendlier terms with stockholders and laborers. Propelled by her December 1945 *Forbes* article, she acquired a reputation for helping companies interact with female stockholders, employees, and customers. Yet new clients did not come easily as the PR field grew crowded with new entrants, including ad agencies with precious little real PR experience.[27]

She landed several clients in the early postwar period, including the New York subway system, but her most important client became the Budd Company of Philadelphia, a manufacturer of railroad passenger cars. Owner Edward G. Budd paid Soss $30,000 per year to initiate "a woman's program" that entailed making women more comfortable with trains, as passengers, investors, and workers. Though Budd passed away in 1946, Soss continued with the company and was upgraded to the firm's public relations consultant. She remained "interested in the woman's angle" when it came to her position, but her "responsibilities [were] not confined to that," as she explained to an executive at *Life*. She worked with *Vogue* on a piece that equated Budd's fashionable trains with summer travel and women's fashion in early 1947 and placed an article in *Railway Age* that May entitled "Budd Company Seeks to Interest Women in Railroads."[28]

Soss endeavored to broaden her client base, and unflinchingly pitched herself as an expert on women-related public relations. She once tried to convince International Harvester that she could help make its annual reports more attractive to "Mrs. Average Stockholder." That was important, she argued, because women had a different "psychology" than men and reminded them that "about half of the stockholders in this country are women." She knew that was true even at International Harvester, although it was a prototypically masculine company that manufactured farm equipment. International Harvester responded, but not enthusiastically. It's quite possible its management agreed with the fictional board depicted in *Fortune* that told a female directorial candidate: "I trust you will forgive my observation that it seems somehow more appropriate for a woman director to serve with a dairy company than with a drop-forge manufacturer."[29]

In any event, Soss replied to Dale Cox, International Harvester's PR director, with a letter that amply demonstrated her mastery of the craft of public relations—and sealed a meeting. The win would prove fleeting, however, as they ultimately chose another consultant for the account. While she successfully signed with companies like Budd, she felt the odds were stacked against her elsewhere, in part because of her gender. Such experiences increased her resolve that corporate America needed some help.[30]

Women, Soss claimed, had a better ethical sense than men. They were "the only hope American business has left" because those in charge of corporations were "terrified of the government and they're scared to death of any change." She professed astonishment that executives were not "more appreciative of what we women are doing for their own good. After all, Mother knows best." She believed that "the men do have Mom complexes" so all she had to do to turn them into "putty" was "to prove . . . that we're not trollops." Women, she believed, would "humanize the corporations." At times, though, Soss hinted that such problems had a cultural component and not just a genetic-biological one. Some men, like her husband Joe and certain CEOs she liked, were just fine. Age undoubtedly played a factor in her view also, noting "that where there is a young president he is more stockholder-minded and more 'woman-minded' than when the president is approaching the pension age."[31]

$ $ $

As Soss worked to refine her niche in the hyper-competitive PR world, the NYSE's popular image began to undergo a metamorphosis. The institution finally began scrubbing the stains its reputation suffered in the Depression years by broadcasting its noble role as a bastion of capitalism in the deepening Cold War. In Spring 1947, the NYSE embarked upon a mass media advertising campaign, the largest undertaken in its long history. Advertisements in the leading magazines of the day, such as *Time, Look, Collier's,* and *The Saturday Evening Post,* hammered home the message that shareowners truly owned the companies in which they invested, a sentiment the rising "gadfly" held dear. The ads also emphasized that shareowners were a varied bunch who came from all walks of life. With the headline, "Stockholders' Meeting," the text of one advertisement read, "They come from everywhere . . . from every income group, from every community. They are women as well as men, employees as well as executives, farmers as well as businessmen. They are typical stockholders, the owners of business."[32]

The NYSE sought to convince the American public that share ownership constituted a mainstream characteristic, and hence to persuade more Americans to enter the market and start paying commissions and other fees to Wall Street's brokerages, many of which remained financially strapped. As Exchange officials knew, equity investors remained few and even fewer generated commissions from habitual trading.[33]

Hoping to build a better image of the stock market and bring more equity investors into the fold, the NYSE encouraged newspaper and magazine reporters to carry glowing stories about the power of stockownership. The Exchange had maintained a press bureau since the early 1900s, which tried to plant positive stories in the media about the NYSE. But in the early postwar period, it succeeded in getting the word out, in part because it augmented its public relations work with advertising, and in part because the exigencies of the Cold War elevated the public perception of Wall Street's work.[34]

Listed companies in the 1940s also were working on burnishing their images. Increasingly, they drew on the image of their little stockholders to make their businesses seem more relatable and to keep regulators at bay. Some, most notably AT&T, had utilized this tactic for some time. In the early twentieth century, AT&T became one of the first corporations in the United States to embrace the emerging field of public relations being advanced by pioneers like Ivy Lee, Edward Bernays, and Soss's mentor Harry Reichenbach. "Ma Bell" anxiously sought to improve its image, lest the mammoth company fall victim to antitrust legislation. By running extensive magazine and newspaper articles extolling its large base of small shareowners, AT&T hoped to show that power and profit accrued to the average American. Widows made unconvincing monopolists and the dividends they routinely received made AT&T seem like a grand tool for dispersing riches across the land. Breaking up the company, therefore, would be politically and economically foolhardy. With these arguments, AT&T successfully staved off antitrust actions until 1982.[35]

Likewise, U.S. Steel, which frequently suffered labor troubles in the early 1900s, leveraged the emerging public relations field to ameliorate its troubles. It ran a popular weekly radio show and proudly advertised in newspapers, magazines, and pamphlets the size of its shareholder base. Soss recognized Steel's PR strategy of publicly touting the depth and breadth of its shareholder base while giving mostly lip service to the concept of investor ownership. But she absorbed the messages of the advertisements promoted by the NYSE and listed firms like Steel. She began thinking of herself as an OWNER in Steel and naturally, and deeply ironically, started acting that way.

$ $ $

In May 1947, stockholder season again reached its peak as most non-financial corporations held their annual meetings in the late spring. To attend her second U.S. Steel shareholder meeting, Soss trekked from her Manhattan home to the Union Club in Hoboken, New Jersey.

That Steel held its annual meeting in Hoboken irritated her. She knew full well that the company's headquarters sat downtown, in the Empire Building at the intersection of Broadway and Rector Street. It had been the company's headquarters since 1901, when

J.P. Morgan created the massive company by amalgamating two big steel producers with Andrew Carnegie's eponymous steel company. Like most interstate corporations of its vintage, U.S. Steel incorporated in New Jersey and held its annual meetings on the west bank of the Hudson River. Though not a requirement, this tradition held up in part due to institutional inertia but also, as Soss suspected, to dissuade stockholders from attending. Hoboken in the early postwar period remained crime-ridden and gritty, hated even by its native son Frank Sinatra. After being booed off stage at his performance at the Union Club in February 1948, the same venue where Steel held its annual meeting, Sinatra vowed to never return.[36]

Soss hoped she could one day make the same vow—moving these meetings out of Hoboken would later become one of her top priorities. She knew her rights as a shareholder attendee, but her thoughts on changing corporate policy were in the early stages. Petite, blond and beautiful, she was also razor sharp—and when provoked, scathingly acerbic in her criticisms. U.S. Steel, as the nation's first billion-dollar company, was quite a force—but so was Wilma Soss. She'd claim in later years that there was no special plan for this meeting—listen to the speeches, understand the procedures, learn the dynamics of the room. All in silence. But when the time came, she'd decide to speak—and if one moment, one singular event, can mark the transition from New York businesswoman Wilma Soss to *Wilma*, a name that carried its own American cultural weight, it'd be this.[37]

While Steel continued to do well financially, Wilma believed the company could be doing even better, particularly with their stockholder and customer relations. She felt strongly that corporations needed to engage more vibrantly with both male and female stockholders. Companies like U.S. Steel, she recognized, needed to do a better job of burnishing not just their images, but also their underlying substance.

Gavel in hand, Chairman Olds called the meeting to order. For a short time, the meeting proceeded without interruptions. The few stockholders present sat quietly and listened, sometimes taking notes. "All of a sudden," Wilma recalled, "I was on my feet. I couldn't have been more surprised." She began to make an impassioned speech, articulating reasons why management needed to name women to their board of directors. Women, she began, outnumbered male shareholders in the company. "U.S. Steel is a woman's company," she declared, with five percent more women shareholders than men.[38]

Given that statistic, it was logical, Wilma argued, that women should be on the board. A share of stock meant part ownership in the company. That was what the NYSE advertisements blared and what U.S. Steel's PR apparatus conveyed. Given the many women owners of Steel, Wilma asked management, "Why isn't there a woman on the Board of Directors?" Without waiting for an answer, Wilma continued, "Women are not represented in a company which is financed by their capital, and which does business in an economy in which women have a plurality of the vote."[39]

Women, Wilma insisted that day, would no longer tolerate being stockholders "in name only." Besides, U.S. Steel could richly benefit from a woman's point of view, Wilma believed. Management therefore needed to make room on the board for women and do so quickly if they wanted to improve the company.[40]

Some of the small shareowners in the room, including several men, enthusiastically applauded Wilma's passionate speech. One wonders if they clapped out of admiration for Wilma's pluck or a genuine feeling of solidarity with her message, or perhaps a little of both. Whatever the reason, Wilma felt further emboldened when she heard the applause. She went on, and told Olds and the board of U.S. Steel:

> It may interest the gentlemen on this board to know that there is being born in this room today the Federation of Women Shareholders in American Business. And they will call upon the steel industry and ask for representation in the business they own. It is my hope that you will not wait for the steel industry to be called upon, but that the United States Steel Corporation will take some leadership in the matter.[41]

Recalling that moment four years later, Wilma explained, "No one could have been more surprised than I was when I got to my feet that morning and said what I did." But Wilma was a clever, talented publicist, and a little lady taking on U.S. Steel with a pittance of stock certainly made for a good David-versus-Goliath story. The fact that she was a woman taking on many Goliaths on the Steel board made the story even better.[42]

General Motors Annual Meeting, 1953. Photo by Dan Weiner – Brackman Associates. 424 Madison Ave. NYC. Wilma Soss Papers, AHC collection #10249, Photo Folder – accretion number: 81-12-21. American Heritage Center, University of Wyoming.

She was familiar with Forbes' Investors Fairplay League and her decision to form a similar organization may not be as surprising as she made it appear. In later recollections, however, she made it sound as if divine inspiration had hit her during that meeting: "*I didn't choose to be the head of the woman's economic-suffrage movement; I was just sitting quietly in my seat, brooding over my one share of stock, when the woman's economic-suffrage movement chose me.*" Whether she owned one share or five, or five hundred, Wilma was a very small stockholder and yet she demanded change, starting with the appointment of a woman director. Her PR career had prepared her to stand up and speak with confidence under any circumstance: "I am accustomed," she once said, "to handling heads of industry, conferring, of course, with top management, having mature men work under me and employing male secretaries."[43]

Wilma saw herself as a suffragette for women's economic rights. While women had progressed during the war in some spheres, Wilma believed more progress was needed.

Wall Street, for example, remained very much an old boys' club. Through the 1940s, a woman had never ascended to membership of the New York Stock Exchange (NYSE) or the American Stock Exchange (AMEX). In the nineteenth century, Victoria Woodhull and her sister Tennessee Clafin had started their own brokerage firm but had not become members of an organized exchange. By the mid-twentieth century, while some brokerage firms like Merrill Lynch and J.S. Bache were beginning to hire women, members of what were still called the "fairer sex," faced a rather difficult path. Companies listed on the exchanges (like U.S. Steel, General Motors, and AT&T) rarely hired women in executive capacities and almost never selected them to serve on their boards.[44]

Wilma came to see herself in a heroic light, fighting for the underdog little stockholder, both male and female. She later told *The New Yorker* magazine, "Spontaneous combustion started me. Steel always seems romantic to me." She added, "The whole thing came out of my subconscious. Was it the voice of Joan of Arc or the ham in me? I don't know."[45] Her speech at the Steel meeting, though perhaps not as impromptu as she later portrayed it, launched her career as a professional corporate activist or "gadfly"—an investor who stood up, literally and figuratively, for stockholders' rights. Wilma and the Federation of Women Shareholders in American Business (FOWSAB) would embrace many stockholder causes over the years, some that perhaps seem minor (like changing meeting locations to more convenient places) and some that may seem significant (such as combatting excessive executive compensation, demanding more transparent management, insisting on more women on boards of directors, etc.)

Wilma and her Federation colleagues were not the only ones fighting for such reforms, but they were among the earliest and most vocal.

By the mid-1950s, Wilma was one of only a handful of faces of corporate shareholder activists that management instantly recognized when entering the meeting room. For decades, Wilma played the thorn in management's side, and not just that of U.S. Steel. Over the ensuing years and decades, the executives and board directors of many other public companies found themselves provoking the ire of Wilma and her colleagues. Most members of that small group of prominent shareholder activists were men. Wilma became the most well-known female activist in the country, rivalled later only by Evelyn Y. Davis, who found an unusual calling to shareholder activism a few years after emigrating to the United States as a Holocaust survivor.

"Corporate activist" and "gadfly" were probably the most common words used to describe Wilma, but she preferred the term *gladfly*. *The New Yorker* once referred to her as "the liveliest and most combative lady capitalist we know." Some saw her as crazy; others, as an astute feminist advocating financial autonomy for women. Perhaps some truth permeated all those depictions, including Wilma's laudatory view of herself and her optimistic view of the potentially uplifting role of the *gladfly*.[46]

Wilma became well-known for her enthusiasm for shaking up corporate America, even if she was not always immediately successful. Photographs of Wilma, invariably standing up tall at annual stockholder meetings, wagging her finger at the nation's biggest executives, graced newspapers and magazines across the country. A few short years after rising at the Steel meeting, Wilma, with her larger than life personality, and her dedication to empowering small investors, became the inspiration for a successful Broadway play (1953) and then a movie (1956), *The Solid Gold Cadillac*, starring Judy Holliday and Paul Douglas. Soon after, Wilma launched her own radio show on NBC, *Pocketbook News,* in which she dispensed commentary and advice in the cause of increasing financial literacy. But in May 1947, all that lay in the future. Wilma was already successful, but she was just beginning to embark on the shareholder activist path that would rocket her into the national spotlight.[47]

$ $ $

Although a pioneer, FOWSAB was not America's very first female investor organization. In the heart of the Great Depression, Cathrine Curtis launched Women Investors in America and served as its national director. Curtis, like Wilma, was a highly unusual woman for her times. Not only had she been a Hollywood actress in the days of the silent film, she also had formed in 1919 her own studio company, which only a few women around the world then could boast. The formation of Cathrine Curtis Company revealed Curtis' deep interest in business, which her father had nurtured in her when she was growing up in Albany, New York. Innately intelligent, Curtis benefitted in her early years from private tutors and attendance at New York University in an era when few women went to college. Discussing her film company, Curtis said, "I'm fond of business, so I decided on this venture—or maybe you'd call it adventure." The *Los Angeles Times* reported, "It would appear that Miss Curtis inherits the business faculties of her father, who is George Taylor, a retired New York capitalist." Her father's business connections likely played a role in Curtis' film company receiving the financial backing of some on Wall Street, including several NYSE members who agreed to serve as directors on its board.[48]

In 1919, the *Los Angeles Times*, which a month earlier had
referred to her as "an adventurous lady," portrayed Curtis as a
confident woman who shattered expectations. With the headline
"Cathrine Curtis Prefers to Drive," the article detailed how she drove
herself in "her Marmon roadster" from Los Angeles to the Coeur
d'Alene mining district in Idaho to film on location there. The
high-end automobile of its era, the Marmon enjoyed a reputation for
speed. Curtis, "president and executive manager of the film corporation which bears her name," was, in the newspaper's words, "a skilled
driver" who once "entertained ambitions to set a cross-continent
record for a woman driver."[49]

Given Curtis' entrepreneurial tendencies and her business savvy,
it is not surprising that she went on to found Women Investors of
America, Inc. (WIAI). The organization's objectives, delineated in
the company's 1935 charter, were numerous and broad. "Investors"
notably did not just mean investors in common stock. The objectives
were "to provide a non-partisan, non-profit making agency through
which the women of the United States may be aroused to *the realization of the stake they hold in the nation's wealth and prosperity*, whether
they be wage-earners, property owners, or homemakers; to support
legislation which has for its object the protection and preservation
of industry; to oppose legislation which is economically unsound;
to revitalize recognition of the basic American distinction between
sovereignty and government, and to protect investments by seeking
to preserve the underlying values thereof." Curtis' fame, as well as the
fact that she had become a lecturer on financial matters, helped her
to secure the directorship of the new organization.[50]

Unlike FOWSAB, WIAI did not focus on building up women
as stockowners or increasing their presence in corporate America.
Moreover, despite the allegedly non-partisan nature of the organiza-

tion, WIAI did evince an anti-New Deal, conservative Republican slant. Its "platform, as outlined in news dispatches, raises a suspicion that there is more than the protection of women investors behind it." Indeed, in addition to conducting financial education seminars, the WIAI also targeted the New Deal by, for example, protesting President Roosevelt's unpopular and unconstitutional court-packing scheme in 1937.[51]

Serving as national director of WIAI gave Curtis a platform to speak on topics of financial literacy as well as politics. For a short time prior to the creation of WIAI, she hosted a biweekly radio program, "Women and Money," that aired on the American Broadcasting affiliate WMCA in New York City. On the show, which ran from early 1934 until February 1935, she dispensed financial advice along with political commentary, much as Wilma would later do on NBC. At a time when the stock market remained depressed, albeit above its rock bottom levels of mid-1932, Curtis instructed women listeners on how to invest, something she had learned from her father. After corporate executives canceled the show, which she attributed in part to her gender, Curtis founded not only WIAI, but also the Women Investors Research Institute. In her efforts to spread financial education to women, she often spoke to small gatherings. In one talk, entitled "Your Investment in America," delivered to clubwomen in Montclair, New Jersey in 1935, Curtis berated men who chose to keep the women in their lives in the dark about finances. Curtis found that deeply ironic, given that women spent more than 80 percent of consumer dollars in the country and owned a significant percentage of the nation's wealth.[52]

Whether it was the anti-New Deal messages or the financial advice or the combination thereof that some women found appealing, Curtis' WIAI boasted roughly 300,000 members spread across 28 states by 1939. As the world moved towards war, however, Curtis diverted some of her attention to increasing isolationist sentiment in the United States and helping form the Women's National Committee to Keep America Out of War. She invoked women's special role as mothers as justification for the movement.[53]

Wilma formed FOWSAB while WIAI still existed. While Curtis beat Wilma to the punch, twice, with her association and radio program, Wilma would ultimately prove to be much more impactful, if only because her career stretched so much longer. But she also excelled in an area Curtis all but ignored: cultivating allies, that is the male gadflies already on the scene when she burst through the doors.

$ $ $

Lewis Gilbert and his younger brother John had been America's leading advocates of the rights of minority stockholders since the early 1930s. They had been fighting for many of the reforms that also came to animate Wilma. When speaking of his efforts, Lewis Gilbert later recalled, "I realized the time was right to get something for us, the shareholders."[54]

Although they came to espouse many of the same stockholder causes, Wilma and the Gilbert brothers came from different worlds. Wilma was truly a small shareholder, holding in 1947 only a few shares in a single corporation. Although she was very talented, she would never make a fortune and once admitted that she was "probably the poorest of the *glad*flies."[55]

The Gilberts, by contrast, came from a very wealthy and tight-knit family. Thin with a Roman nose that often supported spectacles, and wavy brown hair that grayed with grace as years passed, Lewis Gilbert grew up in a spacious apartment on Park Avenue in

New York City. Along with his younger brother John and his older sister Margaret, he enjoyed all the perks that came with considerable wealth. John would later comment, "I was born with a silver spoon and polished it." Lewis was equally blunt: "Fortunately I did not have to work for a living." He did, for a brief time, work as a reporter, but Lewis's point was that he did not *have* to work. Their family had grown wealthy in the mid-1800s, with their grandparents on both sides founding profitable sole proprietorships, one a woolen mill and the other a chain of general stores. Both began investing in corporations in the 1880s, just as corporations in the United States began to increase in size and influence. The Gilbert children were the beneficiaries of a significant amount of inherited wealth from those investments, enough that they could live off the dividends alone.[56]

Lewis Gilbert, a well-bred and self-assured man who never married, came into his self-appointed role as a stockholder "crusader" after being treated rudely at a stockholder meeting in 1933, much like what Wilma would later experience at Steel.[57] At just twenty-five years old, he already had inherited some stocks, including shares in Consolidated Gas Company, which eventually merged into Consolidated Edison. Eager to "see what the company was like," he decided to attend one of its annual meetings.

> I'd never attended a stockholders' meeting, so I expected to be welcomed cordially and to be treated like one of the owners. You can see how naïve I was. The meeting was a disgrace. After the chairman had wasted an hour reading the annual report, which of course, had already been mailed to the stockholders days before, I got up to ask a question, but before I had a chance to say anything, one of the officers sitting in the back of the room made

a motion to adjourn. It was seconded and passed in no time.

Years later, Gilbert remained bitter. "There I was, a part owner—I held ten shares—and I had been treated like a tramp by these people, who were my employees. I was horrified."[58]

Gilbert recalls that as he left that stockholders' meeting, he could "feel a resolve harden within me. I would quit my reportorial job on the paper. I would fight this silent dictatorship over other people's money," a reference to Louis Brandeis' famous tome. "I would devote myself to attending the annual meetings of companies in which I owned stock. I would establish a new avocation, devoting all my time to the cause of the public shareholder." As he left the subway and walked west from Lexington Avenue to his family apartment on Park Avenue, Gilbert vowed to "study corporation law like they did in the old days, watching the great legal minds as they went through their paces at the annual meetings and learn to argue against them in defense of shareholder rights."[59]

Gilbert felt this calling to shareholder activism during the heart of the Great Depression, a time of great disillusionment with big business in the United States and a time of enormous hardship, with one-third of the nation "ill-clad, ill-housed and ill-fed" in President Franklin Delano Roosevelt's famous words. The stock market the year prior, in 1932, had hit its nadir. Consolidated Gas' managers, far from feeling a responsibility to communicate with their worried stockholders, seemed to convey the exact opposite message, judging at least by their behavior towards Gilbert that day.

Other publicly traded companies at the time also struggled to identify what, if anything, they owed their shareholders by way of explaining their business decisions. Many companies in the early part of the twentieth century, before the New Deal, rejected the notion that they ought to fully disclose financial data, even to their own stockholders. Some feared that disclosure could enable competitors, so annual reports often were barebones, a few pages of general information. During the New Deal, though, a series of new securities laws required companies to disclose relevant financial and other information to the public on a timely basis. In addition to an annual report, for example, public companies of a certain size, and all listed companies on national exchanges, had to file with the Securities and Exchange Commission (SEC) a Form 10-K, with more detailed information, and quarterly information, via Form 10-Q. At the time Gilbert went to his first stockholder meeting in 1933, the SEC was still a year from formation.

For a small stockholder like Gilbert to have the audacity to ask questions constituted an unwelcome novelty in the eyes of management. Even fourteen years later, when Wilma stood up at the Steel meeting and delivered her impassioned speech for more women on the board, challenging management at a stockowners' meeting remained unusual behavior. To some, questioning management reeked of disrespect. Wilma and the Gilbert brothers, of course, saw matters differently. They not only had the right, but also the moral duty to interrogate management about company operations. They also felt they had a duty to advance the voices of small shareholders like themselves.

The contempt Gilbert experienced at that 1933 Consolidated Gas meeting convinced him that someone needed to champion shareholder rights. Since he had the time and the inclination, he assumed the task of restoring what he called "stockholder democracy," and eventually recruited his brother John to the cause as well. As *The New Yorker* magazine later reported, "Being of independent means, he [Lewis Gilbert] can spend as much time as he pleases at his chosen work," advocating for stockholder rights and corporate reforms. Gilbert found it stimulating and fulfilling, as it gave his life meaning. He once noted, referring to himself in the third person, that the noted theater critic for *The New York Times* "Brooks Atkinson enjoys the theater. Lewis Gilbert enjoys annual meetings. It's as simple as that."[60]

During the Depression years, Gilbert passionately advocated for companies to keep executive salaries and pensions in check, as he believed corporate executives should not rake in large amounts of money when dividends to stockholders were being cut, and in some cases, eliminated. With this reform agenda in mind, Gilbert confronted at annual meetings some of the nation's top business leaders.

In 1937, Gilbert attended the annual meeting of Bethlehem Steel in Wilmington, Delaware to protest the salary of its legendary chairman Charles M. Schwab, who at the time was paid $200,000 a year (roughly $3.9 million in 2021 dollars). At the next year's annual meeting, in April 1938, Gilbert proposed that if the company cut its dividend to stockholders, Schwab should either serve without pay or at least suffer a ten percent reduction in salary. *The New York Times* called the meeting "stormy." For the first few hours, Schwab did not speak. But then he gathered his thoughts. The room drew quiet as he began speaking slowly and deliberately, emphasizing that he had devoted his life to Bethlehem Steel. "I intend to continue to devote what few years are left me to the company," he added, "if the directors are willing." Schwab, however, adamantly refused to concede to Gilbert's proposal. "I do not intend to give way to the suggestion of serving without pay," Schwab declared. He defended himself, claiming "This company owes me a debt which it can never repay."[61]

According to some accounts of that meeting, Schwab also told Gilbert that he was "hard up," and indeed, he was. He had made a fortune as head of Bethlehem Steel—estimated at its height somewhere between $25 and $40 million dollars. But he had squandered that fortune through a combination of high-stakes gambling, the ravages of the Depression on share prices, and an opulent, Gatsby-like lifestyle featuring lavish residences in Loretto, Pittsburgh, and Manhattan.

As long-time residents of New York, Gilbert and Wilma were familiar with Schwab's mansion on the Upper West Side. Located at Riverside Drive and West End Avenue between 73rd and 74th Street and dominating the entire block, "Riverside," completed in 1906 with no expense spared, stunned those who saw it. Schwab's chateau strategically overlooked the Hudson River, with beautiful views of the Palisades as well. The mansion boasted more than 50,000 square feet and 75 rooms, all decorated exquisitely, with a European flair. The outside was equally resplendent. By the time of the 1938 annual meeting, though, Riverside streaked towards foreclosure, so Schwab, descending into debt, needed his salary from Bethlehem Steel as much as any down-on-his-luck puddler needed his $5 a day job.[62]

Roughly one hundred stockholders attended that day, a large number in that era, and most of them vigorously applauded Schwab when he spoke of his contributions to the company. Gilbert remained silent, as did three other minority stockholders. Schwab was not done. He addressed Gilbert directly: "This suggestion [of taking no pay] is the one sad thought in my sixty years of business experience. Will you, Mr. Gilbert, withdraw it?"

"As a personal favor?" Gilbert asked.

"Yes," Schwab responded. Gilbert, knowing he had been defeated, replied in gentlemanly fashion, "As a personal favor, I withdraw the suggestion." The stockholders, most of whom over-whelmingly favored management and loved Schwab, clapped vigor-ously a second time.[63]

Schwab rested back in his chair, satisfied, and said somewhat chidingly to Gilbert and the audience, "Only by kindness, encour-agement, not by criticism, can we become successful." He told stock-holders that the current President of Bethlehem Steel, Eugene Gifford Grace (1876-1960), was "the ablest man in the industry," and hence deserving of stockholder approval. Schwab concluded, "And now let us be harmonious and merge ourselves into one great family." The tussle ended up meaning little in practical terms as roughly a year after Gilbert's challenge, Schwab died in debt with only a small apartment. Riverside lay in foreclosure, and an era had ended.[64]

With a talent for self-promotion that rivalled Wilma's, Gilbert often retold the story of his confrontation with Schwab to magazine and newspaper reporters, with Gilbert playing the role of Robin Hood on behalf of small stockholders who wanted their company run frugally and efficiently. He also related it in his 1956 book *Dividends and Democracy*. Curiously, Gilbert always omitted one salient detail from the story. He was not the first to question Schwab's pay and his relevance.

Two years prior, in 1935, he had joined two other small stockhold-ers to protest Schwab's pay. One of them, the widow Mary Gallagher, insisted that it was immoral for Schwab to reap such large compen-sation as the company struggled. Indeed, that year, the combined pay of Chairman Schwab, President Grace, and Vice President R.E. McMahon almost equaled the company's stated profits. Gallagher warned, "No wonder Father Coughlin preaches about blood money. He knows what he is talking about. There is too much of this. Here we are without a cent, while you men store up millions. Mr. Grace should know there are no pockets in shrouds." Leopold Coshland, a stockholder from New York, bluntly suggested that "there comes a time when a man outlives his usefulness," and introduced a resolution that would have capped the salaries of Schwab, Grace, and McMahon to a percentage of annual profits had it passed.[65]

Gallagher, livid about the perceived injustice of Schwab's pay, faded from the scene, never again making headlines. Gilbert would take up the torch against Schwab's compensation, periodically allying himself there and at other annual meetings with Coshland and other disaffected stockholders.

By 1947, Schwab had been dead for less than a decade, but his beloved Riverside mansion already had been sold to a developer. A year later, its demolition made room for apartment buildings.

About that time, the Gilbert brothers discovered Wilma. Determined to put her own imprint on the annual meeting and put forward her own agenda, albeit one that often coincided with the Gilberts', Wilma joined Lewis, John, and other gadflies in the realization of something powerful—ownership of a single share of stock gave them certain rights, including the right to participate in the annual stockholders' meeting. It gave them a venue to publicize their causes and convince other stockholders to align with them. Ever optimists, they believed they could leverage their one share to effect positive change, one company at a time. Garnering media coverage of their showdowns with management on annual meeting days was critical. Perhaps they could embarrass management into changing their ways or amass enough support from other shareowners to effect change.

The notion of corporate democracy, though, was not as far-fetched as it might seem today. In postwar America, individual retail investors, not institutional investors, dominated the stock market. The 1940s and 1950s was the era of the individual investor and hence a time when a stockholder activist was likely to arise from the retail ranks. Whether activism could be successful, however, was a different story.

Before Wilma joined the fray, the Gilbert brothers had not experienced many wins. Lewis insisted that he and his brother had made much progress, but the record tells a different tale. There was, however one notable achievement. Thanks to the Gilbert brothers, stockholders had a potentially powerful tool at their disposal by the time Wilma announced the formation of FOWSAB. SEC Rule X14a-7 (now Rule 14a-8), the so-called "town hall rule," allowed stockholders to put their own proposals on the proxy statements that management sent before each annual meeting.[66]

Many managers opposed the rule, with one arguing that "the SEC is daydreaming if it thinks it can make a modern company run according to the principles of Athenian democracy." Managers did not fight back too hard, though, because they understood the rule could not dislodge them. They could oppose stockholder proposals with statements of their own and even if a resolution passed, it was merely a request. Management was not legally bound to implement it.[67]

After the SEC announced the townhall rule in 1938, Lewis Gilbert liked to uphold it as "the small stockholders' Magna Carta." Prior to its passage, small stockholders found it extraordinarily difficult to introduce a resolution at an annual meeting as they had to assume the onerous and expensive task of notifying all stockholders of the proposed resolution prior to the meeting. X-14 changed all that by shifting the responsibility from the shareholder to management. If a stockholder wished to bring forth a resolution, the company needed to include it in the proxy statement that it had to distribute to all stockholders before the meeting. X-14 could have been a game-changer, as it meant that ordinary stockholders had not much to lose by offering a resolution. But there was also not much to gain as most stockholder resolutions lost, in part because management reserved the right to vote the many proxies that shareholders failed to return.[68]

Wilma was the type to see the glass as half full, not half empty. Maybe, just maybe, if she could get the Federation of Women Shareholders in America off the ground, she could affect meaningful change. An old adage on Wall Street was a "man's word is his bond." Wilma believed that. She had given her word at that 1947 U.S. Steel meeting she was forming FOWSAB and that's exactly what she would do.

3

PINNACLE OF POWER

*As a woman who for years has competed in the business
world, I would be the first to agree that the American
woman has almost unbelievable economic power, but
American women, like women of all civilized nations, do
not use the influence their economic power gives them.*

—Mary Roebling, one of FOWSAB's founders.[69]

Wilma "had not planned to be the Carrie Chapman Catt of
women investors," noted *Kiplinger's* in 1949. "But," after the
U.S. Steel 1947 meeting, "the press picked up on her words. Reporters
besieged her for details. Women wanted to join." True to her word,
Wilma quickly formed The Federation of Women Shareholders in
American Business, Inc. (FOWSAB). By September, the non-profit
organization was firmly in place, chartered with the approval of none
other than Justice Ferdinand Pecora, who had headed a damaging

investigation into Wall Street in the early 1930s. The three officers of the new corporation were President Wilma, of course, Vice President Ruth Bryan Rohde, and Treasurer Mary G. Roebling.[70]

All three of the Federation's founding officers were civic-minded and interested in advancing women's roles as investors and participants in "corporate democracy." Rohde and Roebling were well-known, highly talented and from opposite sides of the aisle. Remembering some of the lessons of the suffrage movement decades earlier, Wilma knew that unity for the cause was critical for success.[71]

Born in 1885, Rohde was the daughter of the famous orator and politician William Jennings Bryan, who failed three times in his quest to become President of the United States on the Democrat/Populist ticket. His 1896 "Cross of Gold" speech, decrying the effects of the gold standard on American farmers and ranchers, remains one of the most moving pieces of political rhetoric in American history. Like her father, Rohde had a gift for public speaking and a deep interest in politics. Like her mother, Mary Baird Bryan, one of the few women lawyers in the country in the 1880s, she possessed a keen intellect. Elected to Congress in 1928 as a Democrat, Rohde staunchly supported various women's issues while pioneering new roles. She was the first congresswoman to serve on a major congressional committee, the House Foreign Affairs Committee, and later, in 1933, the first woman to fill a significant diplomatic post, Ambassador ("Minister") to Denmark. Most recently, prior to the formation of the Federation, she had served, at President Roosevelt's behest, as special assistant to the State Department, tasked with helping draft the United Nations' charter.[72]

Although twenty years younger than Rohde, Roebling was also self-assured, smart, and confident. She became one of the first women in the country to head a major urban depository institution when named president of the Trenton Trust Company during the Depression. Roebling passionately advocated for equal rights, and it is easy to see why Wilma's particular cause piqued her interest. Notably, though, for Roebling, the Federation was a way to advocate for the value of the free enterprise system, a core belief. Her hatred of communism was equally as strong.[73]

The Federation, however, came to be dominated by Wilma. Roebling and Rohde quickly gained additional serious responsibilities in other areas of their professional lives, in part because their talents had come to the attention of President Harry Truman. In 1949, just two years after the Federation formed, Truman made Rohde alternate delegate to the United Nations General Assembly. In 1950, Truman appointed Roebling to the Citizens Advisory Committee on Armed Forces Training Installations, a job requiring extensive travel to the country's military bases to assess conditions. He named Roebling in part because the Committee lacked any female members to that point. Deeply committed to the military, especially women's roles in the military, Roebling in 1951 joined the Defense Advisory Committee on Women in the Services. Shortly thereafter, in the mid-1950s, Roebling became the first female governor of the American Stock Exchange and, in later years, served on the Citizens Advisory Council to the Commission on the Status of Women, as well as the Task Force on International Private Enterprise.[74]

The very title of the Federation reveals how plugged in Wilma was to the times and to the thoughts of some business leaders. The name was "Federation of Women *Shareholders*," not "Women *Stockholders*." In 1947, the term "stockholder," not "shareholder" or "shareowner," remained the most common word to describe owners of equities, but a few prominent members of the financial community, like brokerage firm partner Edward F. Hutton and editor B.C.

Forbes, sought to change that. Wilma later conceded that the term "shareowner" would have been even better in her organization's title, as "owner" conveyed to many a more active investor role than the passive term "holder."[75]

Wilma planned to run FOWSAB for only three months before turning over control to somebody else, ending her "sabbatical," and returning to the PR game. She ended up running the organization for the rest of her life, despite the fact the position was unpaid, and in fact at times drained money out of her pockets. It may simply have been the case that Wilma, who served as president and later "Chairma'am," could not find anyone else to run FOWSAB—she was the first to admit that "pioneering isn't easy"—and that she could not obtain a PR gig that interested her, like the one she pursued at International Harvester in 1947. Either way, she loved what she was doing, and the position gave her Wall Street clout and paid speaking opportunities.[76]

Moreover, so many women called her to voice their support after they learned about her U.S. Steel speech that Wilma could not answer them all personally. The outpouring of support, which came from female engineers, lawyers, and students, as well as housewives, compelled her to stick with her announcement. "I had produced a Frankenstein's monster," she later admitted. To back off "would be putting beans up people's noses."[77]

Questions of the organization's scope loomed large. In 1949, *Kiplinger's Magazine* reported, "In a sense, the federation still is feeling its way," but added that it had "decided what it is and what it is not and has worked out a beginning program." The Federation decided that the organization would be "open to any woman who is a stock or bondholder, a savings-bank depositor, an insurance policy holder, or beneficiary, a business or professional woman. Admittedly, this takes in a large part of the country's women." Conversely, the organization was not "an investment advisory service. It is non-profit, non-political. Men may not join." (Later, men were allowed and even welcomed into membership, in tune with Wilma's emphasis on unity being critical to FOWSAB's success.)[78]

At the top of the organization's goals was to get "more women on boards of directors and in policy-making positions," which the organization prioritized "as a measure of economic democracy." Wilma often asserted that women should be on boards in proportion to their percentage in the shareowner ranks. Though often voiced with passion, it's likely she saw that goal as an attention grabber rather than ideal corporate policy. The Federation also sought to increase female attendance at stockholder meetings.

Some of the other parts of FOWSAB's initial program focused on improving corporate standards of reporting and engagement with shareholders on the whole. *Kiplinger's* reported that the Federation sought "better corporation reports, written without mumbo-jumbo, and more post-meeting reports to absentee stockholders," long a Gilbert reform proposal. Another plank in FOWSAB's platform, cumulative voting, also had been advocated for years by the Gilbert brothers. As the magazine explained, "For example, if a woman owns 25 shares and five corporation directors are to be elected, she could cast 125 votes for one candidate or 25 for each of five candidates. Or she could split the 125 among two or three candidates, as she chose." Or, as Wilma more pithily put it, with cumulative voting, shareowners could "bunch" their votes if they wished. In 1954, nineteen states and all national banks mandated cumulative voting. By 1963, thanks in part to FOWSAB, around two dozen states supported it, with additional ones considering the mandate. The three states, however, with the most corporate charters, New York, New Jersey, and Delaware, remained opposed.[79]

The Federation also adopted as part of its program the quest to impart "better economic education for women." *Kiplinger's* added, "Beyond this, Mrs. Soss thinks the Federation may become an economic suffrage movement similar to the political suffrage movement of the first two decades of this century. She is not eager to launch such a crusade but feels that business, by its refusal to recognize women, leaves no other choice." As Wilma explained, "They forced labor to organize; now they are doing the same thing to women."[80]

Expressing confidence that the Federation could make significant progress, Wilma invoked the large number of women investors in leading stocks as evidence of women's potential power. "Why, there are 398,000 women stockholders of the American Telephone and Telegraph Co as compared to 194,000 men . . . Women hold 45 percent of the stock of Standard Oil of New Jersey; 49 percent of the Pennsylvania Railroad, 52 percent of General Motors . . . They control 50 percent of the country's risk capital, pay 42 percent of the income taxes, and make up one third of the working force." Wilma concluded, "We should not be asking, we should be telling them what we want, making our money talk. Here we are struggling to improve the economic status of women when there are six million women stockholders who could unlock the door of opportunity for women by using their votes in industry. I don't know why this should be a new thought, but it seems to strike a lot of people that way." In fact, it was not a new thought, as others, like Cathrine Curtis, had tried to hammer home to women investors their potential power.[81]

But Wilma added her PR power to the message, just as the *zeitgeist* became friendlier thanks to the advent of the Cold War.

Wilma, like Curtis, drove herself to achieve fame. Wilma's PR mentor Harry Reichenbach once described "Fame" as "one of those fascinating women with a past. But she is such a brilliant, scintillating creature that the public eye is dazzled with blind admiration and never peers into the shadow behind her to find out who she is, where she comes from or how she arrived at the pinnacle." Thankfully, we know how fame came to Wilma. She created it, step-by-step, until she considered herself a "star."[82]

$ $ $

A key part of Wilma's fame came from FOWSAB's "Economic Bill of Rights," a manifesto outlining ways to promote women's economic liberation. Indeed, FOWSAB's Economic Bill of Rights harkened back to the broad-based demands advocated by women's rights advocates in the nineteenth and early twentieth centuries. The Declaration of Sentiments signed at Seneca Falls in 1848, insisting on equal rights for women, contained sixteen "sentiments" in total. The sentiments started with the lament that women lacked the right to vote:

- He has not ever permitted her to exercise her inalienable right to the elective franchise.

- He has compelled her to submit to laws, in the formation of which she had no voice.[83]

Wilma placed a lot of her own faith in the power of the corporate ballot and the reforms it could bring. Therefore, FOWSAB's "Economic Bill of Rights," which Wilma helped write in 1947, evoked the spirit of the "Declaration of Sentiments" while focusing more narrowly on economic, financial, and corporate changes. Specifically, FOWSAB's Bill sought to fulfill several aims:

1. To secure women's representation in the executive personnel and management of the companies in which they own stock.

2. To encourage larger attendance by women at stockholder meetings.

3. To encourage more regional stockholders' meetings so that the vast army of housewife stockholders can have an opportunity to attend.

4. To keep women better informed about their rights, privileges, and responsibilities as stockholders and legislation which will affect them directly or indirectly as stockholders.

5. To make the study of economics a required part of the educational curriculum for women.

6. To make it possible for women who have a financial stake in our private enterprise system to express themselves and be heard nationally on matters pertaining to women's, and their families' interest and economic welfare.[84]

It was a shrewd move to position FOWSAB as being in favor of positive things, like rights, rather than standing opposed to men who may or may not have deserved their wealth and status. The 1848 Seneca Falls Declaration perhaps had erred with being combative, listing all the ways "he" had hurt "her." Wilma was herself full of sunshine, and with the savviness of a PR professional, she knew how to be persuasive. As Charles Schwab had told Lewis Gilbert, "Only by kindness, encouragement, not by criticism, can we become successful."

Wilma amplified this positivity in various speeches, positioning FOWSAB's mission in terms of freedom, specifically, the freedom to assemble, communicate, discuss, report, vote, and live free of "fear and reprisal." In specific campaigns, like that for the secret ballot, she emphasized that FOWSAB "is for a free economic vote and opposed to an instructed or coerced vote." She also made clear that FOWSAB was "PRO-STOCKHOLDER," not "ANTI-management nor labor." FOWSAB was "the ONLY group who fights for women AND stockholders."[85]

Wilma carefully established common ground with her audiences before moving on to specifics, especially on controversial topics. Her position paper on the women's liberation, consumer, and environmental movements brilliantly exemplified that rhetorical strategy. Wilma started by noting that stockholders were people, not statistics, and like other people they wanted "to breathe fresh air, drink clean water, drive safe cars, eat healthful foods and, in general, improve the quality of life." Then she spoke her mind. Consumers and environmentalists should have a say, but their movements should not be "used as a cloak to destroy mass production, . . . [which] produces dividends . . . [and] has given us the highest standard of living for the most people." Moreover, "REAL liberation" for women consisted of "control over their money and capital."[86]

$ $ $

Soon after Wilma and her Federation started demanding that women be appointed to more boards, some companies and business organizations named women as directors. New York Life Insurance Company, for example, appointed to its board Mildred McAfee Horton, former president of Wellesley College and, during the war, head of the Women Accepted for Voluntary Emergency Service (WAVES), a unit of the U.S. Navy Reserves. The Committee for Economic Development (CED) named Sarah Blanding, president of Vassar College, to its board. *Kiplinger's* credited Wilma (not her Federation) as "the somewhat surprised initiator of these developments," although it is unclear whether women like Blanding and Horton might have been appointed to those boards regardless of Wilma's crusade. In any event, the number of women serving on corporate boards remained infinitesimal, and many business leaders resisted Wilma's suggestion. As *Kiplinger's* reported, "Several corporation presidents have said to Mrs. Soss, '*Make* us put a woman on our boards, and we will.'" The magazine, however, seemed to be in Wilma's corner, opining, "The chances are that she will, and they will."[87]

Meanwhile, besides advocating for more women on corporate boards, Wilma also pressed for a goal of hers since 1946—inducing U.S. Steel to move its meeting location away from Hoboken. In October 1948, Wilma went to her third U.S. Steel meeting: "I decided Hoboken must go, and I told them so." The reaction was not as cordial as her experience the year before. As Wilma recalled, "It was at that meeting that I stopped getting the sort of tender applause big strong men like to hand out to dear little women flushed with pretty anger." The more negative reaction, however, was not a deterrent. As corporate executives would begin to understand, Wilma was stubborn in her demands, and, like the Gilbert brothers, willing to endure continued rejection of her proposals in the hopes that one day they might get passed. At the very least, Wilma, ever the publicist, understood that putting forth a proposal would garner media attention, and even more attention if it were presented in a captivating way.[88]

Therefore, at the U.S. Steel annual meeting the following year, 1949, Wilma upped her game, dressing in a costume for the event—a media-grabbing tactic Harry Reichenbach surely would have endorsed. She donned one of her mother's old dresses, appropriate for a U.S. Steel meeting in 1901, not 1949. The Gay Nineties costume, which included a wool dress with bustle, a small fan, checked spats and a lorgnette "created a sensation . . . all over the country" after it went out on the AP photo wire.[89]

Her garb, which included "a bunch of violets from which protruded a small American flag," also landed her on primetime TV, in costume, on a show called "We, the People" that aired at 9 p.m. on 10 May. The 30-minute talk show ran on the CBS radio network from 1936 until switching to CBS television in 1948 and 1949 and then to NBC TV until 1952. Highly rated at first, the show's popularity peaked in August 1948 when ex-Soviet spy Elizabeth Bentley appeared to beseech her fellow spies to flip or be ratted out.[90]

Wilma was no shrinking violet, and the publicity-seeking side of her knew how to recognize an opportunity. She well knew the strategies of the Gilbert brothers, who occasionally would wear something salient to an annual meeting to attract attention. Not to be outdone, Wilma added a tag line: "Gentlemen, my case. I have suited my costume to management's ideas of stockholder relations." The old-fashioned dress was not just meant to tell management that they treated women shareholders in a non-modern way; Wilma also wanted to convey that management behaved in a generally outdated manner by continuing, for example, to hold the annual stockholder meeting in Hoboken.[91]

Some shareholders reacted negatively to the stunt. One stock-holder, who had come to Hoboken from Brightwaters, Long Island that day, mocked Wilma as "Mrs. Apple Soss," thinking her performance was unbefitting the gravitas of an annual meeting. Another stockholder, Neal Grootegood, from Mineola, took Wilma's attire more good-naturedly, slyly remarking that he certainly endorsed costumes and that he hoped the attractive gadfly would come to the next one in a bathing suit. Reporter Andy Logan from *The New Yorker* remarked, "There are undoubtedly a number of captains of American industry who wouldn't care what Mrs. Soss wore if she would just stay away."[92]

Wilma made an impression at that 1949 meeting. She did not, however, come anywhere close to getting management to change its ways. Although more than one half of individual shareholders in Steel were women, women present at the meeting and those sending in their votes in proxy did not support her *en masse*. Nor did the men, or the wives of U.S. Steel execs like Mrs. Olds. No "lady" was elected to the board of directors that year and the resolution proffered by FOWSAB to relocate the annual meeting to New York City met overwhelming defeat—8,889,042 shares to 558,802.[93]

Wilma and the Federation clearly faced a tough road ahead. Just as the Gilbert brothers struggled, FOWSAB, too, found little to brag about. But Wilma was becoming famous in the process and victories would come. Some 2,000 stockholders booed Wilma in 1949 for asking Standard Oil of New Jersey to move its annual meeting to New York City from Flemington, in the wilds of New Jersey. In 1951, however, management agreed to the change and later also agreed with Wilma's idea to rotate venues regionally.[94]

Wilma could be stubborn and relentless. While she and the Federation began to spread their attention to other companies, she couldn't let Steel go. There was still work to be done and she refused to give Olds and the board the satisfaction. So, on February 27, 1950, when Steel convened a meeting for stockholders to ratify its pension agreement, she trekked yet again to Hoboken. By that time, Wilma was beginning to coordinate more with the Gilbert brothers. Reporters would sometimes refer to them as the "Gilbert-Soss trio" or the "Gilbert-Soss clan." But the Gilberts rarely went to meetings together; if Lewis went, John would attend a different meeting, often on the same day. So another stockholder, James Fuller of Hartford, joined in on the fun with Lewis Gilbert and acted "in cahoots with Mrs. Soss", as *Life* magazine would later report.[95]

The meeting that day in the winter of 1950 could have been a quick one, because the union agreement was already a *fait accompli*. The company had amassed sufficient proxy votes prior to the meeting to ratify the deal, so the meeting was a mere formality. Approximately 350 stockholders showed up anyway, but even if everyone present voted against the proposed measure, it would have still passed. That knowledge, though, did not deter Wilma, her Federation colleagues, or the Gilbert brothers.

The meeting was notable in several ways. First, for a special stockholder meeting to attract 350 stockholders was unusual. A few years earlier, a regular annual meeting of a large corporation would not have attracted so many. Second, of the stockholders present, a majority were women, many formally and informally part of the Federation, now three years old. They showed up in conservative attire—no costume for Wilma that day. Like her colleagues, Wilma dressed in a dark, professional suit, with a silk blouse and a pillbox hat. Wilma did not always wear costumes to meetings, but she almost invariably spoke at them, and was usually depicted as "leaping to her feet" when she wished to make a point. Sometimes sweet and sometimes sassy, Wilma knew how to put on "a really cracking good show," as one hardware dealer described it. "The liveliest and most combative lady capitalist" around magnetically attracted reporters eager for a good story. Third, the meeting was contentious—more than the earlier meetings Wilma had disrupted.[96]

Life magazine correctly sensed the tension in the room that day and the rising militancy of the stockholders present. The article began with the lede: "No doubt about it American business was beginning to take on some of the more frightening characteristics of a matriarchy. What happened at a U.S. Steel stockholders' meeting in Hoboken, N.J. on February 27 proves it." The article hailed Wilma as the "most articulate spokesman" for the women present in the room and noted Wilma's disapproval of the fact that the company, in which she now owned five shares, had brokered a deal with the Congress of Industrial Organizations (CIO) without consulting stockholders in a meaningful way. She was not just concerned with that pension agreement; she and her Federation colleagues raised numerous issues that day. The company's public relations policies needed vast improvement. As she complained, "We might be nationalized because they [Steel's public relations policies] are so poor." Wilma's comment was prescient, as the company later would temporarily be taken over by the government during a steelworkers strike in 1952.[97]

Wilma kept jumping to her feet with additional criticisms. It infuriated her that Chairman Olds received an annual salary of $164,200—in her mind, that was excessive as it took funds directly out of stockholders' dividend checks. She was also upset that U.S. Steel had set aside $50,000 for Olds when he retired and had also promised $50,000 each to two other executives in their pension agreements. Gilbert and Fuller also grilled Olds about the pensions. Olds was apoplectic and by the time the meeting ended, he reportedly "was hoarse and arm-weary from banging his gavel, one stroke of which had broken his watch."[98]

Olds experienced something new—stockholders taking an active interest in the operations of the company they owned. The number of people attending that meeting—and the noise they made—was one indication, but so, too, were the sheer number of proxies Steel received prior to the meeting. Historically, many stockholders—small and large—would not bother to send in their proxies. But this time, Steel collected proxies representing a majority of all shares. That doesn't mean more than half of all stockholders sent in their proxy votes, but it does represent a meaningful level of involvement. Steel shareholders across the United States were taking more interest in what management was doing, and potentially might hold managers accountable. As Gilbert reprimanded Olds that day, "You forget the shareholders own U.S. Steel, not the Board of Directors."[99]

Steel's management, in turn, tried to be more polite to shareholders and offer the appearance of caring about their concerns. While Steel kept its Hoboken location that year, the company did offer a token measure—offering free bus service to its Union Club meeting site and free lunch to attending shareholders. Publicly traded corporations in the United States would eventually be required to have well-developed stockholder relations departments (sometimes called "investor relations"), but at mid-century, companies like Steel, although aware of the need for public relations, were just beginning to think of investors as another group to cultivate.[100]

$ $ $

Testifying before the SEC in 1952, Wilma claimed that her organization had a broad swath of members, representing different income groups and professions: "Our members consist of large and small—chiefly small—stockholders . . . Many are widows. Some are employee stockholders. Some were active in the women's political suffrage movement and now are pioneering in the exercise of women's economic suffrage." She explained that FOWSAB aimed to facilitate the banding together of women shareholders "so as to help preserve the right of free enterprise, increase the productivity of our private enterprise system, and to combat influences detrimental thereto."[101]

When pressed, she remained intentionally vague about the size of FOWSAB's ranks. Her populist appeal and vivacious personality were not enough to make the organization a mass movement. Contemporary observers, however, could hardly have guessed—between the newspaper headlines, magazine features and chatter in and outside the workplace, FOWSAB was larger than life. Author Joseph Livingston characterized the "Mrs. Soss point of view" as "radically different form that of Jackman [at Forbes' League] or Javits [of the United Shareholders of America]." He explained, "She is a corporate suffragette. She argues that women own a large share of the nation's wealth. They ought to be represented on boards of directors."[102]

If Mr. Livingston had seen the day-to-day of Wilma's brainchild, however, he might have offered a different review. Wilma initially ran FOWSAB out of her apartment on lower Park Avenue. All the paperwork shared the space with Wilma, Joe, and Wilma's aging mother. She kept her work on FOWSAB rather quiet at first, fearing infiltration by "powerful forces" not enamored with the idea of a pro-stockholder organization. As a result, FOWSAB required written recommendations and cash-paid application fees before accepting anyone as a member.[103]

Wilma played advertising and PR consultant for FOWSAB too, contacting various "clubwomen program planners" and publications, including Life Magazine. By its second annual meeting in 1949, FOWSAB boasted members from 23 states, although only a few were "real frontline troops who regularly take part in the excursions to stockholders' meetings." Wilma would eventually garner publicity for her Federation in outlets as diverse as Mademoiselle, American Banker, and the Commercial and Financial Chronicle by making sure her media contacts were well greased with free tickets to FOWSAB events. She also supplied authors and editors with all sorts of information for their stories, including a remarkable paper called "Poor Little Rich Girl vs. Enfranchised Lady Shareholder," and a series of bio blurbs on "Women of Achievement." Sometimes her efforts panned out. Other times, not so much. Life, for example, needed more "dramatic pictures" of "a picturable and newsworthy event to pin our coverage on" and Newsweek dragged its feet so long the reporter felt it necessary to write Wilma a long apology. Time dallied, and ultimately demurred. Another reporter, for The Reporter, relayed that "the Editor didn't buy the idea." The manager of Ladies' Home Journal urged Wilma to provide "specific factual material" to back up claims about female wealth ownership that reporter Sylvia Porter made, citing FOWSAB, in a syndicated newspaper article.[104]

When good press appeared, Wilma thanked the appropriate editors and writers and tried to plant seeds for additional stories. She was also keenly interested in how the articles were received. Ruth Moore, author of an article on FOWSAB in *Kiplinger's* called "Women Own American Business," told Wilma that the magazine had received "quite a bit of response" to the article and that "several readers who said they were interested in joining the federation have asked for your address." She talked Moore into sending 68 copies of the article to Wilma's closest friends and business associates, including gadflies like Lewis Gilbert, former PR clients like E. S. Evans, and FOWSAB officers like Mary Roebling.

Via FOWSAB, which described itself as "as American as apple pie," Wilma tried to influence corporate policy privately, through back channels. For instance, she tried to induce Chairman McCormick to talk International Harvester into issuing post-meeting reports to all shareholders instead of providing simple transcripts only to those who requested one. Every month, she sent out several dozen letters to board chairmen on FOWSAB letterhead. At the bottom came the reminder that "if you are a stock or bondholder, a savings bank depositor, an insurance policyholder or beneficiary, a business or professional woman, or a consumer YOU are a shareholder in American Business." She enjoyed using "dollar green type" in FOWSAB communications. The medium was the message, reminding women shareholders "to use their economic franchise more intelligently and MAKE THEIR INVESTMENT DOLLARS TALK in a world where money does the talking but women have been mighty mum!"[105]

Wilma never disclosed the number of dues paying members of FOWSAB to the press or even its own members, ostensibly because some members objected. Wilma stressed instead the quality of the membership, which included attorney Helen Lehman Buttenwieser, niece of New York's Depression-era governor Herbert H. Lehman, Roebling, Rohde, and so forth.[106]

Wilma did admit that she wished many more women would join FOWSAB. Some reporters estimated membership at 1,500, and others at over 1,000, but internal records show that both estimates were much too high. Some members were businesswomen who believed in shareholder activism, some were widows looking for guidance and protection, and some were younger women with feminist views. At first, guests had to pay to attend FOWSAB programming but were expected to become members if they wanted to continue to attend.[107]

FOWSAB, like Wilma herself, had reached the pinnacle of its power by the mid-1960s, a period when men and women approached the seemingly almighty Wilma on the radio with personal matters, including landlord-tenant, lemon automobile, and patent disputes, if they could tie their concerns in any way to stock prices, "better shareholder relations," or "more women in the management ranks."[108]

But behind the scenes, FOWSAB remained humble. Wilma, a secretary (sometimes volunteer, sometimes paid), a revolving door of officers, and any other volunteers Wilma could scrounge performed three major functions for its members.[109]

The first was informational and educational. For example, it sent out a monthly Calendar of Stockholder Meetings to help members to schedule their attendance. Despite the name, the calendars were more like briefs that provided members with background on the company and FOWSAB's interactions with it.[110]

Meetings often featured speakers well-known on Wall Street, including John Kugel on the threat of another depression, A. W. Zelomek on the changing nature of the U.S. stock market, William H. White on stock market analysis, and John W. Shulz on stock market forecasting. By 1953, FOWSAB offered an impressive array of workshops, eventually branded "Money Matinees," starring various "guest conductors" who helped members to better understand investment policies, market timing, value investing, and portfolio management.[111] FOWSAB also sponsored lecture series. In 1952, FOWSAB ran a six-lecture series, featuring Professor Edward F. Willett of Northeastern University, E.F. Hutton's Gerald Loeb, value investor Benjamin Graham, and monetary expert Franz Pick, at Carnegie Recital Hall. Events like these would continue throughout

FOWSAB's tenure, including an All-Day Woman Investor's Clinic held annually at the Waldorf-Astoria. By the mid-1960s, FOWSAB events drew hundreds of attendees.[112]

FOWSAB's second function was inspirational. Wilma firmly believed that young couples were critical to the future of shareholder democracy, so she encouraged their participation in FOWSAB and the stock market by offering a lecture series on Friday evenings, with reduced rates for husband-and-wife tickets, "in order to make it possible for many young career people to attend." Wilma also sent off Christmas or New Year's cards every year to remind people of her exploits and encourage their involvement in the next fight against poor management. Correspondents like Evelyn Kovacs of Trenton, New Jersey, credited FOWSAB with inspiring her "club" to purchase shares in "companies [with] women as major stockholders." Similarly, a "youngster" inspired by FOWSAB complained to her representative in Congress when a proposed bill threatened to exclude her from annual stockholder meetings, citing an instance when she, as the owner of two shares, had spoken out at the meeting of a large power company.[113]

FOWSAB's third function was to agglomerate corporate voting power. Wilma often went to meetings armed with her one share, plus hundreds of proxies. Many were from FOWSAB members but some also came from "quite a number of male stockholders who have seen her in action and admire either her principles or simply her spirit." FOWSAB pamphlets and membership letters carefully instructed interested members to cross out executives' names on proxy forms and to write in "Wilma Soss or her nominee." Such actions were revocable, the literature noted, and every stockholder's right. "It is to be hoped," read one missive from 1954, "that future proxy forms will provide a convenient space for stockholders to name their own proxies."[114]

By 1950, Wilma was able to vote over 10,000 shares at the U.S. Steel meetings, an impressive number were it not for the fact that they amounted to only 0.033 percent of the corporation's shares then outstanding. Some proxies were simply turned over to Wilma's discretion, but other shareholders wanted FOWSAB to take specific actions. One, for instance, insisted that Wilma "always" bring up "at Annual Meetings . . . the question of women on Boards."[115]

When Wilma could not make an important stockholder meeting, she dispatched emissaries from FOWSAB's ranks. Beatrice Kelekian, whose portfolio dwarfed that of Wilma and FOWSAB combined, was a trusted and vocal representative of the Federation, attending meetings Wilma could not and serving as a board trustee until 1966. At its peak, FOWSAB had folks around the country willing to fill-in for the boss. Stella Sterne, for example, often went to CBS meetings, even in Los Angeles, if Wilma was tied up elsewhere. Some companies deliberately scheduled their meetings in hopes of deterring Wilma's attendance but were rarely successful. General Electric, for example, held their 1966 annual meeting on an early morning in Schenectady, New York. She showed up, in a lynx-trimmed stole and matching beret no less, to berate management.[116]

FOWSAB, a tax-exempt, non-profit, non-partisan organization, owned shares itself and by its second annual meeting held three shares of U.S. Steel. It also accepted gifts of stock but did not, by its by-laws, make specific investment recommendations. It was a "protective association" with "NO HIDDEN MASTERS," and not an extension of some brokerage. Eventually FOWSAB came to own modest shareholdings in AT&T, CBS, Ferro, GE, GM, International Paper, International Products Corp., Ogden, Philadelphia Reading,

RCA, Singer (which purchased General Precision Equipment, FOWSAB's original holding), Standard Oil of New Jersey, Union Carbide, and U.S. Steel. All except the U.S. Steel and some Woman's Bank shares were gifted to FOWSAB. In keeping with Wilma's buy and hold strategy, they were not sold until the bitter end.[117]

The gadflies never amassed enough shares, or proxies, to effect a corporate takeover. They did, however, find themselves in the middle of one of twentieth century America's most notable corporate fights. Just as Laura Partridge seized control of a fictional conglomerate General Products in the movie *The Solid Gold Cadillac,* Wilma and her Federation would find themselves fighting for control of the New York Central Railroad—a fight later commentators would call the "Battle of the Century."

4

PROXY FIGHTS AND SOLID GOLD

*No woman is free or independent who does not
exercise control over her own money.*[118]

—Wilma Soss

After the war, the fortunes of General Motors (GM) roared. From Chevrolet to Cadillac, GM began churning out record numbers of automobiles as the economy shifted into its peacetime gear. With the NYSE encouraging listed companies like GM to promote share ownership, the number of GM shareowners rose sharply from roughly 420,000 before World War II to almost 500,000 by the end of 1953. The trend continued as the decade wore on and GM routinely sent press releases to the major newspapers. The *Los Angeles Times*, for example, wrote a glowing article in 1954 emphasizing how the burgeoning GM shareowner rolls represented the "broad cross section

71

of the nation's social order . . . Those possessing owner interest in GM are farmers, students, pensioners, families in all age groups, widows and widowers, housewives, professional men and women, wage earners, representatives of virtually every economic group."[119]

On the exact same page, the paper also ran a story headlined, "500,000,000th GM Auto Will Be Gold Plated." GM officials knew that the company was on the verge of producing its 500 millionth vehicle, and they made a concerted effort to celebrate the milestone. It would be a Chevrolet, perhaps because the Chevrolet was widely seen as more of a middle-class car than the luxury Cadillac. It would be manufactured as impressively as possible—a "special gold car," management decided, would be "a fitting monument to one of the outstanding milestones in automotive history." As the *Los Angeles Times* related, "a complete set of metal parts, including 314 pieces of metal trim and accessories and more than 300 screws, nuts, bolt and rivets used to hold the parts to the car, were gold plated."[120]

$ $ $

To a nation weary from war and Depression, the concept of a gold-plated car must have seemed like a fairy tale. If GM could manufacture a gold-*plated* Chevrolet, couldn't they also stamp out a "*solid gold*" Cadillac?

On the evening of November 5, 1953, almost a year before that gold-plated Chevrolet rolled off the assembly line, the play *The Solid Gold Cadillac* debuted at the Belasco Theatre in New York City. Directed by George S. Kaufman, from a screenplay written by Kaufman and Howard Teichmann, it quickly became a hit, running in theaters around the country for more than three years. Hollywood adapted it into a movie, a classic of Hollywood's Golden Age, starring the beautiful A-list actress, Judy Holliday.[121]

The play centered around Laura Partridge, whose character evolves over the course of the story into a vibrant champion for ordinary stockholders. Her character appears to have been based on Wilma and her exploits in shareholder activism after the war. Ever humble, Wilma repeatedly claimed the play was based on her life; the playwrights never denied this. From the time she left her Detroit PR job in 1945 to the time the play debuted in 1953, Wilma had blazed into the small, male-dominated world of shareholder activism, and become a household name. People recognized her as someone who stuck up for the small shareholder, the "little guy." A character in her own right, Wilma was relatable and inspiring—not just in the context of a shareholder meeting, but also, apparently, on the stage of a Broadway theatre.[122]

Laura Partridge is a small shareholder who owns just ten shares of a company called General Products (GP). Partridge cares about the company and her investment, as small as it is. An engaged shareholder, she attends GP's annual shareholder meeting only to find that the meeting is about to conclude in rapid time without anything substantial being discussed. Partridge tries to ask a question about the company's annual report and eventually succeeds in being recognized. She inquires about the CEO's reported annual salary, which she finds a tad excessive. The board tries to evade her question and then defends the pay package, but Partridge remains stubbornly persistent. To try to appease her, General Products decides to make Partridge their first ever Director of Stockholder Relations—a blend of the real Wilma's two careers and a position they mistakenly think will prove insignificant.

Partridge, however, takes seriously her new job to serve GP's five million shareowners. Writing personalized letters back to shareholders who contact the company with various questions and concerns, she cultivates strong relationships with many of GP's small stockholders. Eventually, she also uncovers conflicts of interest, and areas where management is not acting in its stockholders' best interests. A proxy fight ensues, and the army of small share owners surprise Partridge by putting her effectively in control of the company.[123]

Proxy contests in the real world remained rare but were not unknown. In 1950, for example, disgruntled stockholders in the Sparks-Withington Company elected their own slate of directors over management protests, the first time that small stockholders had successfully joined forces to assume control of an NYSE-listed industrial company. A proxy fight was the closest thing to Hollywood's version of the Wild West that existed in corporate America. While general laws prevented the use of actual six-shooters and Winchester rifles, just about everything else was fair game—throwing out shareholders, *Robert's Rules of Order*, common notions of "fair play," and anything else that threatened managerial hegemony. Yet in the play, Laura wins, with help from common folk alert to their own interests. As the curtain draws down, the narrator explains, "And so, a few days later, arm in arm with Prince Charming, Cinderella made another trip downtown. Only this time, not in the subway, not in a coach drawn by six white horses, but in a solid gold Cadillac, driven by a solid gold chauffeur."[124]

The play delighted Wilma, who found it flattering someone would find her story and cause worthy of dramatization. She was even more delighted when the play morphed into a movie. The adaptation, launched in 1956 by Columbia Film, featured some tweaks to the main character, changes that made Partridge considerably more glamourous—even more like Soss.

Teichmann and Kaufman depicted Partridge in the original screenplay as a "timid old lady" who somehow gets up the courage to challenge management. Wilma was 53 years old when the play debuted—not old, by any means, but not young either. But she always had been beautiful, with a luminous presence. Now in middle age, Wilma still took pride in her trim figure, fashion taste and the fact newspapers commented on her appearance and dress.[125]

She was far from dowdy, and yet on stage, the person who played Partridge, Josephine Hull, was described by *The New York Times* as "a plump little lady, a long way past sweet sixteen." Sixty-seven years old at the time she assumed the Partridge role, Hull was a character actor well-known and admired for many plays and screen performances, including as the sweet but crazy widow in the movie *Arsenic and Old Lace* (1944), which starred a young Cary Grant, and a few years later as the sister in the comedy *Harvey* (1950), starring Jimmy Stewart, for which she won an Oscar for Best Supporting Actress. The role of Laura Partridge helped further cement Hull's stardom. Sadly, during the run of the play, Hull suffered a series of strokes. She tried to make a recovery, coming back to the stage for a brief stint after a three-month hiatus. It ultimately would prove difficult and she retired from the show, giving her last performance on August 24, 1954.[126]

For the movie, screenplay writer Abe Burrows remade Partridge into a single woman, much younger and prettier, and even more innocent and naïve. The change in marital status enabled a romance to be woven into the storyline. In the revised plot, Partridge winds up falling in love with Edward McKeever, played by the well-known actor Paul Douglas. The fictional McKeever was the former CEO of

GP who patriotically had left the company for a wartime job with the government, only to find the company poorly run in his absence.[127]

Instead of the matronly Hull, 32-year-old Judy Holliday played Partridge to resoundingly strong reviews. Holliday already was a star in her own right, having won a Best Actress Oscar in 1951 for her performance in the movie *Born Yesterday*. As Partridge, Holliday played a zealous reformer and a staunch defender of capitalism. This emphasis may have been intentional on part of the directors, for Holliday had been accused of being a Communist a few years prior. Appearing before a Senate subcommittee in 1953, she disavowed any connection, past or present, to the ideology or proponents of communism. Now in 1956, Holliday happily made a movie promoting capitalist thinking, albeit with a corporate reform bent.[128]

Praising her performance, *The New York Times* raved, "she is knocking the role completely dead." Newspapers noted the contrast in age and weight between Hull and Holliday. In understated fashion, *The Times* drily noted, "There is not much physical resemblance between . . . [Miss Hull] and Miss Holliday." It went on to say, "The type of stalwart female that the fictional Laura Partridge is has no traceable limitations of social status or age. She is the innocent creature who gets her gentle claws set in a man's hide and then serenely but stubbornly rakes him until he helplessly spouts blood and dies."[129]

With the word "Cadillac" in movie theatres across America, GM was quite pleased. GM publicists lent a helping hand to market the film, bringing to the production set a gold-painted Cadillac. On November 5, 1955, the day the special Cadillac arrived for on-site filming on West Fifty-first Street in Manhattan, a GM press agent was on hand to answer questions about how they got the automobile that golden hue. "It's been sprayed with a powdered gold mixed with lacquer," he explained, "same as is used in gilding gold frames." He went on to relate that GM originally had tried a different hue that the producers and camera men rejected as too dark. A reporter inquired, "Could that mean that a solid gold Cadillac wouldn't look like a solid gold Cadillac on the screen?" The GM press agent declined to weigh in but did note that they had experimented with fifteen shades of gold before landing on the color now before them. Moreover, the job of converting the Cadillac to this gold color required over 300-man hours. Explaining that the conversion process cost roughly $600, *The New York Times* cautioned readers that "Shoppers are not advised to ask for it [a gold Cadillac] at neighborhood car dealers." Besides, the gold wouldn't "stay on the chrome."[130]

Meanwhile, Wilma continued to pursue her corporate gadfly work with zeal, even against GM. After GM's Alfred Sloan opposed regional shareholder meetings because he thought his executives' time would be better spent playing golf, Wilma "turned up in golf clothes to drive home the point that stockholders too play golf and would gladly give up their golf game to meet with executives."[131]

Although she never managed to take control of a major publicly traded corporation, Wilma did help at least one takeover attempt succeed. But unlike Judy Holliday's whimsical trip downtown, arm in arm with Prince Charming, the ending to this story wasn't so glamorous.

$ $ $

Somewhat ironically, Wilma loved trains more than autos. She took many train rides between San Francisco and New York as a youth, summering with her mother in the Bay Area but living most of the year with her grandparents in Brooklyn, where she attended school. During the war, she commuted, apparently weekly, on the New York Central from her Manhattan home to her PR gig in Detroit. Among other goods, her client, Evans Products, made passenger busses and other types of work trucks that could switch between roads and rails.[132]

Already by the Great Depression, many railroads were in the process of losing market share to rivals while contending with a hostile regulatory environment. By the 1950s, giant railroads, once castigated as monopolistic monsters, barely remained in business as their share of the intercity passenger market plummeted to ten percent. Even their long-haul freight market share dropped below half for the first time in over a century.[133]

Wilma wasn't ready to give up on railroads just yet. She believed in investing for the long-term. That meant that when a company started going down what she believed to be the wrong path, she did not follow the "Wall Street Rule" and sell out to some poor sap who wasn't paying enough attention. Instead, she suggested to management an alternate path, for the sake of her own dividend income and to help countless other long-term, small shareowners who would not, or could not, attempt to influence company policy or sell out during downturns.[134]

$ $ $

Given her love of trains and shareowner activism, it was inevitable that in 1954, Wilma found herself embroiled in the struggle to control the New York Central Railroad, a corporate governance fight of such uncommon length and intensity that commentators decades afterward would call it the "Battle of the Century." Such a nickname for a mere proxy contest, a rare competitive election for corporate board seats, was a bit of an exaggeration—but what transpired in this governance fight was certainly worthy of the attention.

By the early 1950s, the New York Central owned more than 10,500 miles of track and other assets worth $2.5 billion. Over 100,000 people worked for it and over 44,000 people owned at least one of its 6.5 million shares of stock outstanding. But the railroad's stock had notably underperformed its peers, angering shareholders and particularly individuals who relied on its dividends to pay their grocery and utility bills, the so-called odd-lotters who owned fewer than 100 shares each. U.S. railroads found themselves "caught in a vise," as "they were not entirely free either to increase their earnings or to reduce their costs." That vise squeezed profits and made it difficult to raise the new capital necessary to make needed improvements.[135]

Into this less-than-ideal circumstance stepped Robert R. Young, the so-called "Populist of Wall Street." According to a biographer, Young "waged unrelenting war on the major investment banks, insurance companies, and law firms" in his quest to keep capitalism appealing to the working class—a group more familiar to Young than his corporate raiding would suggest.[136]

Growing up poor in Canadian, Texas, Young learned to be shrewd at an early age. His first job was a rather menial position at DuPont. But by penning a harsh critique of the company's advertising practices, and offering solutions, he worked his way into a treasurer's office position.[137] He would later take his understanding of corporate finance to General Motors, becoming an assistant treasurer earning $35,000 a year. But Wall Street long held an allure, and Young joined an investment company, Equishares, in 1929. Here, he made a personal fortune shorting the market before the Crash. Capital in hand, Young set out on a series of corporate takeovers.[138]

Young's strategy for takeovers was to win public opinion so that the odd lotters would turn their proxies over to him. In the case of New York Central, he couldn't communicate with shareholders directly because corporate incumbents, his foes, controlled access to their addresses. But there were other ways—Young placed advertisements that lamented that railroad stockholders had "no voice in their management" and called for reforms. Like Wilma, he also ran an organization, the Federation for Railway Progress, and regularly railed against monopolists as well as communists and closed shop labor unions. "You need only look here," Young told a U.S. Senate committee, "to find the devices by which a small group of men have assumed control of many of our great corporations." He knew that the governance game was rigged in favor of insiders and incumbents. As Young explained, through "the use of intimidation of employees, the ins have an almost insurmountable advantages over the outs." Young saw himself as one of the "outs," an outsider trying to muscle his way in to save the railroad, and the small investors who had stuck with the stock.[139]

The New York Central, often simply called the Central, enjoyed a rich history long before Young, or Wilma, got involved. The railroad formed in 1853 to consolidate the ten short railroads connecting Albany to Buffalo. In 1867, Cornelius Vanderbilt purchased control of the line, which soon became a key component in a complex network of rail lines that connected New York City to Chicago. When Vanderbilt died in 1877, he owned 87 percent of the Central's stock and bequeathed it all to his son, who would later sell half his interest to J.P. Morgan. Thereafter, directors in the pocket of Vanderbilt, Morgan, and their heirs controlled the Central. Various shenanigans ensued, all terribly interesting but too numerous to detail here.[140]

What's key to the story, and to Young's involvement, is this: Before the stock market collapsed in October 1929, the Van Sweringen brothers, Oris and Mantis, formed a new transportation holding company called the Alleghany Corporation. Its assets ranged from bankrupt railroads like the Missouri Pacific to real gems like the Chesapeake & Ohio railroad (C&O). In 1937, after the Depression had taken its toll, Young and two partners bought the remnants of the Van Sweringen empire, including 43 percent of the Alleghany Corporation.

This move made Young an enemy of the Morgans, who felt they had a right to *all* assets in distress. As white-shoe financial aristocracy, they saw Young as an inconvenience—someone bold and brash, who would eventually learn his place. When the upstart refused to cooperate, Morgan interests made a move for the C&O. The tussle stressed Young to the point that his mental and physical health collapsed, but he gathered his strength and embarked on what would be his first proxy fight.

During the contest, Young developed many of the techniques, like open letter appeals to small shareholders, that he would later employ in the contest for control of the Central. By soliciting a superior bid for a C&O securities sale from Chicago investment bank Halsey, Stuart and then threatening, as a stockholder, to sue any director who voted to go with the Morgan bid, which would have cost the company an additional $1.35 million, there was little room for the Morgan sides to make their case. They were livid at the loss, of course, but its implications were far more concerning. If competitive bidding for securities issues were to become the norm, an old, comfy way of getting rich would all but fade away.[141]

The battle for the C&O greatly bolstered Young's tough competitor reputation on Wall Street and solidified his standing among many small stockholders as a fighter against entrenched interests. By early 1942, Young was in firm control of Alleghany and its crown jewel, the C&O. It would, however, become a Pyrrhic victory. Both entities became embroiled in a jurisdictional dispute between the New Deal's Securities and Exchange Commission (SEC) and the old railroad regulator, the Interstate Commerce Committee (ICC). Although the outcome of the regulatory turf battle was hardly a victory for Young, his reputation gained when it became clear that many of the Alleghany's operating roads had improved financially under his leadership.[142]

In 1945, Young considered buying Pullman, America's premier manufacturer and operator of railroad sleeping cars. He rightly feared competition from the airline industry, realizing airlines were bound to benefit from the technological improvements induced by the war. But perhaps Young could utilize the upheaval to his advantage. He used a government decree forcing the separation of Pullman's manufacturing and operating companies to launch a bid for control of the service side of the nationwide sleeping car business.

When Young lost traction in the bitter battle with railroad interests, he resorted to mass advertising to garner public support. The most famous of Young's ads proclaimed that "a hog can cross the country without changing trains—but YOU can't!" It was a smashing PR success because, while it ran in only a few newspapers, the message struck such a chord that soon thousands of other newspapers were picking up on the story and discussing Young's ad.[143]

Unfortunately, the PR success wasn't enough. In 1946, Young realized that he was not going to be able to buy Pullman, so instead he went after his leading opponent in the struggle for it, the New York Central. Its stock, recently as high as $35 per share, had dropped to just $13 as the year ended. By January 1947, Alleghany owned about four percent of New York Central's stock, far more than the Vanderbilt interests then owned. By the time Young officially lost his bid for Pullman that March, he owned 400,000 shares in the Central, which shrewdly offered him two board seats, subject to ICC approval. During the ICC hearings, Young and his expert witnesses attested to the importance of directors owning significant stakes in the businesses they directed, noting that in 1920, the Central's board members had owned nineteen percent of the company, but by 1946 they owned less than two percent. It was of no avail as the ICC determined it would be unlawful for Young to run Alleghany, the C&O, and the New York Central.[144]

$ $ $

By the time Young had exhausted his ICC appeals in May 1948, Wilma had firmly entered the gadfly game and gained years of important experience before Young launched his second bid to control the Central in 1954. Her most important contribution to corporate activism in those days was the establishment and development of FOWSAB, which amplified and focused Wilma's corporate voting and PR soft power. But it was her charisma, knowledge, and wits that mattered most, which she brought in full to the second battle for the Central.

Young turned his attention to the Missouri Pacific, which was still trying to reorganize after its bankruptcy, and bided his time while the Central's new president, William White, tried to engineer a financial turnaround. He also quietly brought his personal and corporate ownership of Central stock to over twelve percent.

Young moved on the Central again in 1954. He made sure Alleghany and the C&O were held in friendly hands so that he could become the CEO and board chairman of the Central without ICC interference. He also met with White and promised to keep him and his right-hand man, offering lucrative stock options to guarantee a "yes."

The Central's board rejected Young's overture without much consideration. In doing so, they assumed that because most of Young's shares were sequestered in a trusteeship administered by Chase Bank, a proxy fight would be impossible. The facts were right; the conclusion wasn't. Young rallied numerous non-Morgan-affiliated stockholders, some quite substantial, to his banner, and a proxy fight began.[145]

While nobody was injured during the ensuing "battle," the conflict was eerily similar to the Cold War, then in full swing: phones were tapped, hidden microphones were planted, and security experts were hired to conduct counterintelligence. Both sides also engaged in a propaganda war, with most effort directed towards the state of New York, home to 14,000 of the Central's 44,000 shareholders. In addition to Robinson-Hannagan Associates, a major PR firm in New York, the Central hired Georgeson & Company as its professional proxy solicitor.

Young and his supporters felt no need to hire a PR firm, but they did engage a professional proxy solicitor, Kissel & Company. Also on Young's side were the gadflies, especially Wilma after Young proposed Lila Bell Acheson Wallace of *Reader's Digest* for a directorship and credited Wilma in helping inspire that decision. In a final PR coup, he recruited for the board another member of a group near and dear to Wilma, an odd lotter, who previously served as a train engineer and owned just 80 shares of Central stock.[146]

But the key to the contest seemed to be the 800,000 shares in the Chase trusteeship, which Chase could vote, or not vote, as it saw fit. Young controlled the votes of over one million shares, or eighteen percent of the company, enough, he believed, to ensure victory, especially if he could vote the shares held by Chase. As such, Young arranged for the C&O to sell the shares to a pair of Texas investors friendly to Young.[147]

Prodded by the Central, the ICC started a probe into the sale, but Young was hardly the one to investigate.[148] The Central, which acted as its own transfer agent, refused to transfer the 800,000 shares to the Texans. Noting that the transaction was perfectly legal, the ICC refused to investigate Young any further and the Texans sued the Central to complete the share transfer. Dumbfounded, the Central then claimed that Young could not lawfully control two of the Central's subsidiaries, so he could not lawfully control the Central itself. Legal, consulting, and publicity fees piled up on both sides. The Central spent almost $900,000 in the fight, and Young over $1.3 million. As his legal victories piled up in the weeks before the May 26 meeting, the fees were looking like a good investment.

In a different theatre of the war, Wilma informed the SEC that FOWSAB would introduce three resolutions at the Central meeting in May. Most notable was the secret ballot, so shareowners, especially shareowner-employees, could vote without fear of reprisal. Young backed her, eventually telling Congress that in a proxy fight there must be a secret ballot to ensure fairness.[149]

Even the SEC got involved, on the grounds that New York Central common stock was listed on a major stock exchange. The SEC's rules and procedures on information disclosure were woefully inadequate in the event of a hostile takeover attempt. How could it vet off the cuff statements made to reporters or in the question-and-answer period after a speech? Naturally, Young and his allies were more than happy to bend the rules as much as possible without drawing the SEC's wrath.[150]

The SEC would later update its rules such that public statements need not be submitted to it beforehand. It also ruled the use of fronts, like Young's Texas buddies, impermissible. In the meantime, the SEC could do little to tamp down on the escalating media war, which peaked before the annual meeting when *Fortune* ran an article highly critical of Young that the New York Central illegally mailed to stockholders. It paid $7,000 in fines for its transgression—the best money spent in the entire saga, according to White. Young tried to fight back through advertisements, but the SEC blocked some outright and made him tone down others. It also made him backtrack on claims that the Central would pay dividends of $8 per share under his leadership, music to the ears of stockholders who had received no dividends between 1932 and 1942 and only sporadic payments thereafter.[151]

Attacks and counterattacks continued until the day of the annual meeting. "Both sides are guarding their proxies," *The New York Times* reported, "as if they were hordes of diamonds." And the gadflies, it warned, were ready to "make railroad history" by bringing on the "hubbub and whoop-de-do."[152]

Young went into the meeting with independent stockholders on his side by a two-to-one margin. Professional advertisers polled by *Time* magazine were certain that White would prevail. After agreed upon preliminaries, Wilma took her turn to speak, praising the nominations of Wallace and Young for the board, as well as cumulative voting. White, having little patience, tried to get her to sit. Worked into a frenzy that "startled" even her own "adherents," wagging her right index finger while calling for an end to White's "Alice-in-Wonderland procedure," Wilma audaciously climbed onto the speaker's platform. A uniformed police officer was called in and removed her from the hall.[153]

During voting, rumors swirled that the infamous 800,000 shares would be voted for management, or perhaps not at all. None of this was true, but Young wanted to win by more than 800,000 votes so that Central's current management could not tie up the election in the courts. For three weeks after the meeting, three law professors counted the proxies behind closed, guarded doors.

In the end, Young won big, even without the contested 800,000 shares nominally owned by his two buddies from Texas. White conceded and the Central dropped all remaining lawsuits and protests. Young, who paid himself a dollar-a-year, and his crew took over and immediately waived all director fees until a dividend of at least $2 per share could be paid to stockholders. Wilma was almost as elated as Young. She had made a big splash at the meeting and played a role in getting a woman on the board of a major corporation.[154]

$ $ $

By 1954, investment guru Benjamin Graham believed that thanks to the actions of the gadflies and Young, "stockholder participation" stood poised to develop "into a really effective safeguard of ownership interests." But the delicate alliance between rational capital and activist zeal soon soured as Young's victory proved fleeting. The Central had gone bankrupt amidst the proxy fight, a fact White and his crew forgot to mention. Young had spent years and a fortune on a worthless asset. Even with the aid of Al Perlman, the railroad operations wizard who had taken the Denver & Rio Grande Railroad out of bankruptcy and into a dividend-paying dream, there was little hope for the Central. Some fancy accounting created enough paper profits to drive its stock price just shy of $50 a share but 1957 brought recession to the entire railroad industry and increased competition from the New York State Thruway and the nearly completed St. Lawrence Seaway.[155]

Wilma and Young fell out during the 1955 Central stockholder meeting because Young reneged on his promise to implement cumulative voting and managed to banish Wilma from the main meeting room through a simple "lottery." During the meeting, Young, unchecked by Wilma, behaved in an imperious manner, "resorting to freewheeling parliamentary techniques" to get his way as *The New York Times* put it. "Tycoons rise and fall," Wilma reminded FOWSAB members in a letter that proved eerily prescient. "After the smoke of dispute clears away, that which is good, that which is true, that which is right, endures forever."[156]

Fearing a repeat performance, Wilma hired a bodyguard, professional wrestler Emma Maitland, and a lawyer to attend the 1956 Central meeting with her. All three wore white gloves and Maitland carried Wilma's megaphone, which Wilma used whenever anyone cut her mic, and threatened to use it to "conk" anybody who dared accost Wilma.[157]

While Wilma protested, Young faced a spate of stockholder lawsuits related to his use of the Allegany's resources to win his proxy fight. Other lawsuits dating back to the Van Sweringen era also troubled Young, who was not so spry anymore, or as wealthy as he once was. As the Central's stock fell to $13.50 a share and its dividends sank back to zero, Young fell into depression once again. On January 27, 1958, he took his own life in the billiard room of his mansion in Palm Springs.[158]

Nobody will ever know for certain why Young committed suicide as he left no note, but Wilma via *Pocketbook News,* her new weekly, coast-to-coast NBC radio show, helped to spread the legend that a letter from a widow impoverished by the drop in the company's stock was the final motivation. By 1958, Wilma was clearly disillusioned with Young and offered proof positive of his negative influence on the company, and railroads generally, by noting the big run up in railroad stock prices following news of his demise.[159]

In 1964, Wilma attended the Central's annual meeting in Chicago wearing black satin Pullman pajamas and a black veil to mourn the death of passenger rail service in America. The Central's directors, she noted, *flew* to the Chicago meeting. For at least another decade, Wilma still occasionally waived the bloody shirt of the "Battle of the Century" in her radio broadcasts and showed up at another meeting for the Central barefoot because the company's dividends were insufficient to buy a pair of shoes.[160]

While R. R. Young's railroad empire faded away, Wilma, bolstered further by the success of *The Solid Gold Cadillac*, achieved fame, if not quite fortune. In addition to numerous newspaper and magazine cover stories, like the 1966 *Life* magazine feature that awarded Wilma the title of "Queen of the Corporate Gadflies," she appeared on television several times.

Moreover, her *Pocketbook News* radio program aired nationally and posted large enough numbers, estimated at 3.2 million at one point, to keep her on NBC weekly until 1980.[161]

Wilma also delivered public speeches to pretty much any group that asked her to speak. In 1949, for example, Wilma spoke about "Today's Woman in Finance" before the Municipal Bondwomen's Club of New York and then early the next year in George Shaskan's 12-lecture series, "Investment Planning for Women." In 1963, she took part in a panel presentation at Bryant College in Rhode Island that was widely praised because, according to the college's

Vice President, Charles H. Russell, it "was beautifully balanced" and Wilma "added a wonderful element of humor in addition to important commentary and information." The college's PR director, Gertrude Meth Hochberg, called Wilma "one lovely, lively gal!" who shed her "light on the dark places in the stock market!"[162]

In 1971, Wilma gave a "marvelously invigorating talk" before the National Council of Jewish Women. "I have heard nothing but raves about your metal personality," its president wrote, "which shone through your every word." Wilma also spoke at Harvard, the University of Pittsburgh, and Columbia University. Her Harvard talks were held at the Bull and Bear Club, one of the many student organizations then active at the law school. She also trekked to Chicago at the invitation of a gathering of a shareholder group, with about fifty directors from twenty some corporations in attendance. She was also listed in *Who's Who in America* and was regularly invited to the New York Stock Exchange's Christmas Party.[163]

By the mid-1960s millions of investors and businesspeople knew of Wilma, if not through press coverage of her gadflying antics or FOWSAB then through *The Solid Gold Cadillac* or *Pocketbook News*. Even rival female financial writers conceded that Wilma had "reached great heights of usefulness and service in the realm of women and money." Two years later, her longtime colleague Beatrice Kelekian retired from the FOWSAB board "after long and valued service." FOWSAB's and Wilma's influence was seemingly assured.[164]

But nature—remember that Wilma was born in 1900—and the forces of reaction would start to work against her. Little men like Young, and little women like Wilma, most corporate executives believed, were mere usurpers bent on trickling off power from those with a right to rule. Corporate activists had to be put back in their rightful place, cut down to size and swatted down by their natural superiors. Though the "Battle of the Century" had passed, there was no shortage of fights that lay ahead.

5

CAMELOT COME
AND GONE

Don't let it be forgot, that once there was a spot, for one brief shining moment, that was known as Camelot.

—Alan Jay Lerner as quoted by Jacqueline Kennedy in *Life Magazine* shortly after her husband's assassination.[165]

JANUARY 20, 1961
WASHINGTON, D.C.

On a bitterly cold late January day, a young and seemingly vigorous President John F. Kennedy wore no overcoat as he delivered his inaugural address. Many in attendance stuffed their hands in their pockets to try to keep warm. An intense snowstorm had blanketed Washington, D.C. the day before, creating havoc in the nation's capital and causing many of the pre-inaugural nighttime festivities to be canceled. Observers noted that the weather had not been so terrible for an Inauguration Day since 1909, when the famously well-insulated William Howard Taft took the oath of office.[166]

While some braved the snow-laden streets of D.C., millions of Americans watched from home. Kennedy's inauguration was the first presidential transition broadcast in color. Americans far from the nation's capital, for the first time, experienced details previously reserved for the Washington class—the velvet red stairway, down which a young optimist traveled to stand before the nation; the contrast of Old Glory draped against the Capitol's marble white; the iconic baby-blue coat and pillbox hat adorning the soon-to-be First Lady, working their hardest to shield her from the cold.

Color televisions, though, were not yet common enough for everyone to see the splendor. Many Americans still relied on their less expensive black and white sets to watch the inaugural address. Others listened in, as so many had in the past, on the radio, that stalwart and still-common feature of American homes.[167]

By Kennedy's inauguration, *Pocketbook News* was in full swing. Wilma did not cover politics for its own sake, but she tried to help her listeners understand how politics could influence the economy, the stock market, and all offshoots of her "economic suffragette" cause. As the 1960 election approached, she noted that "hard times are the great unifier," so Democrats pined for deflation and recession. The Republican administration, by contrast, was "stepping hard on the gas to give the go-ahead to the economy."[168]

Few predicted at the start of the 1960s just how revolutionary the decade would be, as movements to pull America out of Vietnam, advance civil rights, and challenge attitudes about sex all gained momentum. In her long list of predictions for the 1960s, "more televisions will be in color than in black and white" was perhaps Wilma's only example of foresight.[169] While she likely had strong views on hotly debated topics like birth control and abortion (she had strong views on almost everything), Wilma stayed away from commenting on either subject, to keep FOWSAB and her radio show about money, not politics. After all, her crusades to get women on corporate boards were controversial enough.

$ $ $

On December 14, 1961, Kennedy authorized a Presidential Commission on the Status of Women. "If our Nation is to be successful in the critical period ahead," he contended, "we must rely upon the skills and devotion of all our people." Kennedy carefully emphasized that he was not suggesting all women *had* to work outside the home—in fact, he actively deplored "those economic conditions which require women to work unless they desire to do so." But, Kennedy noted, "women should not be considered a marginal group to be employed periodically only to be denied opportunity to satisfy their needs and aspirations when unemployment rises or a war ends." Almost two decades older than Kennedy, Wilma remembered clearly what had happened at the end of both world wars, when the women who stepped up to work for the war effort were unceremoniously dismissed to make room for returning veterans. In 1961, in the throes of an escalating Cold War, President Kennedy affirmed that "women have basic rights which should be respected and fostered as part of our Nation's commitment to human dignity, freedom, and democracy." These were not empty words, as the Commission helped to push passage of the Equal Pay Act of 1963 and the Civil

Rights Act of 1964. Mary Roebling, longtime president of Trenton Trust Company and short-time treasurer of FOWSAB, played an important role in achieving those reforms as part of the Advisory Council for the Commission on the Status of Women.[170]

During his presidency, Kennedy contended with several international crises, including Vietnam, the Bay of Pigs, and the Cuban Missile Crisis. Like President Kennedy and his predecessor Eisenhower, Wilma remained concerned about the spread of communism, but never aligned herself with the antics of Republican Senator Joseph McCarthy in the early 1950s. She was a moderate, more interested in economic policies than politicking. What she saw herself doing for her country (to borrow Kennedy's words) was teaching Americans, through FOWSAB and her radio show, how to share in the fruits of capitalism. Wilma believed in competitive capitalism, a la Adam Smith, and eschewed socialism, communism, and other -isms that espoused the forcible redistribution of wealth. She sought equality of opportunity, and she very much wanted everyone to have a fair *chance* of improving their financial status.[171]

By the early 1960s, Wilma owned stock in more than fifty corporations, and continued to expand her holdings as the decade progressed. She only owned a share or two in some companies—just enough for the shareholder meetings. Prudent, diversified investment in the stock market was an effective way for ordinary citizens to methodically build wealth, but also a means of participating in the governance of American corporations. Wilma encouraged all stockholders to exercise their shareholder rights, and even developed a Shareholder Bill of Rights. While Dr. King exhorted African Americans to go to the ballot box and tap into their political power, Wilma urged everyone to find their voices as active shareholders to wield more economic power.[172]

Wilma ratcheted up her activist tactics to match the changing times, although she never lost her sweetness and *joie de vivre*. As protest movements swelled, she, too, became more strident in her demands. When new to the gadfly game in the late 1940s and 1950s, Wilma tried to catch flies with honey, rather than vinegar. Like the cheerful Laura Partridge, Wilma in her younger days tended to exude a little faux naivety along with her ever-present warmth and vivaciousness. While she tried hard to press her reform platform and could be tough, she for years carefully avoided unnecessarily alienating those she wanted to persuade to her side, including little shareholders, board members, and CEOs. In the 1960s, as cultural norms changed, at least to some degree, and her reputation waxed, she realized she could get away with a bolder approach. While avoiding controversial topics like birth control, she could speak out with more verve at shareholder meetings and stop taking "no" for an answer when it came to corporate board seats.

Wilma often arrived early at meetings and took a seat in the front row. There's no record of her ever sitting further back than the third. Here, she'd gird herself for battle by rifling through proxies, annual reports, and newspaper clippings "like a frontier marshal checking the chambers of his six-gun." "The chairman's gavel scarcely has smitten the lectern before she is on her feet asking a question," one reporter noted with admiration, "usually one the chairman does not wish to answer." If he evaded, she kept at it, like any good reporter, while trying to walk that fine line between advancing her agenda and getting tossed out.[173]

The chairman also had to walk a fine line. He needed to show at least some respect for shareholders' right to express themselves, but also had to ensure that the meeting proceeded in an orderly fashion. Disrupting a meeting was a misdemeanor, but what constituted a disturbance was not well established. Some suggested that the mere act of showing up at a shareholder meeting in costume, a veiled reference to Wilma, should be considered a disturbance. Others, however, thought that the chairman had to declare behavior out of order and warn the shareholder to desist before the shareholder could be asked to leave. If the shareholder refused to leave on request, then a motion to eject the shareholder should be entertained and, if it passed, reasonable force to remove the shareholder could then be used. What was reasonable depended upon the circumstances, but lawyers advised that any physical ejection "should be particularly careful in the case of a woman." While her gender did not protect her from being carried out, Wilma leveraged that bias to the hilt.[174]

"Her customary tone and manner set my teeth on edge," reporter John Brooks confessed, "but I can't help recognizing that, because she does her homework, she usually has a point." Even her costumes exuded relevance. For example, when companies issued particularly obscure proxy statements, Wilma wore to the meeting her Sherlock Holmes deerstalker's hat and carried a large magnifying glass. However attired, Wilma, like the Gilberts, invariably showed up at meetings "clutching in her right hand three pounds of bylaws, proxy forms, SEC regulations, and lists of the shares she represents at the day's meeting," plus, of course, *Robert's Rules of Order*.[175]

Wilma argued that following parliamentary procedure separated her from the hecklers and that *Robert's Rules* was "the accepted foundation stone of an honest, democratic annual meeting." According to one business attorney, the gadflies "rise to make obscure parliamentary motions to or to make motions to amend proposals contained in the proxy material, hoping to have them voted on in their amended form." While most believed this was appropriate, "confusion and wasted time" could result, leading some to argue that the rules of order should be simplified. Intent on stopping Wilma from making yet another point of order, Irving S. Olds of U.S. Steel once accidentally smashed instead of his gavel, his own watch, which he had placed on the lectern before him to keep track of time.[176]

Wilma's style at the microphone was described as "savagely positive." When General Electric CEO Ralph Cordiner tried to evade her questions at the 1961 meeting in Syracuse, Wilma lectured him on American corporate law: "You are not an act of God. You are a form of labor, and you are running for election in a very grave time." Stockholders rarely spoke to corporate bigwigs like that, but it was just another day at work for Wilma.[177]

When a board member of another major corporation claimed that he would punch Wilma in the nose if she were a man, she retorted that "when we stockholders pay over one hundred thousand dollars a year to an executive, we expect brains, not brawn." Such confrontational scenes were not sporadic but rather common events in Wilma's life during the shareholder meeting season, which typically ran from March through June, with most banks, though, holding theirs in January. "Few directors like to admit that the Gilberts and Mrs. Soss are remotely effective," one reporter noted, but the facts said otherwise.[178]

Undoubtedly, Wilma's embrace of stronger tactics at corporate meetings also emanated from sheer frustration of spending more than a decade on the shareholder meeting circuit with little major or enduring to show for it. By this time, she had stood up at literally hundreds of meetings, often in out-of-the-way places, scolded boards for their lack of vision, and tried to mobilize sleepy shareholders to her cause. Major victories, though, had remained elusive. True, five women she advocated for board positions finally had secured them and she successfully goaded several corporations to move their annual meetings to places more accessible to average shareholders. She also had generated powerful discussions within the SEC and corporate America about the need for secret balloting. She took heart that she was making a difference but pined to make more substantial progress—notably with FOWSAB. FOWSAB's membership had not grown by leaps and bounds; a low number, she feared, would smack of failure and signal irrelevance. Even after allowing men to join, FOWSAB's ranks remained embarrassingly thin. In truth, Wilma had succeeded not in creating a mass organization, but an executive women professional network. Some of the highly talented women who belonged to FOWSAB were among those Wilma was pressing corporations to put on their boards of directors. These were women who were encouraging each other on, seeing each other's potential and wanting the corporate world to tap into their talents.[179]

To a great (and maybe a flawed) extent, Wilma's and FOWSAB's identities were intertwined. In Wilma's eyes, if America were to have more women on boards, secret shareowner ballots, and increased corporate transparency, it was up to her to deliver, with help from the handful of other active professional stockholders. Perhaps taking a cue from the non-violent resistance movements of Mohandas K. Gandhi and Dr. King, she even proved willing to be carried out of meetings when corporate titans refused to let her talk. She was stubborn, but admittedly, so were they.[180]

$ $ $

Media coverage of Wilma's activism remained avid through the decade. *The New York Times*, *The Wall Street Journal*, and other national papers frequently reported on her activities. Some of the nation's biggest magazines, like *Cosmopolitan* and *Life*, featured her in flattering stories.

In April 1963, Wilma scored a major coup—a profile by *Cosmopolitan* in an issue themed "Where the Money Is." Beneath the cover's scarlet masthead sat President Kennedy and his wife. His slim, black tie, identical in shade to Jackie's dress, stood boldly against the background's matte white. A puff piece within called "Money and the Presidency" detailed the President's surging popularity and discussed, cautiously, his family's great and reportedly ill-gotten wealth. Several prominent figures wrote on money for this issue. Ayn Rand of *Atlas Shrugged* fame outlined the distinction between "money-makers" and "money-appropriators" in "The Money-Making Personality"; Bob Hope tried to bring comic relief to Cold War tensions, detailing his tour of Russia in "Moscow Wants My Money!"; and Don and Gael Forst, notable in the journalism industry, wrote on a topic the slyly astute were making an art form: "Income Tax Loopholes." A lengthy piece by author Richard Gehman, entitled "Guardian Angel of Shareholders," glowingly covered Wilma's proselytizing efforts on behalf of small shareholders, particularly, the "ladies."[181] Contributor to *The New Yorker* and *Cosmopolitan* and biographer of Frank Sinatra, Jerry Lewis, and Humphrey Bogart, Gehman hailed Wilma's leadership of FOWSAB. He saw her as the "guardian angel" of little shareholders, even though, as he implied, CEOs and boards saw her more as the angel of death.[182]

"With a megaphone for her trumpet, this diminutive blonde's mission in life is to blast at the walls of big business," wrote Gehman. "Tycoons tremble," he said, "at the name of Wilma Soss, who utilizes the stockholders' meeting as a battleground to champion the rights of the small shareholder." He described Wilma as "a sprightly, pretty, and—to the average board chairman—needlingly nerve-racking lady who has spent the last seventeen years of her life raising her voice, which can become as strident as that of a mongoose, in stockholders' meetings, trying to get big-company executives to act in a democratic manner." He noted that Wilma didn't always get her way, but she did have her successes. Gehman gushed, "She has probably done more than any woman alive to get stockholders rights that are theirs, but which all too seldom are given them by the big companies." According to Gehman, "Mrs. Soss is in Carry Nation's tradition, and in Lucy Stone's, and in that of all those women of history who have trumpeted that their place is not in, but away from, the home."[183]

Gehman's comparisons were apt and made by others, including a couple from California, who called Wilma in 1959 to urge her to become the next Carry Nation by breaking down the door of the negotiations between Big Steel and Big Labor. Six-feet tall, Nation fervently supported abolitionism and after ratification of the Thirteenth Amendment in 1865 began crusading for temperance. Wielding an ax and quoting from the Bible, Nation destroyed bars to convince people of the evils of alcohol. Wilma never had been involved in the Prohibition movement, nor was she outwardly religious. And, fortunately for corporate boards, she tried to not get into fistfights.[184]

Gehman's comparison of Wilma to Lucy Stone was a bit more relatable. A leading abolitionist and early suffragist, Stone helped persuade Susan B. Anthony and others to join the cause of women's rights. "I'm a Lucy Stoner at heart," Wilma said in a separate interview. She sometimes referred to herself as the head of the "corporate suffrage movement" and *Newsweek* likened her to Susan B. Anthony.[185]

Just as Stone had pioneered, Wilma jumped in early on shareholder reform. The Gilbert brothers had plotted a path, but no prominent women were seen on the trail until Wilma arrived. Some of the companies she focused her ire upon had recently suffered scandals that hurt profits, share prices, and thus, shareholders. This was all particularly regrettable, she thought, for it was entirely avoidable. Wilma believed women in a corporate setting could serve as moralizing influences. If more women sat on boards and in executive positions, she reasoned, corporations would stop tolerating unethical and illegal behaviors. She saw it as her duty to chastise company boards and CEOs to make them see the error of their ways. She demanded accountability at the highest levels and would focus her fight on ways to end the ever popular pastime of corporate fraud.

$ $ $

At the 1960 CBS annual shareholder meeting, Wilma showed up with a mop and pail, to "clean things up." CBS recently had suffered terribly from a series of scandals involving the rigging of the country's most popular quiz shows. In the 1950s, Americans fell in love with the quiz show format and were hooked on programs like *Twenty-One* and *Dotto*. Even Eisenhower, when he was President, allegedly never missed his favorite program. But the simple joy this format was meant to bring was put on hold, as increasing numbers of contestants reported producers giving the correct responses to favored opponents.[186]

In a 1959 speech to the Pittsburgh Advertising Club, Louis G. Cowan, the president of CBS-Television network and, ironically, the founder of another tainted quiz show, *The $64,000 Question*, tried to control the damage by reassuring the public of the network's high standards. "Network television," he declared, "has the great responsibility of maintaining its integrity in product and in the conduct of its business." While some accusations were unjustified, Cowan made it "abundantly clear that no program should be on the air—quiz or otherwise—that does not meet the standards of fairness," and promised to remove programs from the air promptly if "sufficient evidence" proved they engaged in fixing.[187]

In the grand jury investigation, New York assistant district attorney Joseph Stone declared that although "no violations of the penal law had been uncovered," they had discovered "situations of grave public concern affecting the general welfare." Stone stated that the jury had an obligation "to report to the citizens of New York County on the harmful and corrupting influences which they discovered growing in their midst." According to the brief, the public had a "right to know the extent to which it had been duped and cheated," and beyond that, that "television itself [needed] to know facts enabling it to clean its house." He added, "there can be little doubt that the presentation would lead to legislation and regulation designed to prevent a recurrence or continuance of such fraud."[188]

According to Stone, the quiz shows represented "a tawdry hoax perpetrated on the American people by a group of corrupters." Who had known about this hoax, and on what levels? And even if top management didn't know, shouldn't they have? Would secret ballots filed by proxy help "clean its slate" by allowing for the ouster of poor management? Anonymity, Wilma pressed, would let people reveal their true preferences, without fear of retribution. Companies like CBS might ignore her demands for the secret ballot, but she would keep trying. And she would keep trying to get more women on boards, a just cause in her view, as the simplest means to lift corporations up morally, and in turn, financially.[189]

Wilma Soss as Sherlock Holmes. Photo by Tommy Weber. 202 East 39th Street, New York, NY 10016. Murry hilly 5-5151. Number: 9638 C1-6, Wilma Soss Papers, AHC collection: #10249, Photo Folder – accretion number 81-12-21. American Heritage Center, University of Wyoming.

$ $ $

The gavel smashed down at GE's 1961 annual meeting. Wilma was, apparently, out of order. Chairman and CEO Ralph J. Cordiner tried to reign in her commentary as she pushed to be heard. Wielding her copy of *Robert's Rules of Order*, she argued her behavior was in line—after all, it was her meeting as much as his.

Cordiner, successor of the legendary "Engine Charlie" Wilson, was a formidable foe, but GE had issues worth discussing. A price-fixing scandal tarnished the company's reputation to the detriment of its millions of shareholders. Wilma had traveled all the way to the Onondaga County War Memorial Auditorium in Syracuse, New York, to make her points. The gavel could only do so much.[190]

GE management had hoped the meeting would be swift, like those of simpler times when the most strenuous part was the stroll to lunch. This meeting, however, stretched over a six-and-a-half-hour period, in large part due to Wilma. "A state of uproar" marked the proceedings, according to a reporter, mainly due to the "frequent bobbing up and down of a small blonde lady stockholder, who addressed the chair in savagely positive terms whenever she opened her mouth."[191]

Speaking into the microphone handed to her on the floor, she warned Cordiner—and the rest of the board—that they reported to the shareholders, and not the other way around: "I am your employer today. I am representing those who employ you." The year under review, 1960, had been an awful one for GE. The company constantly made headlines for all the wrong reasons. GE had been under intense government scrutiny for violating antitrust provisions by colluding on prices in the electrical equipment industry. Trouble began in May 1957, when the Tennessee Valley Authority (TVA) had complained that it had received identical bids on three contracts, bids that were supposedly secret. The ensuing grand jury investigations into price-fixing in the electrical equipment industry, authorized by the U.S. Attorney General, revealed TVA's suspicions of price rigging were true. Chaired by the popular Tennessee Democrat Estes Kefauver, who had become a household name in the 1950s for investigating organized crime, the Senate Antitrust and Monopoly subcommittee held widely publicized hearings over many months.[192]

In February 1960, indictments started to come down. The government charged fourteen manufacturers, including GE, with conspiracy to fix prices and rig bids. Perhaps even more shocking was the number of corporate officials indicted—twenty-eight executives, including several at GE. The government was committed to showing how seriously it took price fixing, for such practices could harm everyday consumers and, worse yet, change how they vote.[193]

During sentencing, Judge J. Cullen Ganey decried the behavior of the electrical companies, saying it was "a shocking indictment of a vast section of our economy"—that these companies had "flagrantly mocked the image of that economic system of free enterprise which we profess to the country and destroyed the model which we offer today as a free world alternative to state control and eventual dictatorship."[194]

Willing to let some of its mid-level officials take the hit for antitrust violations, GE's top executives proclaimed their own innocence, either claiming no knowledge of what transpired or no involvement. They deflected attention onto Raymond W. Smith, vice president and general manager of the transformer division, and William S. Ginn, vice president and general manager of the turbine division. Philadelphia grand juries would indict Smith and Ginn for violating antitrust law, while declining to act against three senior GE officials—President Robert Paxton, Chairman Ralph Cordiner, and group vice president Arthur Vinson.

GE demoted Smith and Ginn and slashed their salaries. Ultimately, GE lawyers and the government made it explicit to the American public that top officials like Cordiner and Paxton were not found guilty of anything. In a prepared statement, Justice Department Attorney Charles Whittinghill announced, "The government does not claim that any member of the General Electric board of directors, including Mr. Ralph J. Cordiner and Mr. Robert Paxton had knowledge of the conspiracies pleaded to in the indictments, nor does the government claim that any of these men personally authorized or ordered commission of any of the acts charged in any of the indictments." Immediately thereafter, with the reputation of its top executives still somewhat preserved, GE entered pleas of guilty and *nolo contendere* to the indictments.[195]

Wilma was not the only one unhappy that GE's top leaders had escaped blame. In fact, Judge J. Cullen, during the sentencing hearing, declared that "the real blame is to be laid at the doorstep of the corporate defendants and those who guide and direct their policy . . . they bear a grave responsibility for the present situation for one would be most naïve indeed to believe that these violations of the law, so long persisted in, affecting so large a segment of the industry, and finally, involving many millions upon millions of dollars, were facts unknownst to those responsible for the conduct of the corporation."[196]

Judge Cullen also promised that "heavy" corporate fines would be levied. Such fines would hurt the companies' bottom lines and likely their share prices, which already suffered during the scandal. The twenty-nine guilty corporations collectively paid close to two million dollars in fines. GE and Westinghouse, the major offenders, had to pay approximately half of the total. Thirty employees would receive fines and jail sentences, and seven ultimately would spend a month in prison. The fact that white-collar employees received jail time for an antitrust violation sent a powerful signal to corporate America—antitrust enforcement was back.

Others felt the clean-up had to go further. Wilma agreed with Judge Cullen's opinion on the culpability of the board of directors. Her questions at the annual meeting, unsurprisingly, were rebuffed. "Are you going to give me double talk or are you going to reply?" she asked sharply at one point. Almost three thousand shareholders attended, and the majority cheered Cordiner and jeered Wilma when she attacked his leadership.[197] A reporter for *The Washington Post*, Bernard Nossiter noted that "if the majority shareholders were angry with GE's role in the multi-billion price-fixing conspiracy or the fact that the value of their stock had dropped from almost 100 to nearly 60 since the conspiracy ended, they didn't show it."[198]

Cordiner seemed to retain his magic touch. A master showman, he smiled confidently as he reminded shareholders that the company's stock, while it had taken a recent beating, was still way up from where it had been ten years ago, before he and others had taken the helm of the giant conglomerate. Applause rippled through the audience.

Seeking to defuse the harsh criticisms launched by Wilma and her small but vocal cohort, Cordiner emphasized that GE's decentralized model, the key to its success, entailed costs. Most importantly, the executive team couldn't be on top of every little thing that occurred at every level. As he explained to the shareholders before him, "you delegate pricing authority in a far-flung organization. A few highly trusted employes [sic] make a mistake. No one person can guarantee the acts of 250,000 employes [sic] at all times. All you can do is teach. We failed." Most shareholders, or at least those in the room, seemed to buy the explanation.[199]

That afternoon, Cordiner resoundingly won reelection for another term as chairman, and was also appointed the company's president. Nothing Wilma could have said would have prevented the outcome. Wilma knew Cordiner controlled the proxies but, aided by fellow GE critics, at least she had let management know that not all shareholders approved of their behavior. She would be back, dogging management at many more GE meetings. If nothing else, the 1961 meeting convinced Wilma even more of the need for the secret ballot and proxy reform. If the votes of absent shareholders hadn't automatically fallen under the sway of Cordiner, more shareholders might have been inclined to vote against him. And if the ballot were secret, there'd be less hesitation in casting the votes.

In 1956, the U.S. Senate Banking & Currency subcommittee called Wilma to appear to explain the secret ballot. Corporate elections, once secret, became open at about the same time that U.S. political elections finally became secret in the late nineteenth century. As Wilma argued, "without a secret ballot no stockholder resolution can pass unless recommended by the management." Ergo, "it is the foundation of corporate democracy in more than name only" and became a major plank in the activist reform platform by the early 1950s. "Suppose you are [a] bank trust officer," one advocate explained, "and vote your proxies to oust a director. If so, there is always the fear that your bank would lose that company's business." Some corporate executives were inclined to "snoop," as Wilma discovered firsthand when the president of Republic Steel asked specific shareholders to revoke the proxies they had given to Wilma.[200]

$ $ $

In the spring of 1965, with stockholder season in full swing, Wilma and FOWSAB had a very active agenda, hopping from one annual meeting to another. They tried to be strategic, making sure they hit the ones that would generate the most attention, or ideally, where they could have some success. As in prior years, Wilma coordinated to some extent with the Gilbert brothers. Often, they showed up to the big meetings together, and implemented a premeditated strategy. Wilma and the Gilberts would intentionally sit on opposite sides of the room to make management feel like they had to contend with activists swarming them from all quarters.

On May 12, 1965, Lewis Gilbert, Wilma, and some of their followers attended the annual shareholder meeting for Communicate Satellite Corporation—or "Comsat," for short. Authorized by the Communications Satellite Act of 1962, Comsat incorporated the next year and issued shares in a much-hyped IPO that Wilma likened to that of Ford, which experienced a quick pop followed by a decline in the market to half the offering price. The Comsat situation was even worse, she noted, because the company's prospectus indicated that profits would not be forthcoming until 1967 and even then, were not assured.[201]

Comsat launched its first satellite in 1965 but its finances aroused suspicion. Chairman Leo D. Welch presided over the meeting at the Shoreham Hotel that year. Wilma and the Gilberts already had garnered headlines that spring for tangling with boards at other meetings. Welch, well aware of the trio, couldn't forget the prior year when their speeches made the meeting drag on for over nine hours. He would be better prepared this time, hiring ten Pinkerton agents to police the gathering.[202]

A private security guard agency founded in 1850, Pinkerton reveled in its reputation for quelling labor unrest. Infamously in

1892, Andrew Carnegie and his deputy Henry Clay Frick used the agency to end an ongoing strike at the Homestead Steel Works. Nine steelworkers were killed in the clashes. Now, the Pinkerton guards at the Comsat meeting were by no means as threatening as those who stormed Homestead—but their presence made the backdrop far more intimidating than the norm for a gathering of shareholders.[203]

Wilma seated herself in the hotel auditorium, attired in bright Bermuda shorts, yellow knee boots, and a huge yellow hat to match. At least some of the 1,700 shareholders present had been there the year before, and many recognized her, even in the outrageous outfit. As the meeting began, managers realized that Wilma and Gilbert seemed intent to follow the pattern of aggressive questioning that they had used the year before. Gilbert stood up, forcefully inquiring how many shareholders had named him as their proxy. Chairman Welch said he would find out, but that didn't end Gilbert's pestering. Wilma, too, started in, demanding to be recognized. Welch refused, saying he would call on her at a later point. Her question was whether shareholders had received proper notice prior to the annual meeting, but her intent, it seems, was to prod the board. For five minutes, pursuing this procedural point, Wilma and Gilbert proceeded to create "bedlam," as the *Los Angeles Times* later reported. The Pinkerton guards were called in. Gilbert went quietly, with a guard at his elbow and another grabbing his briefcase. Wilma, however, refused to budge and had to be carried out. "AT&T-ism!" she shouted. "I'm going to sue," she said as she was dragged out, kicking up her heels and waving her hat at the crowd.[204]

Wilma was livid, as was Gilbert. Both believed they had the right to be in that meeting, and both felt they had been badly mistreated. Gilbert told reporters it had been "the most disgraceful annual meeting in the United States"—and that was a lot coming from a man who had been to thousands of shareholder meetings in his long career. Wilma, after checking the doors of the auditorium to see if the guards had left one unlocked, fumed some more: "They have no right to resort to police state methods like this."[205]

Eventually, Comsat execs let the duo back in, perhaps presuming that the "hecklers" had learned their lesson. Wilma got right back into the swing of things. She wanted to know whether the two lawyers currently on the board ever did any legal work for Comsat. It was an intelligent and fair question—she was trying to gauge any potential conflicts of interest. The board didn't even know, or at least, that's what they claimed. "I suggest you find out before the next meeting," she replied.[206]

With the discussion still focused on the nomination of directors, Wilma proceeded to question the absence of some board members. One of the missing directors was Clark Kerr, president of the University of California. Getting in her digs, she quipped, "I'm sorry Mr. Kerr is too busy at the University of California to be here, but then we don't have free speech at Comsat meetings either." Otherwise, the meeting proved uneventful. From an agenda perspective, all twelve directors up for reelection won their seats on the board again, and two proposals brought forth by small stockholders failed to gain traction.[207]

The next day, photographs in many of the major papers showed a matronly woman looking distraught and disheveled as she was carried out of a shareholder meeting. In some of the pictures, it was hard to make Wilma out too well—she was a blur, as photographers had a hard time capturing the "bedlam" as it unfolded.

Wilma herself, though, was proud, not embarrassed, about her forcible removal from the Comsat meeting. Her threat of a lawsuit was just that: an empty threat. Wilma could be angry for a brief time, but her sense of humor always resurfaced. That December, the Christmas card Wilma widely sent out featured the picture of her being tossed out. Her holiday greeting read: "Bottoms up for the New Year. Heads up for Annual Meetings!" She would observe about herself years later, "If you can laugh at something, it seems the best way to show how ridiculous it is."[208]

Wilma always liked to make a scene, but found it was taking more effort to be noticed. Costumes weren't enough anymore. Resistance to her new tactics was to be expected, but even some within FOWSAB wondered whether Wilma's theatrics had gone overboard. Beatrice Kelekian, Vice President of FOWSAB, would resign a year later, citing Wilma's penchant for histrionics.[209] But on that May day in 1965, Kelekian, who attended the meeting, was more critical of Comsat than either of the ejected gadflies. "Welch ought to have his face smashed in," she yelled to reporters, adding, "And if there was a red-blooded man in that meeting, he would have."[210]

While reporters covering the 1965 annual meeting focused on Wilma, Lewis, and to some extent Kelekian, another shareholder activist named Evelyn Davis was also present. Davis would prove to be the biggest disruptor of annual meetings going forward, far exceeding Wilma's theatrics.

A little of what was to come shone through at the Comsat meeting. Smoking her cigar, Davis goaded the gadflies on. When she got her turn on the floor, Davis proposed that Comsat impose an age limit on board members. It was an interesting idea, a way to prevent them from serving forever, as shareholders rarely ousted board members via the ballot. She was not a vocal advocate for civil rights, but in arguing for more director turnover, she raised the point that "we don't have a Negro on the board." She seems to have brought the issue up primarily to target the Comsat managers who had thrown out Wilma and Gilbert. "If we had one [African American on the board]," she added, "maybe minority rights of stockholders would be looked after."

Davis, it seemed, had an answer for everything. Loud, brash, and scathingly acerbic, she'd become a lightning rod at these annual meetings. Though opinions about her were strong, and stretched far in every direction, one fact remained undeniable: Evelyn Davis did things her way—and *only* her way.[211]

6

QUEEN OF THE
CORPORATE JUNGLE

*Power is greater than love, and I did not get where
I am by standing in line, nor by being shy.*

—Evelyn Y. Davis, founder, Shareowner Services, Inc.
and editor, *Highlights and Lowlights*.[212]

APRIL 28, 1959
NEW YORK COLISEUM, NEW YORK CITY.

The rain and gray skies on IBM's annual meeting day didn't dissuade a record crowd from descending upon the New York Coliseum, the sprawling convention center that had opened just a year earlier on Columbus Circle. Among the roughly 2,450 shareowners packed into the meeting that day was the thirty-year-old Evelyn Y. Davis. Sporting a black cropped cut, reminiscent of the early century's "flappers" with a sixties edge, the perpetually serious Davis was not one to exude cheerfulness. But beneath her stern expression was an enthusiasm, one shared by several in the room. Today was her first shareholder meeting—an introduction to the forum she'd soon come to torment.

Evelyn Yvonne DeJong would gain the Davis name in 1957, when she married a wealthy accountant in Washington D.C., William H. Davis III. Wholly without love, the marriage lasted two years. "A little settlement" of "a few hundred thousand dollars" came to her as part of the divorce. With an inheritance from her father, a neurologist and long-time professor at Johns Hopkins University, Davis had come into fairly substantial wealth.[213]

She relocated to New York to start a new life, albeit with her ex-husband's last name and much of his savings. She embarked on a new career as an active equity investor, a pesky corporate gadfly inspired by the archetype of one Wilma Soss. Well before Davis entered the New York Coliseum to attend IBM's meeting, she knew of Wilma. Davis was a fan of *The Solid Gold Cadillac* and avidly followed news reports of the real-life Laura Partridge.[214] This April meeting would be the first time Davis would get to witness Wilma, and her newsworthy antics, live and in person.

The trio of Wilma and the Gilbert brothers often targeted IBM, but their gumption that day was something to admire. As Lewis Gilbert would relate, "The role of the minority shareholder is not for the timid." The experience intoxicated Davis as it had the Gilberts and Wilma, although she didn't say much and shook "like a leaf" on a windy day. Despite making only a small comment regarding IBM's dividend, Davis got her name in *The New York Times'* review of the shareholder meeting. "Evelyn Y. Davis," as she liked to be called, was on her way to becoming a celebrity.[215]

$ $ $

Just as Wilma appeared from seemingly nowhere in the late 1940s, the "unstoppable" Evelyn Yvonne Davis made a similar entrance in the late 1950s. A sign of the times, Davis took everything up a notch, exhibiting behaviors more aggressive and acerbic than Wilma's or those of other professional gadflies. Much to the frustration of CEOs around the country, Davis accumulated shares in roughly 120 corporations and became a regular—or a "professional" or "independent" as she preferred to be called—at their shareholder meetings.[216]

Learning from Wilma's displays, even down to the tactic of wearing costumes to shareholder events, Davis quickly mastered the art of raising hell at annual meetings. Strong, determined, and smart, she delighted in stinging top executives with harsh rebukes of their decisions—often while flirting with them. The tactic earned the attention of journalists but induced many to question if gadflies were "crackpots" or "crusaders."[217]

In her early thirties when called to corporate activism, Davis was younger than most other professional shareowners. The Gilbert brothers and Wilma were in their sixties, as were most in the FOWSAB crowd. But Davis brought to the fray big money and equally big ideas about how management should behave toward shareholders like herself. Drawn into the fight by Wilma, and likely the NYSE's "Own Your Share" marketing campaign, Davis took the notion of share *ownership* to heart and unabashedly demanded a say in corporate decisions.[218]

Unlike Wilma, Davis cared little about appointing women to board positions. A jealous sort, Davis exhibited what would later be called the Queen Bee syndrome—other women could advance only after she did, and she often disparaged those ahead of her. On more than one occasion, she complained that the typical woman executive given an ounce of power acted as if "it weighs 1,000 pounds."[219] Davis, instead, inveighed against excessive executive privileges—whether in the form of favored charities that executives connived to fund with money from "their" company, pay-for-nothing schemes offered to loyal friends, or other machinations for diverting profits from small shareowners.

Corporate donations to charities particularly bothered Davis. As the corporate social responsibility (CSR) movement gained steam in the 1960s and 1970s, economist Milton Friedman also critiqued the growing practice. In his eyes, money diverted to charities rightfully belonged to shareholders, either as dividends or corporate assets.[220]

Davis went further in her criticisms, accusing corporate bigwigs of using charitable donations to support their mistresses. Some top brass, she contended, ensconced their lovers into paid charitable positions funded with corporate donations. As a shareholder, Davis didn't want *her* money supporting some mistress, or any other executive perks. She didn't care so much if CEOs were unfaithful to their wives—she cared that she and other shareholders were getting fleeced, without their consent, in the process. Many shareholders and executives didn't know quite what to make of such criticism, and some thought Davis crazy for alleging such a thing. The salacious accusations, though, distracted from her better points, like the need to reign in executive salaries and vote people with new ideas onto boards. But Davis didn't care what anyone thought. She believed in the validity of all her points and took pride in being well-informed and savvier than most regarding how business operated. As she was quick to remind, "no one knows corporate America better than Evelyn Y. Davis."[221]

$ $ $

After her first appearance at the IBM annual meeting, Davis made up her mind to dominate future shareholder meetings and began preparing herself for a starring gadfly role. The top priority was improving her communication skills, in part by reducing her still prominent Dutch accent. She enrolled in a public speaking course at a YMCA in Manhattan. At the time, such public speaking classes were hot among the career-minded, fueled by renewed excitement over Dale Carnegie's influential book *Public Speaking: A Practical Guide for Business Men*, first published by the YMCA in 1915. About the same time that Davis took her class at the Y, other aspiring businessmen, like Warren Buffett, spruced up their own speaking skills in similar programs around the country. Davis credited the class with giving her the confidence to speak frequently and loudly at shareholder meetings for decades to come.[222] Davis also studied security analysis at the New York Institute of Finance. With the added self-assurance that came with more financial knowledge and improved speech, Davis "fell into" the gadfly life "like a fish in the water."[223]

"I WAS BORN TO RAISE HELL" read one of Davis's favorite sweaters. She wore it to some shareholder meetings to burnish her reputation. When not using sweaters as billboards, she often donned costumes that accentuated her slim figure. In 1970, in a rather notable case, she stripped down to a bathing suit at a GM meeting and strutted around the auditorium brandishing an American flag.[224]

At a 1971 Comsat meeting, the 41-year-old wore tight hot pants then in vogue. Coined by *Women's Wear Daily*, the term "hot pants" was reserved for very short shorts "worn by sexy, proud women," as *Jet* magazine proclaimed. A few months after Davis broke the business dress code, James Brown debuted "Hot Pants (She Got to Use What

She Got to Get What She Wants).” As the song title proclaimed, Davis believed in mustering all her beauty and brains to try to get what she wanted. As she once told a reporter, “I have absolute power at those stockholder meetings,” adding, “And, yes, I enjoy having power over men.”[225]

Observers rarely saw the connection between what Davis wore and what she said, and often they were right. Unlike Wilma, Davis wanted to call attention to her beauty, and if she could get reporters covering the stockholder meeting to mention not just her points, but her pants, so much the better. She even went so far as to sometimes give reporters her body measurements, hoping they would include them in the story.[226]

Despite such vanity, Davis made many substantive points. Some, like curbing executive secrecy and abolishing staggered election of board members, were in line with those advocated by Wilma and the Gilberts. But Davis’s overall approach was harsher, coarser, and more self-absorbed than that of Wilma, who generally displayed a happy demeanor even when ill-treated. Davis exuded everything but that, and often appeared angry and anti-social. She remained reclusive throughout her life, which may explain why, as much as she admired Wilma and thought of her as a close friend, she never joined FOWSAB. Davis wanted all the attention for herself, so she founded her own company, Shareholders Research, Inc., which purported to render investment advice.[227]

Meanwhile, Davis tried to make herself *the* advocate for small shareholders. Most of the media referred to Wilma, not Davis, as the “Queen of the Corporate Gadflies.” But Davis coveted that title for herself. To reinforce her royal status, Davis introduced herself at a Twentieth Century-Fox annual meeting as “Cleopatra, Queen of the Stockholders.” The aura of nobility seemed to fall flat, as one observer recalled her as a "cigar-smoking *femme fatale* with a Viennese accent."[228]

Wilma didn't seem to mind Davis's claims to greatness, but other shareholder activists were less forgiving. At the same Twentieth Century-Fox meeting, another activist, the actress/song-writer Gloria Parker, walloped Davis in the eye when she wouldn't relinquish the microphone. While shareholders who wanted to talk sometimes needed to literally battle for the microphone, such in-fighting did little for the small shareowner.[229]

Shareholder meetings could, and sometimes did, turn ugly. At a meeting for American Airlines, one shareholder, angry at Davis's monopolization of the mic, knocked her to the ground. She needed five stitches to staunch the flow of blood from a cut to her ear. But just one hour later, she attended another annual meeting for the New York Times Company telling reporters, "The show must go on!"[230]

Even Wilma and Davis occasionally butted heads, metaphorically speaking. At a meeting for Morgan Guaranty, each demanded that Chairman Henry Alexander recognize them first. Alexander deferred to Wilma, explaining, "I will recognize age." Wilma was thirty years older, but she didn't want to be seen as old. The comment didn't sit well with Davis either, who yelled back, "What about beauty?"[231]

Despite such incidents, Wilma and Davis always remained friendly. Davis and the Gilbert brothers, however, was a different story. John and Lewis often agreed with Davis's underlying criticisms of management, but they feared that Davis's rants and efforts to monopolize the stage might give shareholder activism a bad name—that she might delegitimize the whole movement. Berating CEOs for outsized executive compensation packages was a fair complaint, but deriding Chrysler CEO Lee Iacocca for his weight was not. By all accounts, Davis was brash and outspoken, unafraid to use coarse language and lewd tactics to gain press attention. Criticizing Davis, John Gilbert once remarked, "She'll harangue the chairman . . . She uses vile language. I'm a gentleman. She's not a lady." Yet he conceded that amidst some of her wackier remarks, Davis often had valid points. As Gilbert said, "when the devil is right, she's right."[232]

Davis often came across as wild, unpredictable, and just a bit crazy. And to say she had a big ego would be an understatement. She once suggested to a reporter to headline the story about her: "I Was Gifted With Both Extraordinary Beauty and Extraordinary Brains and I've Used Them Both to My Utmost Advantage."[233]

She was notoriously difficult to get along with. She made enemies easily and was often alone. Yet Davis and Wilma got along well from the get-go. Wilma welcomed Davis into the activism fold and seemed to accept her, along with her eccentricities. In an odd way, it made sense that the two would click. Wilma got along with almost everyone, Davis with almost no one. It wasn't just that Wilma was kind and big-hearted—she knew how to wield some measure of power in the shareholder meeting room. Davis lusted after this kind of influence. She desperately wanted to learn from Wilma how to get the leaders of the biggest companies in the world to listen to *her*. [234]

Unlike Wilma, Davis mostly sought self-aggrandizement, not the protection of small shareowners from poor management: "The main thing . . . is to keep my name out in front." She wanted to make more money for herself, both from her investments and by leveraging her fame, but she also wanted publicity just for the attention. According to one of her ex-husbands, "To say Davis loved publicity would be a massive understatement. She lived for publicity."[235]

Evelyn Y. Davis prepares to light up an AT&T stockholder meeting at Kingsbridge Armory, April 1964. Photo by Ed Clarity/NY Daily News Archive via Getty Images (#97257651). Used with permission by Getty.

$ $ $

In 1963, however, Davis found herself getting recognized for all the wrong reasons. While Wilma got positive press from various media outlets, including *Cosmopolitan,* which touted her as the "Guardian Angel of Shareholders," Davis garnered press of a different sort. Just as her gadfly fame was hitting new highs, she found herself at the heart of a prostitution scandal. Much more than equity research, it was alleged, took place in her company headquarters at 525 Lexington Avenue, the Sheldon Towers Hotel.[236]

New York City vice cops had gotten wind of her "office" room antics and organized a sting in which an undercover officer called Shareholder Services to see what Davis might offer. Asking for

"Yvonne," Davis's middle name, turned out to be "code for another type of up-and-down that wasn't on the Dow Jones Average." When officer Donald Smith asked Yvonne about her services, Davis allegedly quoted him twenty bucks for "twenty pages of typing," and fifty dollars or more for "fifty pages of typing," if dinner was included.[237]

Smith followed up, going to Davis's hotel room to see what would happen. After his arrival, Davis immediately disrobed, and Smith promptly took her into custody. The evidence was fairly clear, and Davis was soon convicted of solicitation. Judge Abraham M. Roth, however, displayed leniency, waiving the usual thirty-day jail sentence on the grounds that Davis's public humiliation constituted sufficient punishment.[238]

In later years, however, Davis denied adamantly that she had engaged in prostitution. "It's all garbage," she told one reporter when asked about the episode. She claimed that she had been set up by powerful CEOs whom she had ticked off over the years, and this was her retribution. The evidence seems incontrovertible—but perhaps, too, she knew something about the philandering of certain CEOs.[239]

Davis's scandal was not lost upon fellow gadflies, especially the Gilbert brothers, who saw it as further proof of Davis' instability. Davis was worth millions; why would she engage in this behavior? The Gilberts sometimes taunted Davis about the conviction, going so far as to mention the anniversary of her arrest in a preamble to their comments at a public shareholder meeting a year later. Wilma was kinder, never bringing it up, at least not in public, which may be an additional reason Davis continued to adore Wilma, her motherly figure in the gadfly world.

Despite the scandal, or maybe to some extent aided by the notoriety, Davis plowed on, endeavoring to burnish her reputation as *the* shareholder activist. The "Bad Girl of Corporate America" and the "Vamp of Wall Street," pinned on her by the media, were badges of honor, not reasons to step aside. Still, the sobriquet she loved the best was "Queen of the Corporate Jungle."[240]

Davis continued to take cues from the career trajectories of Wilma and the Gilberts. Wilma had her own radio show and essentially ran FOWSAB. The Gilberts published their own annual compendium of what transpired at important stockholder meetings. Davis concluded that she needed her own outlet, opting for a newsletter targeted to CEOs and presidents.

In 1965, her publication entitled *Highlights and Lowlights* ("H and L") debuted. She served as editor, publisher, and author. The commentary ranged all over the place, from informative news about annual meetings, the stated purpose of the publication, to corporate gossip, to political analysis, to details of her personal life. In one issue, she even wrote about her recent facelift. A reader called H and L "wildly idiosyncratic"—it certainly was.[241]

Somewhat shrewdly, Davis demanded, and got, a royal ransom for a subscription to *Highlights and Lowlights*. At one point, it cost $480 for one short issue. She'd later raise the price to $525 per issue, with a minimum order of two copies. Many prominent CEOs subscribed, in part, to keep their names out of any negative stories that Davis might have in mind. In any event, Davis loved to exert this control and *Highlights and Lowlights* stayed a big money-maker for decades.[242]

In a late 1990s interview, Davis claimed to make $600,000 in annual revenue from subscriptions to her newsletter. She made no excuses for the steep price tag. "People ask why the price is so high," she once remarked. "They pay for the name," meaning her own. She went on to explain, "Like this is an Yves Saint Laurent suit I'm wearing." The implication was clear: just as a fashionable woman is willing to pay for the quality of a pricey suit, a smart CEO is willing to pay for the "quality" news provided by Mrs. Evelyn Y. Davis.[243]

The gadflies, though, saw through her *Highlights and Lowlights* bit. John Gilbert called it "a form of blackmail," explaining how "[Davis] calls [the CEO] up and says, 'Hello, darling, how many copies?'" Even though the CEOs "don't really want them," they respond, "All right," because they know she has them in a tough spot. CEOs evidently worried about ticking off Davis, for her writing and antics knew no limits. She didn't always play fair, and that loosened many a purse string. One wonders, though, if the subscription came out of their own pockets or corporate accounts.[244]

$ $ $

Davis, Wilma, and former FOWSAB officer Beatrice Kelekian would travel to Toronto in April 1971 for IBM's annual meeting. CEO Tom Watson had been sidelined by a heart attack in November 1970, requiring him to turn over control of the company for several months. By February, he was back on the job, but for how long nobody knew. Many shareholders believed that Watson was key to IBM's continued success and were nervous about how the company would progress if Watson ultimately stepped aside. Shareholders had a right to know the succession plan, and about the health of the CEO. Management, though, didn't appreciate the probing.

At the meeting, a reporter for *The Wall Street Journal* noted that Wilma, Davis, and Kelekian asked "most" of the questions. Davis led off, asking Watson to affirm or deny the rumor that he was about to step down due to health reasons. It was rebuffed. Wilma, ever focused on the mission, demanded the board appoint the well-qualified "Mrs. Patricia Roberts Harris," former Ambassador to Luxembourg. Watson surprised Wilma by announcing that IBM was already considering Harris, along with a few other women, for the board. It was an interesting response on a couple levels—not just that Harris was on IBM's radar, but also that IBM management seemed to have come to an internal understanding that it needed to appoint at least one woman to their board soon due to outside pressure, presumably from the gadflies. Wilma was thrilled: "Does that mean that we will have a woman on the board in the next year?" Watson's answer must have delighted her: "We will bend every effort towards that end."[245]

She could have left it at that—for once, her persistence had resulted in a big win. But she went on to scrutinize the economic wisdom of a member of IBM's current board, William McChesney Martin, former chairman of the Federal Reserve and former president of the NYSE. Watson declared Wilma out of order. As she refused to stand down, Watson called upon three Pinkerton guards (one, a woman) to physically escort her out of the building. Attired in a safari outfit replete with helmet and Bermuda shorts, Wilma was "half carried" out by the two male guards. She seemed to take this second IBM ouster in stride; the two guards, however, complained to the press that Wilma scratched their hands.[246]

Davis largely stayed out of the fray, perhaps sensing this was Wilma's fight and not hers; perhaps also because she seemed to like Watson and may have wanted to stay on his good side. A few years earlier, Watson had instructed a bodyguard to protect Davis from "possible harm at the hands of a glowering male stockholder incensed over her efforts to monopolize the meeting." Clearly, Davis's relationships with the CEOs she taunted were complicated. They were sometimes willing to tolerate her—a decision seemingly in the interests of both parties.[247]

Davis was unafraid to solicit favors from management. When she decided to buy a car, she demanded that an automobile manufacturer personally deliver it to her. While Chrysler dilly-dallied with her injunction, the CEO of Ford Company readily complied, handing her the keys to a Ford car during a press conference, as to not incur her infamous wrath. The car that appeared on Davis' driveway was not, alas, a Cadillac of solid gold—it was a Ford Mercury Topaz, hue unknown.[248]

$ $ $

Most people didn't know what to make of Davis. She could be shockingly lewd in shareholder meetings. Even at a time of loosening mores, she pushed the boundaries of respectability, and she seemed unpredictable. Most of all, she projected a deep unhappiness. For decades, she was reticent to disclose publicly that she had survived the Holocaust, imprisoned for a time in two concentration camps after the Nazis arrested her in her native Amsterdam.[249]

Only the people closest to Davis, and there weren't many, knew this secret. Davis avoided media questions regarding what she and her family had experienced during the Second World War—she preferred not to discuss it. As psychiatrist Viktor E. Frankl, himself a survivor of the camps, once noted, former prisoners often would remark: "'We dislike talking about our experiences. No explanations are needed for those who have been inside, and the others will understand neither how we felt then nor how we feel now.'" It's possible Davis held a particular reluctance to mention her experience, as her immediate family had all survived.[250]

Many people never guessed that Davis had been a prisoner during the war. She did not belong to the Jewish faith; by the time she lived in Manhattan, she identified as Episcopalian. But Davis indeed remained haunted by her experiences as a child. Ex-husband Jim Patterson recalls, "Her memories of her family's arrest by Nazis in Amsterdam . . . remained painful her entire life. She shared this pain with me and I am living witness to the brutality she lived through and struggled with from surviving the Holocaust." Those who knew Davis's past may have had some inkling about how her wartime traumatic experiences shaped her, and arguably, indirectly led her into activism.[251]

$ $ $

Born in Holland in 1929 to a Jewish mother (Marianna) and a Protestant father (Herman DeJong), Davis was a Jew in the eyes of the Nazi regime that seized the Netherlands in May 1940. She never knew Anne Frank, but the girls were the same age, and both lived in Amsterdam at the time of the invasion. Their experiences would wildly differ, in large part because Davis hailed from a prominent family. Much later in life, Davis wrote that she had been born "on the wrong side of the ocean but the very right side of the tracks." Recalling her privileged upbringing in a luxurious twelve-room house, Davis explained, "we had two maids and a French governess. Then the war came and that was it." Davis's father was a celebrated neurologist, and her mother, a noted psychologist. The family's prestige didn't save them from suffering during the Holocaust, but it helped them survive. It was a lesson Davis seemed never to forget: your power and connections could be the difference between life and death.[252]

In 1942, while Davis's father delivered a lecture in the United States, Davis and the rest of her family were rounded up. But unlike the Franks, the DeJong family managed to get on a list of select Dutch Jews who two permanent state secretaries had deemed worthy of saving due to their perceived outstanding contributions to Holland. The list began only with two people and their families. Interceding, a Hague bureaucrat wrangled a pact with the Nazis to save them from slaughter. When the news leaked about this safe list, other prominent Jews across the Netherlands clamored to get on it, too. The SS seemed to have acquiesced to the idea of an exclusive list because it would help prevent some Jews from going into hiding. You had to be present to apply to be on the list, and you needed influential non-Jews to vouch for why it was important to the country that you be saved. In total, roughly 600 to 700 Dutch Jews made the list. A wide range of professions was represented—among them, celebrated lawyers, doctors, orchestra members, scientists, and politicians, along with their families. They became known as "the Barneveld Group" due to the fact that they initially were interned in the Castle De Schaffelaar in Barneveld (often simply called "Barneveld Castle"), a town on the outskirts of Amsterdam.[253]

For Davis, her brother, and her mother, living in Barneveld Castle was a far cry from the lifestyle they had enjoyed in their own home. But relative to the fate befalling others, it was luxury. There were no starvation rations or grueling forced labor. They even were allowed to bring some of their possessions with them, such as porcelain dinnerware, grooming tools, and other comforts of home. Castle residents like the DeJongs tried to retain elements of culture in their daily routines, putting on musical performances, going to school, and taking care to maintain their personal appearances. As one Barnevelder recalled, being incarcerated in the castle didn't stop the men from shaving every day, and women from doing their best to style their hair according to the most up-to-date fashions. But the castle, and the nearby De Biezen mansion, grew increasingly crowded and the food more limited. Along with the imposition of rations, men and women, who initially were allowed to live in castle rooms with their families, were divided into barracks. While the once privileged residents tried to preserve an air of dignity and a sense of individuality, slowly, everything was being stripped away.[254]

In the fall of 1943, things got much worse for Davis, her family, and the rest of Barneveld. An eyewitness recalls, "the German Army stormed in and they sent us to Westerbork. That put the fear of God into everybody because Westerbork was where most of the Dutch Jews went before they were carted off on trains eastwards." The survivor further noted, "It was in Westerbork that one began to realize things were really bad. The food was adequate but monotonous, there was lice everywhere, scarlet fever, dysentery, polio."[255]

Westerbork was a transit station for those destined for death camps like Auschwitz and Sobibór. Davis and the other Barnevelders watched the selection of other Jews, some of whom the Barnevelders personally knew, for transport. Although spared the same fate, the fact that the group had been sent to Westerbork signaled that the Nazis were not likely to uphold the pact much longer.

Teenage Davis picked potatoes and followed harsh orders, but she remained with mother Marianna and brother Rudy while her father waited out the war in the United States. Being in the Barneveld Group at Westerbork didn't protect Davis and the others from the sadism of the German guards. A fellow Barnevelder, Steven Frank, recalls how as an eight-year-old child, he ventured too close to a barbed wire fence at Westerbork, and guards let loose one of their Alsatians. Bitten badly all over his arms, legs, and thighs, Frank learned to keep as far away as possible from not just the fence, but also the guards, a lesson Davis, a few years older, also seemed to have learned.[256]

During a mortar attack, shrapnel tore into Davis's leg, and she bore the scars the rest of her life. In September 1944, as Allied armies threatened to liberate the Netherlands, the Nazis moved the Barneveld Group to Theresienstadt (also called "Terezin"), an over-crowded work camp and ghetto in Czechoslovakia. Theresienstadt originally housed Jewish prisoners from Moravia and Bohemia but by then it served as a transit camp for Jews destined primarily for Auschwitz. Theresienstadt was a nightmare for Davis and others sent there. It was not, however, an extermination camp—just hard toil on thin rations with the constant threat of violence from the guards and their dogs. The camp was unusual in its "self-administration" style. Prisoners, not the SS, decided which inmates would be on the next transport for the death camps. Often who you knew determined if your name appeared on the list.[257]

Among those sent to Theresienstadt were "Jews with merits" from all over Europe. Viktor E. Frankl, who would later write the international best-seller, *Man's Search for Meaning,* drew on this experience. Before being arrested and deported, Frankl headed the department of neurology at Rothschild Hospital in Vienna. Notably, both Frankl and Davis's father, Herman DeJong, were in the same profession and the same specialty—Frankl practicing in Austria, DeJong in Holland. It is possible that the DeJongs and Frankls even knew each other, either before the war, or during it.[258]

While a prisoner at Theresienstadt, Davis and her family, along with the rest of the Barneveld Group, were housed in barracks separate from the rest of the camp. Davis worked in a factory, cutting mica, a hard mineral used to make heat resistant glass. She recalled,

"It was terrible, very cold and dirty." But she somehow got through it. "I was fifteen years old," she once said, "and as a sort of mental escape, I started to fantasize about the director of the factory, who was a Czech Nazi. I got a crush on him, like you'd get a crush on a professor at school. And, honest to God because I had this crush, it got me through the camp." Davis added, "I'd look forward to going to the factory because I'd see this guy. Nothing happened: I was still an innocent girl. But it made the whole thing bearable for me." She concluded, "Ever since then, I've had infatuations with what you'd call very prominent authority types. See? That has kept with me the rest of my life." "*Prominent*" carried a very precise meaning in the concentration camps—it meant you had a stronger chance of being one of the saved because you had "merits."[259]

For Davis to find a will to live by fantasizing about a Nazi factory manager might sound crazy. Holocaust research, however, suggests that many teenage girls employed similar coping mechanisms. The experience of teenage women in the camps led to particular expressions of post-traumatic stress syndrome ("PTSD")—a condition not yet recognized in the 1950s. Writing decades later, in the 1990s, discussing a phenomenon he called "concentration camp syndrome," scholar Herbert Bower explained, "It does not seem inconceivable that some victims, and far more so the children among them, incorporated the aggressive, punitive and antisocial super-ego of their persecutors with far-reaching results in their future lives."[260]

$ $ $

In May 1945, less than a year after the DeJong family arrived at Theresienstadt, Soviet troops liberated the camp. Davis recalls, "My mother told me that if the war went on another week, we all would have perished." Davis and her family likely received assistance from the Red Cross, which probably facilitated their exit into Switzerland. From there, Davis and her brother Rudy relocated to the United States, where Davis's father still resided. By this time, Dr. DeJong was a professor at Johns Hopkins University. Marianna chose to return to Amsterdam and by 1952 the couple had divorced. Rather than being angry at her father and seeing him as abandoning her during the war, Davis resented her mother instead. Just as she later blamed her mother for her prostitution scandal, Davis also labeled her (and her Jewish heritage) as the cause of the family's wartime suffering.[261]

Davis saw herself as Dutch, not Jewish. Although a Holocaust survivor, she did not identify with many of the other victims. In her mind, Jewish refugees from Germany—like Anne Frank and her family—had brought the Holocaust to her doorstep in Amsterdam.[262] As a once wealthy Dutch citizen and then a Barnevelder, Davis seemed to have seen herself as above the rest. When the war ended, she wanted to reclaim the privileged life and status she once had enjoyed. Her neurosurgeon father had successfully rebuilt his life in the United States. Unlike the hordes of displaced persons roaming Europe after the war, Davis in 1945 had a new home to go to, one now devoid entirely of her mother.

Davis's life changed rapidly after her liberation. In the spring of 1945, she was a prisoner in Theresienstadt, fearing imminent death. A year later, she was leading a rather typical American teenage existence, attending high school in Catonsville, Maryland. During that period, she did not receive any sort of psychological counseling. The thought, common among Holocaust survivors and mental health professionals, was that immersion into ordinary life would be the best therapy. In June 1947, Davis graduated high school at age eighteen, right on schedule—but this milestone only masked the emotional difficulties she was still experiencing.

Frankl once quoted German philosopher Gotthold Ephraim Lessing as saying, "There are things which must cause you to lose your reason or you have none to lose." Frankl interpreted this to mean "An abnormal reaction to an abnormal situation is normal behavior."[263] Given what she had been through, Davis was not crazy for having difficulty adjusting to life in the States; she would have been crazy *not* to have been troubled.

Like many survivors, Davis felt profoundly unhappy and couldn't figure her way out of it. Nevertheless, Davis plowed on, moving to the next step expected of someone from a well-to-do family: college. In 1947, she enrolled at Western Maryland, stayed for a semester, and then enrolled at George Washington University, intent on studying business administration.

Years later, Davis would refer to herself as a member of the "GW Class of 1951," but she never graduated and seems to have been expelled from both schools for inappropriate relationships with professors.[264]

Davis did not think of herself as a financial feminist, yet in some ways, she was. Compared to Wilma's brand of action, it was much more focused on the individual—Davis herself—than the group. Wilma saw herself more as part of women united; women's control over their money, she believed, was the key to better futures. But for Wilma and Davis alike, living in the midst of growing movements that challenged convention, it was the work of the gadfly life that kept them focused. Each fought for a better tomorrow in her own unique way—and each one, whether through radio, hot pants, management reforms or megaphones, left a mark on corporate America it would not soon forget.

7

PROGRESS, PROTEST AND INFLATION

Money represents power to men, but to me it represents freedom.

—Mickie Siebert[265]

DECEMBER 28, 1967
NEW YORK STOCK EXCHANGE,
NEW YORK CITY.

As Muriel "Mickie" Siebert was sworn into New York Stock Exchange (NYSE) membership, the gravity of the moment overwhelmed her. Her hands shook as she signed the register because she was deeply cognizant not just of all the "history in that book," but that she was making history that day as the first woman to ever hold a seat on the NYSE. The book in front of Siebert was massive. She'd later relate, "[it was] about nine inches thick, with the entire constitution of the Stock Exchange written in longhand and the signatures of everyone who's ever been a member. I saw names from the Civil War."[266]

While Siebert was making history that winter, Wilma and Davis were immersed more than ever in their corporate activism. Both did extensive research, dissecting company financials and other information they could get to fuel their grilling sessions. CEOs knew their names and faces, and invariably scanned the auditorium for them before starting their meetings. Increasingly, to help spread the share ownership message, Wilma focused her attention on the NYSE, where she was becoming good friends with President Keith Funston. It is likely that Wilma and FOWSAB carefully watched Siebert's bid for NYSE membership, standing by to move the process along if needed.

It was none too obvious to anyone, including Siebert herself, that a woman would be successful in the quest to obtain a seat on the Exchange. It probably helped that her bid happened during Funston's long reign as Exchange president. He, too, had been an outsider to Wall Street, coming to head the NYSE in the 1950s after a stint as president of Trinity College in Hartford, Connecticut. Funston, along with Vice President Ruddick Lawrence, had been rather forward thinking about potential Exchange reforms, but Wilma over the years did her best to woo them into a deeper commitment. The decision to admit Siebert came down to the entire NYSE, not Funston alone, but the Exchange had to tread carefully due to the passage of Title VII in the Civil Rights Act of 1964. Title VII prohibited job discrimination based on race, color, religion, national origin, and sex. At first, it looked like the federal government might be rather lax about enforcing Title VII. Notably, President Johnson's Executive Order 11246 made no mention of sex discrimination. While the Old Guard at the NYSE likely breathed a sigh of relief, the

National Organization of Women (NOW), co-founded in October 1966 by Betty Friedan of *Feminine Mystique* fame, inveighed against the omission.[267]

Johnson corrected it in Executive Order 11357 on October 13, 1967. This appeased NOW leaders to some extent, although they soon became skeptical of the Equal Employment Opportunity Commission's enforcement of the new order. While considering Siebert's bid, the NYSE did not yet know how the EEOC would interpret their mandate. Perhaps the NYSE might be better served by opening its club voluntarily, rather than by force. Siebert nervously went to the Secretary of the Exchange, John J. Mulcahey, Jr., to inquire about purchasing a seat. She asked, "Can I buy a seat, or is this just a country club?" According to Siebert, Mulcahey told her, "We can't turn you down for nonbusiness reasons, on the basis of sex, or you could sue every member of the board of governors."[268]

The NYSE remained an unincorporated partnership and members thought of their Exchange as a sort of club. Like other country clubs, it wasn't bound to offer equal access, at least according to some members. But what did the NYSE gain from exclusion? As Wilma would say, the most talented people, regardless of their personal characteristics, should attain power, and Siebert was a well-known, savvy trader who had worked her way up to partnership at Brimberg & Co.

Plus, as Mulcahey well knew, the nearby American Stock Exchange (AMEX) had already opened its membership to women two years earlier. Mary Roebling, of early FOWSAB fame, had served on the board of the AMEX from 1958 to 1962, but was not a seatholder. Arguably not by coincidence, AMEX appointed two women to its membership rolls in 1965: Julia Montgomery Walsh and Phyliss Petersen, both of whom were affiliated with brokerage firms in the

Washington D.C. area. This was exactly the type of trajectory Wilma envisioned when she insisted on the importance of women in the board room. Qualified female board members like Roebling would pave the path for other qualified women to gain prominent business positions.[269]

Of the two exchanges, the NYSE was the more prestigious institution at the time, making its price of membership much higher than that of the AMEX. The NYSE, contrary to prevailing belief, never explicitly prohibited women from joining, a fact that shocked Siebert when related to her by star mutual fund manager Gerry Tsai. Tsai, whose own mother had been a member of the Shanghai Exchange during the war, was correct, but the NYSE reserved the right to reject applicants, even those sponsored by other Exchange members. Political activists like Betty Friedan and financial activists like Wilma and Roebling backed Siebert—so did a handful of male Exchange members. Tsai encouraged her as well, telling her that if she owned a seat on the NYSE and started her own brokerage firm, she would finally be able to earn what she was worth.[270]

A risk-taker like Wilma and Davis, Siebert seized the opportunity and won the seat. Many at the NYSE feared the precedent, expressing concerns of an imminent "invasion." At a Christmas party, an Exchange governor (board member) would ask Siebert, "How many more women are there behind you?" Their trepidation would prove misplaced, at least in the short-term. Only two women followed Siebert's lead and joined the NYSE—Jane Larkin, for a brief time, and Alice Jarcho, who would become the first woman to have a full-time presence on the actual Exchange floor.[271]

Siebert delighted in breaking down a barrier at the NYSE, and she would go on to form her own brokerage firm, Muriel Siebert & Co., which in 1996 morphed into the discount brokerage firm

Siebert Financial Corp. Commenting on her firm's success, she was quick to remark that "[if] you can't play with the big boys, start your own game."[272]

$ $ $

While Siebert began her career as a NYSE seat-holder, Wilma continued to run FOWSAB and devote time to her weekly radio show. For her part, Davis continued to write and publish her wildly erratic newsletter. Many corporate titans undoubtedly wished they both would retire. In her late sixties, Wilma was certainly of retirement age but saw no reason to stop fighting. The much younger Davis would follow her mentor's example and remain on the activism circuit as long as possible. Neither were about to go away.

Mounting social tensions egged them on as the scale and scope of cultural movements intensified. Disillusionment mounted, mainly among passionate young adults, as the Vietnam "conflict" escalated, poverty loomed large, and urban uprisings underscored racial divides. Some protesters took on companies they saw as complicit, like those that benefitted from the Vietnam War, or allegedly aided discrimination in the U.S. and apartheid abroad.

Several demonstrations, like the 1965 storming of Chase Manhattan Bank's headquarters to demand divestiture from South Africa, had a discernable anti-capitalist bent. Neither Wilma nor Davis was supportive of these types of movements, least of all for the threat they posed to their dividends.[273] For similar reasons, the gadflies must not have been thrilled at what happened at the NYSE the morning of August 24, 1967. Shortly after equity trading commenced, protestor Abbie Hoffman, along with a few cohorts, visited the Exchange intent upon some mischief. The Visitors'

Gallery, open since 1939 and popular among tourists, overlooked the trading floor, which teemed with the actions of brokers, specialists, and runners. As security guards warily watched on, Hoffman and his crew leaned over the gallery railing, and proceeded to shower the floor with dollar bills as a sign of their disgust with capitalism and the Vietnam War.

Some startled traders ran to grab the money, while others laughed, and still others steamed at the disrespect to the Exchange. Photographers tipped off about the stunt captured the bills wafting down to the Exchange floor. After his eviction from the Exchange building, Hoffman provided a final photo op by lighting up a five-dollar bill. Hoffman counted the episode a success, later recalling that "We had $200 in dollar bills—enough to look like a lot of money—and we went and threw them down from the gallery of the Stock Exchange." He continued, "Trading stopped for about six minutes; the tickertape stopped—it was great!"[274]

Exchange officials, like President Keith Funston, were unamused. Not long afterwards, the NYSE enclosed the Visitors' Gallery with bullet-proof glass, over an inch thick.[275] With his well-orchestrated protest, Hoffman and the group he, Jerry Rubin, and others recently had founded (the Youth International Party, or "Yippie" movement) garnered attention. Fondly recalling the incident much later, Hoffman remarked, "If you don't like the news, why not go out and make your own?"[276]

Hoffman's dollar bills rained down onto an NYSE that retained its club-like atmosphere. Accompanied women could enter the floor as guests, but they could not conduct business there. Wilma herself had been on the floor, escorted by President Funston, as had other groups of women, like a delegation of librarians curious to see trading in action. Such occurrences, though, remained relatively rare.

Typically, non-members had to observe the frenzied activity from the Visitors' Gallery. That was where in 1953 a young Siebert fell in love with the NYSE, on a tourist trip to New York with two close friends. Exhilarated by the energy, Siebert told her friends right then and there, "Now, *this* is exciting. Maybe I'll come back here and look for a job." She returned home with the ticker tape souvenir that read, "Welcome to the NYSE, Muriel Siebert." Years later, she'd hear the same exact greeting, but its meaning would markedly change.[277]

$ $ $

By 1968, a few months after Hoffman's dollar burning, tensions in the United States were palpable, in part due to growing casualties in Vietnam. At the end of January, Ho Chi Minh's regime in North Vietnam conducted a broad military offensive, targeting multiple key cities in South Vietnam. The "Tet offensive" took South Vietnamese and U.S. forces off guard, leading to high casualties as American forces stemmed, then pushed back, the North Vietnamese Army. The U.S. military might have prevailed, but casualties, and questions of the war's purpose, were growing.[278] When news later leaked that U.S. troops had committed war crimes that March, killing civilians in the small village of My Lai, the tide of American public opinion turned further against the war.[279]

On issues other than the few she prioritized, Wilma tended to avoid controversy. She neither disparaged nor praised wartime protestors during her radio show. Rather, she focused on how continued involvement in Vietnam might affect consumers' pocketbooks, and how the war and other geopolitical events might influence the value of the dollar and the trajectory of the stock market. The market roamed in bear territory, reflecting a stalled U.S. economy, which had been dragged down in part by the heavy expenditures required to support both the war in Vietnam and President Johnson's Great Society programs. Throughout 1968, the stock market gyrated, battered by Tet and the assassinations of Martin Luther King, Jr. in April and Robert F. Kennedy in June. On again, off again peace talks, President Johnson's withdrawal from the presidential race in March 1968, numerous urban uprisings, a declining dollar, and the Poor People's March on Washington in June also increased national uncertainty and market volatility.[280]

Through the turmoil, Wilma reminded her listeners that for all stocks, "sitzfleisch," the ability to sit out rough patches without panicking, was key. "It takes money not only to buy stocks but also to afford to *hold* them." As stocks whipped up and down, responding to daily noise, like rumors about the war's status, Wilma told listeners that "successful long-term investors avoid being over-influenced by day-to-day emotions." Wilma's advice matched the attitude of most market participants, as annual stock market turnover, the percentage of shares that traded hands in a year, was typically less than twenty percent in the late 1960s. But investors were human, and it was difficult not to be emotional about the increasingly fragile state of the market, the dollar, and the Union.[281]

In the spring of 1968, sit-ins, strikes, and riots roiled across college campuses, including Wilma's alma mater, Columbia University. Wilma, herself opposing continued American involvement in Vietnam but not an active protester, knew the main issues triggering the unrest at the Morningside Heights campus. Incensing pacifist students, the university maintained a strong ROTC program, and it continued to allow, even encourage, government and defense companies to recruit there. At the same time, the University came under attack for its campus expansion plans. Officials had just announced plans for a new gym, which would require deeper penetration into Morningside Heights, on the border of West Harlem, causing possible dislocation and disruption for many long-time residents.

In April of 1968, protesters, including members of the Student Afro-American Society (SAS) and the radical Students for a Democratic Society (SDS) led by Tom Hayden, an outside agitator not enrolled at Columbia, stormed several administrative buildings and classrooms on campus, and occupied five of them, including Hamilton Hall, a short distance from where Wilma had taken her journalism courses decades previously. After several days of occupation, the NYC police arrested those camping inside the buildings, along with other protesters totaling more than 700.

Most Columbia students were not involved in the protests, and many supported the University. The majority of alumni were distraught that Columbia received this kind of news attention. Campus unrest tarnished the University's prestige by giving the impression that it had been overrun by "hippies," and had lost control of a portion of its student body to the extent that it couldn't operate as usual. The takeover of key buildings stalled administrative functioning; protesters organized lifts of food through windows; and classes had to be cancelled. The headline for a *Life* magazine article that May was "Mutiny at a Great University," and many wondered how long Columbia could indeed continue to be "great" given such anarchy on campus. Chiding the protesters, New York's Mayor John Lindsay inveighed, "The demonstration clearly exceeded even the most liberal perimeters of the right to assemble and dissent."[282]

For that same issue of *Life*, the magazine editors asked five students in Columbia's Graduate School of Journalism to provide their inside perspectives. In the wake of the unrest, many of Wilma's fellow alumni stopped giving to the University. Some never donated again. While infuriating some, the Columbia uprising inspired similar protests on other campuses across the country, which continued as casualties in Vietnam mounted.[283]

Pledging to get America out of Vietnam and to restore law and order at home, Republican candidate Richard Nixon, former vice president in the Eisenhower administration, won the presidency on November 5, 1968, defeating his Democratic opponent, sitting Vice President Hubert Humphrey.[284]

By May of 1973, of course, the nation would be transfixed by the start of the Senate Watergate hearings, investigating the burglary of the Democratic National Committee (DNC) office, in the Watergate complex of buildings in Washington D.C. The burglars turned out to be connected to Nixon's Committee for the Reelection of the President ("CRP", later mockingly called by critics "CREEP"). Nixon's efforts to cover up the scandal resulted in his resignation from office. Impeachment proceedings against him began in February 1974, and he resigned on August 9, 1974. But his greatest crime, in Wilma's eyes at least, was breaking the dollar's peg to gold, a process that began in 1971 and was sanctified by 1973.

$ $ $

Wilma was a natural extrovert, and she loved giving advice to whomever would listen. On *Pocketbook News*, Wilma had that key audience. She spent much airtime discussing the demise of the gold-backed dollar and the subsequent rise in inflation—why it was rearing its ugly head, what to do about it, and how it hurt.

Since 1792, the U.S. government had determined the value of the dollar by setting it equal to a specific amount of gold (and

sometimes silver) and allowing it to be traded freely both domesti-
cally and internationally. That retail gold standard system broke down
during the Great War, and then again during the Great Depression.
Near the end of the Second World War the Allies designed a new
global monetary system at a meeting held in Bretton Woods, New
Hampshire. The result, called the Bretton Woods System (BWS), was
a system of fixed exchange rates centered around the U.S. dollar, convertible to gold at $35 an ounce. The nations that joined the BWS,
basically the entire "free" or non-Soviet world, agreed to accept U.S.
dollars at fixed rates, i.e., so many dollars for so much local currency.
The U.S., in turn, promised to sell gold to the nations in the system
at $35 per ounce, the rate established by FDR during the Depres-
sion's darkest days. The dollar, in other words, served as a substitute
for gold in international trade but holders could trade their dollars in
for gold at a known rate when they saw fit.

Wilma tracked the BWS's demise in excruciating detail, deriving
most of her insights from Franz Pick, a monetary expert whose
analyses she often summarized for listeners before adding her own
thoughts. The BWS was designed to allow member nations to enjoy
the convenience of fixed exchange rates while preserving countries'
abilities to conduct their own monetary policies, i.e., the ability to
raise or lower domestic interest rates to meet output and employment
goals. The BWS worked for over a decade, although some countries,
like Britain, that ran chronic trade deficits, had to devalue their currencies several times to improve their balance of payments (more
exports; fewer imports). Countries running trade surpluses, like West
Germany, faced the opposite problem, and had to raise the value of
their currencies in U.S. dollar terms several times. When the West
Germans revalued the mark in 1961, Wilma called it a "monetary
coup" that few Americans, even bankers, understood. In 1957, after

the French devalued their franc for the eleventh time, Wilma noted that the twenty percent reduction was good news for Americans traveling to France or interested in buying French products. Longer term, though, it would mean France earned more dollars than it spent and hence had dollars to convert into gold.[285]

The BWS was a boon to the U.S. in the postwar years. Europeans used dollars to rebuild their shattered countries, and American banks were at the forefront. The dollar's place at the center of international trade and finance allowed the U.S. government to borrow and spend large sums. For decades, it seemed that Americans could enjoy both guns *and* butter (military expenditures and consumer goods) without worrying about inflation.[286]

During the 1960s, however, some nations, like France, increasingly converted their dollar holdings into gold, forcing the U.S. government to face difficult tradeoffs. After Kennedy's narrow victory in 1960, he was constrained in the economic policies he could affect. For example, he could not lower interest rates as promised without threatening a run on gold, which would go against his sound dollar pledge. Ike was already pulling U.S. troops back home from abroad to limit government spending and save gold, Wilma noted. "There is a Dictator in our land," she noted. "That Dictator is: GOLD." Kennedy would ignore the dictator, however, and reverse the flow of U.S. "advisers" back into southeast Asia.[287]

It ultimately fell upon the U.S. Federal Reserve to defend the dollar-gold peg by raising domestic interest rates even when the domestic economic situation weakened, calling for lower rates. When the pound sterling, a key international currency, fell in value in 1964, the British raised their interest rate to seven percent and the Fed responded in kind, raising America's domestic interest rate to four percent to keep dollars flowing into the U.S. and protect the U.S. government's gold supply. As it was an election year, President Johnson was unhappy with the move—economic slowdowns aren't popular and that's exactly what the Federal Reserve was encouraging.[288]

But the Fed had to act, Wilma explained to listeners, because "money for hire chases interest rates around the world." "Only the threat of war is worse than a monetary crisis," she added, before detailing how the Fed and the central banks of several other countries had helped to support sterling at $2.80. In 1968, the Fed again raised interest rates as part of an accord with European bankers who also sought austerity measures in the form of higher taxes and lower government expenditures. In a fortunate turn for the dollar, riots in France forced the French government to sell off some of its gold hoard, alleviating some of the pressure on the system for the time being.[289]

When the British devalued the pound sterling in late 1967, Wilma noted that government officials had denied the idea to the bitter end, while Pick called devaluation "inevitable." Pick was right, as were his warnings that the devaluation had not gone far enough. "Britain's Chancellor of the Exchequer admitted that at the time he assured everyone that the pound would not be devalued," Wilma told listeners, "He already knew it would have to be done. Such are the duties of public officials."[290]

Many blamed France for the demise of the BWS but, as Wilma explained, France was within its rights to demand gold for dollars. The true culprit, Wilma explained, lay at the twin deficits of government spending and the negative trade balance. "Since 1950," she reminded listeners, "we've spent 32 billion dollars more abroad payable in gold than we've received. Now our real gold stock is less than eight billion calculated in paper dollars."[291]

When President Johnson signed a bill ending the "gold cover" requirement for Federal Reserve Banks, where one dollar's worth of gold backed every four dollars of paper notes, Wilma lamented that "the dollar is no longer as good as gold." She told listeners that "the drums were beating and the flags flying in the St. Patrick Day's Parade on Fifth Avenue. I caught it in front of the Plaza. I looked up at the flag, so proudly we hail. And I began to cry . . ." The drama continued in another episode a few weeks later that began with Wilma claiming that "You are watching the late, late show for the United States in defense of the dollar. The scene of the rescue operation has shifted from Washington with the aid of six nations to Stockholm and the Big Ten with France, the villain or the unsung hero as strict disciplinarian." Her melancholy was fueled in part by her belief that "the loss of our dollar prestige would constitute a victory for the Communists."[292]

In response to German proposals to revalue all the currencies in the BWS, or to abandon fixed exchange rates altogether, Wilma noted the likely inflationary effects of either path. Revaluation of all the system's currency against the dollar, she explained, would have the same economic effect as "devaluation" of the dollar, and that "would be instant inflation." She then explained that those worried about higher prices should go into debt to buy real resources like land and avoid fixed income assets, like bonds.[293]

Wilma wanted a return to the pre-Depression retail gold standard, so she backed de Gaulle's call for a return in 1965, calling it the "pocketbook story of the year . . . of the decade ... possibly the pocketbook story of our generation." While many still equated gold with deflation and unemployment, she said, "there isn't a woman in the world who wouldn't rather have gold in her hands than paper, no matter whose picture is printed on it." She noted that politicians were doing little substantively to alleviate pressure on U.S. gold reserves caused by the redemption of dollars for gold by central banks as part of BWS.[294]

The world, though, went in a different direction, hoping that if central bankers remained independent of political influence, they would generally keep inflation low and steady, which became the de facto goal of policymakers worldwide—a fact that Wilma herself noted in 1966, when delegates from 105 countries appeared in New York City for the annual meeting of the International Monetary Fund (IMF) and World Bank. All Wilma could think about was the fact that "the United States owes more Gold than it owns," while everyone in attendance talked about inflation, and not, Wilma lamented, "*stopping* inflation."[295]

Wilma had a difficult time believing in central bank independence because she knew about periods when the Fed had subordinated itself to the government, as during World War II and the Korean conflict. And on her radio show she had covered the run-in between William McChesney Martin, the head of the Fed, and LBJ, when the president tried to intimidate Martin into maintaining easy money policies. Martin refused but a chastened LBJ did re-nominate him as Fed chairman. Wilma also knew that the Minneapolis Fed unilaterally reduced its interest rate a quarter percent a week before Minnesotan Hubert Humphrey was to be nominated for President at the Democratic National Convention in Chicago. This Wilma took to be a return to the party's traditional easy money policies, a tradition temporarily shrouded during LBJ's reign due to inflationary pressures.[296]

Wilma touted herself as the first and only reporter to notice that neither party in their 1968 convention platforms promised to defend gold convertibility at $35 per ounce as Kennedy and Johnson had.

Meanwhile, the IMF announced it would not index Special Drawing Rights, or paper gold as Wilma liked to call them, to the cost of living. Neither boded well for the dollar or the BWS, which did not outlive the coming, troubled administration of Richard Nixon.[297]

$ $ $

Wilma clearly knew what investors should do to decrease the effects of inflation—take on nominally denominated debt. "It may be better to have a mortgage on your house than to own a mortgage on someone else's in a period of deteriorating money," Wilma told listeners in 1965. Going into debt was even better than buying stocks because stock prices did not always keep pace with inflation, much less exceed it, while debtors could repay their obligations in less valuable dollars. Holding cash in an inflationary period would not do because "what FDIC can't insure you against . . . is the diminishing purchasing power of the dollar." "Even if you put your money under the mattress," she reminded listeners, "it will change in value."[298]

When it came to understanding the causes of inflation, which of course is the first step in successfully forecasting it, Wilma was on shakier ground. She knew that "rising prices cause inflation like wet streets cause rain" but at first she did not understand what caused the rain. Today, economists know that inflation, properly understood, is a monetary phenomenon. Prices rise across the board continuously when the rate of growth of the money supply exceeds the rate of growth of the demand for money. That fact was not well understood early in Wilma's radio career, when inflation was often considered the result of "cost-push," code for workers demanding higher wages. If granted, it was thought, those bigger paychecks would allow workers to bid up the prices of the goods they consumed, thereby causing inflation. Labor negotiations and strikes therefore led to much wringing of the hands and lamentations of woe from a woman ostensibly on the side of the little guys in their battle with Big Business. Wilma, for instance, lamented the fact that by 1959 some 600,000 workers nationwide had won so-called escalator clauses (automatic cost of living adjustments, or COLA) in their labor contracts. And she quoted, approvingly, Roger Blough, Chairman of U.S. Steel, when he argued that "in seeking a cure for inflation, we must not attack the results of inflation—(price increases) rather than the cause—cost increases."[299]

Not until the mid-1960s did Wilma begin to question the orthodoxy and consider the monetary causes of inflation. Specifically, she wondered aloud if trading stamps caused inflation. Retailers, especially grocers, gave trading stamps to customers in an early type of loyalty program. Once a book was filled with the requisite number of stamps, the customer could exchange it with the stamp issuer, of which there were many specialized companies, for merchandise like televisions, row boats, sewing machines, and so forth. Wilma also worried about misleading advertising by the leading stamp companies and defaults, but her primary concern was with the potential monetary effects of the popular stamp programs.[300]

Wilma need not have worried as trading stamps were merely money substitutes, not new sources of cash. But her ruminations were signs of things to come. In 1967, she clearly differentiated between cost-push and monetary inflation when she noted that "some 700 major labor contracts have come up for renegotiations this year resulting in a cost-push type of inflation as well as the type that comes from inflating the money supply." Soon after she told listeners that the 3.5 percent inflation rate, the fastest in a decade, was "fueled not only by the cost-push of labor settlements but by massive infusions of new money into the banking system by our Federal Reserve Board." By 1969, she was citing Citibank to the effect that "most of the blame for inflation" should be placed on an "erratic money policy that has pushed up the quantity of money more swiftly than the quantity of goods and services."[301]

Inflation became a hot topic in the U.S. following World War II because most Americans had grown up during the gold standard era, a period when the price level changed but on average went down as much as it went up. The postwar period was one in which the price level went up more in some years than in others but never went down. Continual increases in the Consumer Price Index (CPI), Wilma explained, meant that a dollar in 1957 could buy only half as much as a Depression-era dollar had bought. American families, Wilma believed, could "beat the CPI" by bargain hunting, doing without some non-essential goods, and choosing cheaper substitutes.[302]

This "creeping inflation" weighed heavily on many Americans, including those in the middle class with modest savings who owned nominally denominated government bonds and life insurance. "A little inflation, like the first cocktail, makes everybody feel happy," Wilma warned, "but inflation which cuts into savings and purchasing power is really just another tax." Wilma claimed that the Republicans had a better record on inflation than the Democrats did, and that most people believed that, so the Democrats raised the specter of deflation during the 1960 presidential campaign. Instead came more inflation and in 1968, 1971, and 1973, the delinking of the dollar from gold.[303]

In 1966, Wilma declared inflation public enemy number one and called it "the cruelest tax of all." In late 1967, she noted that most Americans surveyed stated their number one worry was the value of money, not race riots, draft cards, adultery, or even hippies. And they were right to be worried, as the Great Inflation of the 1970s would prove.[304]

Inflation and government debt were inexorably tied in Wilma's view. "Every deficit," she believed, "comes out of your pocketbook in taxes or inflation." Government deficits caused inflation directly and increased the government's incentive to print more money. So Wilma was a debt hawk too, more of a neoclassical debt pessimist than Keynesian debt optimist. In fact, she claimed that "the Britisher John Keynes got his lowest mark in economics when he entered civil service."[305]

Instead of joining others in applauding Kennedy's inauguration speech, for example, Wilma wondered aloud if "the roar of affirmation would have been the same if [Kennedy's main proposals had been] translated as it eventually will be into pocketbook language such as controls or higher taxes." In 1966, Wilma noted that interest on the national debt ate up twelve percent of the federal budget, a bigger line item than anything else, save defense.

Many believed that inflation was good because it made it easier for deeply indebted governments to repay what they owed. But Wilma espoused what is sometimes called the "fiscal constitution," a doctrine dating back to Alexander Hamilton that held that deficit financing was only "acceptable as inevitable in times of war or emergency." Watching New York City slowly degenerate into bankruptcy only furthered Wilma's debt pessimism and belied the notion that inflation helped governments to repay their debts. First came the downgrade of the city's bonds, which led to higher interest charges. As the Big Apple's deficits climbed higher in response, its bond ratings dropped again, raising its interest costs by millions of dollars per year, which forced it to borrow yet more. Finance administrator Roy Goodman would not find a way out, Wilma predicted, and she was correct.[306]

During the currency crises that periodically struck during the BWS, Wilma for lunch would order *domestic* sardines on rye to "help our balance of payments problem." She was half-joking but always appreciated a laugh. "Everybody's against sin and FOR a stable dollar," she later quipped, "but not everybody agrees on how to achieve" the goal of stopping the "creeping" inflation that had beset the economy since the end of World War II. "Inflation has slowed down for a while," Wilma told listeners in 1960, "but a Department of Labor official admits that inflation is no longer in the creeping stage. It's TODDLING!" "As for the dollar being as good as gold," she quipped after President Johnson signed the bill that allowed banks to limit the gold they held in reserves, "that has become as obsolete as saying '23, skidoo,'" early twentieth century slang for a rapid exit.[307]

$ $ $

All joking aside, inflation left Wilma unamused. Her serious intellect understood that inflation hurt borrowers, consumers, savers, and workers.

The Phillips Curve, the notion pioneered by A.W. Phillips that overly hot labor markets could cause inflation, suggested that high unemployment could slow down price increases. "Full employment," Wilma explained, "means not more than two to three percent unemployed . . . virtually unattainable without inflation." She knew that minimum wage laws increased unemployment, but also realized that because they were not indexed to inflation, any ill effects were soon lost as the dollar declined in purchasing power.[308]

Wilma also knew the Fisher Effect, which she stated as "inflation breeds higher interest rates," affected the interest rates that savers could expect to receive. The effect of usury caps, or maximum rates of interest on loans, however, was to limit lending. "Ceilings on interest that can be charged for mortgage money in many states," she noted in 1968, "will make the money harder to come by," hurting poor borrowers the most.

And Wilma knew that inflation *relative* to other countries drove exchange rates and hence the cost of foreign vacations and imported goods. The dollar was in much demand in 1962, she explained, because inflation in the U.S., while an egregious two percent, was better than the seven to ten percent inflation experienced that year in the Common Market countries of Europe. As a currency weakens, she understood, policymakers should raise interest rates in response. And she knew that inflation hurts the "international trade balance" and thus weakens the dollar, all else constant. She also understood the effects of currency values on trade. Raising the value of the German mark, she noted, would "lower the price of imports [into Germany] and raise the price of [Germany's] exports" and that that would "put a squeeze on profits, hurt foreign sales, and possibly trigger a recession in West Germany."[309]

Wilma also realized that by fixing the price of gold at $35 an ounce for decades, the U.S. government made domestic gold mining unprofitable. The price of everything went up and up but the payout for gold mining companies remained the same. Buying gold stocks, therefore, was really speculating that the dollar would be devalued.[310]

Wilma cared deeply about pocketbook issues hitting everyday Americans, and thus she watched with frustration as inflation ratcheted up throughout the 1970s. She continued to weigh in on the Great Inflation problem on her weekly *Pocketbook News* broadcasts. On that pioneering program, she also discussed a range of other issues, especially investment strategies. With millions of loyal listeners, Wilma's radio show continued to educate the American masses, even as membership in FOWSAB declined and the Great Inflation raged. Even more than the magazine articles describing her antics, *Pocketbook News* kept Wilma in the limelight and showed just how well her Wall Street bets played out.

8

POP ECONOMIST

Once a thing is past, I'm not interested.
I'm always interested in the future.

—Wilma Soss. Once a week for decades. Across America.

W hile Wilma never could quite turn her Federation into the disciplined, mass movement she envisioned, she neverthe-less attracted millions of listeners to her weekly radio show. The show's sheer longevity—running nonstop from 1957 to 1980—was powerful testimony to Wilma's popularity among a varied set of listeners, women as well as men, young as well as old. She was inter-ested in spreading economic and financial literacy, and she took an egalitarian approach to that quest, never patronizing her audience or pandering to them. She was in the business of uplift and believed in everyone's power to learn for themselves and better their overall financial situation.

Titling the show *Pocketbook News* was Wilma's way of saying that it provided relevant commentary that could benefit everyone in their pocketbook (or purse, handbag, wallet, bank, or brokerage account). Just as decades later Jim Cramer geared his television show *Mad Money* to amateur investors, Wilma sought to appeal to ordinary people trying to get a leg up. Unlike Cramer, she weighed in on personal finance/household economics matters and the direction of the broad economy, not just the state of the stock market. She did it all with authority and verve. Her famously loud voice once was likened to a "strident . . . mongoose," and it was jokingly said that "she could do her Sunday afternoon coast-to-coast radio show without the aid of the NBC network."[311]

In everything she said on the air, Wilma proved herself to be much more than "a highly attractive, fearsomely energetic blond lady." She possessed a serious intellect. Although not the best in the math department, she was keenly analytical. The result was a certain wonkiness that held Wilma in good stead throughout her career as a corporate activist and broadcast journalist.[312]

On the air and in shareholder meetings, Wilma often argued for policies on two levels, ethical soundness and profitability, long before the corporate social responsibility (CSR) movement came into vogue. She backed her claims with facts and figures, which gave her an authenticity that even her detractors could admire. She also knew a lot of economic theory, some picked up at Columbia, but much through self-study. Through events at FOWSAB, she listened to many learned talks about the stock market, business trends, and other relevant matters. Her library overflowed with corporate reports, management case histories, and important business tomes, including Benjamin Graham's books on value investing and the lesser known but also important work of Jackson Martindell, including his

1950 *The Scientific Appraisal of Management: A Study of the Business Practices of Well-Managed Companies.* In 1949, after stints in the U.S. military and as economic consultant to Yugoslav dictator Josip Broz Tito, Martindell founded the American Institute of Management and developed a qualitative "management audit" technique to assess the quality of business leadership.[313]

While avoiding mathematics, Wilma came to the right conclusions by reasoning through economic problems in line with theory and informed by experience. Although she cannot properly be called an economist as she did no original work in the field, she worked very much in the tradition of business economics and political economy and her views were quite sophisticated. She was a pop economist able to convey complex topics to a lay audience. Unlike most acolytes of the dismal science, she could find the humor in the driest financial concept and the direst economic situation.

While some of Wilma's humor sounds execrable to the modern ear, we know that they elicited smiles from her listeners because they admitted as much. Many of Wilma's jokes helped to further her agendas, particularly "economic suffrage." According to one of Wilma's more elaborate jokes, a banker lent a lady $1 for a year on the security of a $1,000 bond. After renewing her loan several times, the banker had to ask why she kept borrowing a dollar if she owned a bond worth a cool grand. Well, the woman explained, the bank wanted $10 a year for a safe deposit box. This way, she got the bank to safeguard her bond for only six cents a year *and* had the use of its dollar.[314]

After interviewing baseball legend Ty Cobb about his investment strategies, Wilma wryly noted that "at 71, Mr. Ty Cobb keeps his speculative eye for blondes." She noted at the end of a long discussion of prescription drug prices that "those most tranquil about prices of drugs are the Christian Scientists—they don't touch the stuff." She ended a warning about getting sucked into investment pools by joking that America "could use a 'speculators anonymous' like alcoholics anonymous."[315]

Wilma sometimes played off celebrity news to make a point. When actress Joan Crawford claimed that she was not worth a "sous," for example, Wilma explained to listeners that non-contributory pensions were often stingy with widow's benefits and that Social Security gave little aid to widows who did not have minor children or were too young to retire. In April 1962, Wilma castigated Jackie Kennedy for going to lunch at Buckingham Palace wearing a mink hat, "hurting the milliners and too late in the season to help the furriers." Liz Taylor was just as bad for being spotted in Rome about the same time wearing a Somali leopard hat and coat. When LBJ's daughter Lynda Bird got a job at *McCall's* in 1966, Wilma used the opportunity to explore the business empire of its publisher, Norton Simon. Similarly, Wilma used Jackie's marriage to Greek tycoon Aristotle Onassis to explore the billionaire's portfolio of stocks and productive assets, like ships.[316]

Wilma also liked to describe people with power in business and government. Economist Walter Heller, for example, she described as "tall, slim, youthful looking, urbane and witty. He dispenses the [JFK] Administration's economic line interlarded with humor."[317] Behind all the laughs and glitz, however, lurked a serious intellect that should be understood in detail. Suffice it to say, Wilma could bet the second half of her life on Wall Street because she understood it, inside and out, better than most men.

$ $ $

Although Wilma had no formal training in economics, she knew many of the basic tenets, especially those related to finance, and explained them with great clarity. Occasionally, she shared valuable tidbits like the cheapest way to get a loan, which in 1959 was to post a savings account as collateral. "Your net interest cost may be as low as 1.25 percent," or the difference between the savings rate and the loan's interest charges. She also walked listeners through the intricacies of buying U.S. savings bonds, series E, F, G, or H, some of which made coupon payments or could be sold to other investors and some of which had to be held to maturity. She also explained how federal deposit insurance worked, which in the 1960s was $10,000 per insured bank or savings and loan but warned that it could be several weeks before depositors received all of their money back in the event their bank folded.[318]

Most of the time, though, Wilma supplied listeners with analysis, not information. Although she often quoted experts, she did not parrot back everything she heard but rather combined it with her own insights based on her deep understanding of business economics.

Wilma knew, most fundamentally, that interest rates strongly influenced the "course of the stock market" because sums to be received in the future, from dividends or sales of shares, had to be expressed in current dollars by discounting them by the current rate of interest. So, interest rates and the prices of IOUs and other assets were inversely related. In other words, "bonds . . . went down in price as their yields went up."[319]

She knew, too, that lower interest rates stimulated the economy. "Interest rates have to come down," she told listeners in mid-1968, "to stimulate the homebuilding boom needed to keep us from sliding into recession in early 1969." Wilma also knew about the wealth effect and stated it clearly: "When the stock market goes down, people spend less."

Although she tried to avoid the gratuitous use of jargon, Wilma knew that listeners needed to learn the lingo if they were to keep up with the news on their own. She explained the ins and outs of terms like "liquid," a term for assets that are easily and quickly saleable. When asked if stocks were liquid, Wilma responded that the answer depended on "the quality of the stock and the market for that industry or company," and whether it traded on an exchange or over the counter. And, she warned, liquidity could quickly dry up during a crisis.[320]

Wilma understood that international trade could help consumers by keeping domestic prices down. And she knew that tariffs could trigger trade wars big enough to lead to recession, as during the 1930s. So, she opposed the so-called Christmas Tree Amendment, a protectionist measure for certain domestic industries that attached to a bill increasing benefits for Social Security recipients. "Exports," not limiting imports with tariffs, "are our first line of defense in protecting the dollar," she smartly argued. Before the assassinations, urban uprisings, and Tet offensive changed everything, she believed that "free trade versus protectionism may well" be a major issue in the 1968 presidential campaign. She called tariffs "cry-baby legislation" and accused U.S. Steel of urging its stockholders to whine for special privileges. Later, she called the children's wear trade a "cry baby" industry for seeking protectionist legislation. At the same time, she prayed for "peace on earth," including "the free flow of ideas, of people, of goods and moneys without the barriers of border controls."[321]

Wilma displayed a clear understanding of the theory of rational expectations, the notion that investors trade on expectations, not realities. So "if business does not begin to recover as hoped by the final quarter of the year," she warned listeners in June 1958, stock "prices will be vulnerable for having discounted events that do not occur." Echoing NYSE president Keith Funston, she noted several times that "the stock market is a barometer of economic weather—not a thermometer of the nation's health." It rarely moved in sync with the economy but rather ran ahead of it. "The stock market," she noted, "is always looking ahead at least six months," so when it went "sideways" all that meant was that the future was not yet discernible.[322]

"Statistics used by the government tell us what has happened," she further explained. "The stock market," by contrast, "foreshadows what people think is going to happen and to what extent they are willing to bet their own and others' money on it." Wilma typically explained to her radio listeners the three great presidential reports made every January: the State of the Union, the budget, and the Economic Report. But, she noted, "the stock market is the nation's pulse." It was a leading economic indicator, or, as she explained it, "the stock market is one of the earliest movers in the economy. It feels in its ticker what is going to happen."[323]

$ $ $

On air, Wilma, like FOWSAB, did not make buy or sell recommendations on individual stocks or other investments. Nor did she respond to specific queries. She admitted that if she had "all the answers" she would be "busy making millions" instead of talking. She once said that Thomas Watson, president of IBM, made the most sense of any businessman she had spoken to because he told her firmly: "I never forecast!" Wilma doubtless would have noted the irony in IBM much later naming its forecasting AI software after Watson.[324]

Sometimes, though, Wilma warned her listeners away from tricky strategies, like short selling, which she noted grew in popularity whenever the stock market trended downwards. "But," she warned listeners, "short selling in anticipation of the price going down further is even more risky than buying stocks in expectation of a rise in price" if you do not own the underlying shares. Such naked short selling, as gurus called the practice, could lead to a "whopping loss," she warned. Wilma also warned investors away from the bond market in 1958 because speculators were buying and selling on margin. With just five percent down, and even zero percent at some brokerages, people could make or lose millions in just a few hours. That type of gambling was not Wilma's way.[325]

Conglomerates, or disparate companies thrown together by executives during long bull markets, made Wilma bonkers. "In the 'go go' stock market," as she put it, "conglomerates have been swingers." They might be fun at first, but investors could end up getting burned in the end. Wilma, as usual, was up on the latest and greatest in academic research, citing a study by Sam Richardson Reid of the University of Illinois that showed that the merger of 487 companies between 1951 and 1961 "actually lowered the profit rate."[326]

Other fashionable but tenuous investments, like convertible bonds, also failed to win Wilma's approval. Not long after she warned listeners about convertibles, the Fed raised margin requirements on them from 20 to 70 percent, which made their values plummet. "Didn't I tell you on *Pocketbook News* that the convertible bond market was no place for a widow or the uninitiated?" she gloated.[327]

Wilma also rightly ripped diamonds as reliable investments, urging people to pawn them at reputable, charitable pawn shops whenever they needed a loan. Otherwise, diamonds were just pretty, sentimental rocks that did not pay dividends, were unlikely to appreciate faster than inflation, and could suffer a big loss if new sources were discovered, as they allegedly had been in Yakutsk, U.S.S.R., or if artificial diamond producers started to produce gem quality stones, which they eventually did. "Just how much diamonds are a hedge against inflation," she noted, "is doubtful" as the prices of some carats could skyrocket while others hardly budged. Moreover, it was difficult for individuals to sell them for more than wholesale. Buying stock in DeBeer's, which controlled much of the free world's diamond trade, was a better play.[328]

Wilma also discussed the ins and outs of the super tricky art market. Look for potential big movers rather than paintings likely to barely keep pace with inflation, she suggested. But she later noted that while some pieces of art appreciated in spectacular fashion, like a Monet that jumped in value from $80 to $11,000 to $1.4 million over a few decades, other artworks, even by the so-called masters, sometimes stagnated or even fell in price.[329]

After properly insuring oneself and family, investors should buy bonds first, then stock mutual funds. "Only your surplus money should be put into the stock market," she counseled listeners. Wilma was right in tune with what the NYSE was preaching in its ad campaigns at the time. Occasionally, when the stock market got frothy, the NYSE ran cautionary advertisements with exactly such warnings. Wilma wanted more people to buy stocks, but only if they could afford to do so. At the time, 40 million Americans owned savings bonds while only nine million owned stocks. "Every American should own savings bonds," she argued, "before buying stocks." Stock mutual funds were the next logical step, especially when inflation loomed, and they, like savings bonds, could be purchased via a regular monthly payroll deduction plan.[330]

Wilma preferred the traditional "buy and hold" approach to stock market investment. In other words, she tried to induce listeners to "think in terms of business growth over a span of years and not in stock prices overnight." Timing was often crucial, lest one buy high and sell low. She suggested that life insurance stocks could be purchased for long-term investment at any point, but fire insurance stocks should be purchased only when the companies were losing money and should be sold only when they were profitable because they experienced frequent "hard" and "soft" market cycles.[331]

Well before Warren Buffett became a household name, Wilma, like the original value investor Benjamin Graham, urged listeners to "stick to underlying values—earnings, profits, dividends, business prospects." "Companies that have expanded too rapidly and have too much debt in their capital structure," Wilma suggested, "should be avoided even if many stock market favorites fall in this category." That is precisely the same advice given in market historian Edward Chancellor's *Capital Returns*, published in 2015.[332]

Just because the stock market was up, Wilma repeatedly reminded listeners, did not mean that it would continue to go up. In fact, higher prices often indicated that a fall was imminent. Maybe this time really marked a "new era" as market promoters always claimed, but Wilma doubted it. "About every twenty-five years we have one of these new eras in Wall Street," she noted in 1961, almost fifty years before Professors Carmen Reinhart and Ken Rogoff popularized the phrase *This Time Is Different*. "The first one began before the Civil War." Even if this time *was* different, she added, "sooner or later the old fundamentals will re-assert themselves." It might look foolish not to be on the stock-buying bandwagon "when [positive] psychological forces dominate" but, she assured listeners, "eventually the old yardsticks as to value would reassert themselves."[333]

Wilma liked employee stock ownership programs (ESOPs), especially that of Sears Roebuck, which from modest beginnings in 1916 had grown by 1958 to about $700 million, or twenty-six percent of the giant retailer's market capitalization. She was especially encouraged when Sears recognized their workers' right to vote their shares secretly in corporate elections. She believed that stockownership plus some actual control of corporate management was more "People's Capitalism," the catch phrase of the NYSE, than simple ownership of shares.[334]

Wilma loved the idea of Main Street investors buying shares in individual companies, where they could feel like they held a tangible stake. But she also knew how expensive the commissions on small stock trades were. If an investor like herself bought fewer than 100 shares in a company, brokerage firms penalized that investor, charging what was called an "odd lot fee." It was almost as expensive to buy or sell one share of stock as it was to trade 100 shares. Most people couldn't afford to buy 100 shares of major corporations like AT&T or GE. Wilma bought odd lots all the time, when she grabbed a few shares here and there of various companies to gain entrance into their stockholder meetings. But many Americans simply skipped buying stock because the transaction costs were too hefty.

When some brokers, facing tough times, raised their commission rates, Wilma complained, as she did not want trading fees to impede share ownership. Small stockholders needed to diversify their portfolios and to have easy access to cash when necessary, so higher brokerage fees dramatically cut into their profits.[335]

Frustrated by the high cost of investing in individual stocks, Wilma watched the growth of the mutual fund industry with interest, noting that before World War II less than half a billion dollars were invested in mutual funds but by 1958 over $10 billion had gone "that-away" and more funds were being founded every day. With inflation becoming increasingly prevalent, Wilma reasoned, investors should forego savings bonds, which were safe from default risk but not inflation risk, in favor of stocks, especially stocks easy to buy via mutual funds.[336]

She sometimes, though, had mixed thoughts about the desirability of mutual funds. She was quite alert to the sometimes heavy, hidden fees associated with such funds, and extremely cognizant that past performance was no indication of future results. She carefully covered the commotion caused by the Wharton School's 1962 study of mutual funds, which showed that unmanaged funds did just as well as managed ones on average, despite the much higher cost associated with active management.[337]

Wilma was also critical of stockbrokers, or rather the willingness of Americans to believe that "every stockbroker is . . . an astrologer, when his business is only that of an order taker." "Good security analysis," Wilma explained, was not based on intuition or inside information but rather by "knowing a particular industry, ascertaining the position of a particular company within that industry and analyzing the company's balance sheet." Stockbrokers, she reminded individual investors, were commissioned salespeople, not dispassionate professional investment counselors, even if they pretended to be.[338]

Buying stocks through brokers not affiliated with the NYSE was particularly fraught with danger, Wilma warned. "Remember," she told listeners, "reputable brokers don't usually solicit business over the telephone from people they don't know." Listeners should not fall for "boiler room" scams. They should buy blue chips via an exchange, not penny stocks over the counter, Wilma cautioned. But even then, Wilma warned, stockholders had to beware because the SEC 'was underfunded and federal protections for stockholders had not been strengthened since 1940. "So you see," she noted in late 1958, "it is still 'buyer beware'!"[339]

That went even for bank depositors. After a notorious New York bank robbery and a huge embezzlement scheme was uncovered at a California bank, Wilma reminded listeners of the importance of keeping their cash in federally insured depository institutions. She thought it best to eschew completely the 390 or so uninsured banks, mostly mutual savings banks, and the thousands of weakly insured savings and loans sprinkled across the country, the very thrifts that would crash in the 1980s. For those who kept most their cash at home, Wilma suggested they make sure that the dough was insured in case of fire or theft.[340]

Wilma often got into the weeds, discussing in detail everything from stock splits to how to physically manage stock certificates. Don't sign them and leave them laying around, Wilma warned, because they can be stolen and sometimes could be tough to get back. But, again, Wilma's bright mind really shone when she applied theory, experience, and an intimate knowledge of current events to cast light on the dark corners of the financial world.[341]

$ $ $

On her show, while Wilma did not try to predict individual stock price movements, she did try to predict changes in the macroeconomy and the overall stock market. Wilma correctly predicted that over decades stock prices would rise faster than inflation, on average, due to the growing population and increases in productivity.

Shorter term, however, it was possible for the price level to rise while stocks faltered. Moreover, "uncertainties always give the stock market indigestion." To understand the twists and turns of the stock market, therefore, investors had to understand the business cycle as well as the political atmosphere, the two major sources of uncertainties, a perspective still touted in prominent investment books. Investors could not afford to believe that all trends were likely to be long-lived but instead had to understand the underlying drivers so they could, as Jackson Martindell put it, "take adequate precautions against the whipsawing effects of a sudden reversal."[342]

Wilma sometimes accurately called turns in the economy, especially the end of recessions, but she rarely made bold prognostications. She knew that "indicators of the foreshadowing variety have at times in the past given false signals of trouble" but that leading indicators rarely wrongly signaled recoveries. When asked in June 1958 if the recession that began in 1957 was over, Wilma responded by running down a list of leading and coincident indicators, like employment, freight car loadings, gasoline and oil inventories, housing starts, and retail sales, and responded as the National Bureau of Economic Research (NBER) itself did at the time, in the negative. Only in subsequent months would it become clear that the economy had stopped shrinking in April 1958 and would continue to grow until April 1960.[343]

But Wilma clearly called the end of the 1960-61 recession, in early April 1961. (Much later, NBER, the semi-official arbiter of such matters, declared it had ended in March.) "Already," she said, "we have signs of revival in the economy. Initial unemployment claims dropped two weeks in a row. New orders for durable goods placed by manufacturers increased for the first time in five months. The steel operating rate—still low—is at a new high for nine months. Contract awards for heavy construction are ahead of last year." Plus, stocks were up, as were retail sales and auto sales. Wilma even tracked burlap orders because shippers used the coarse canvas to wrap furniture in transit, making it a leading indicator of furniture sales. Brilliant![344]

Predicting changes in the stock market required an understanding of market dynamics. Here, Wilma wisely sought advice from other experts, as much as she could get, by talking to people like Lewis Schellbach, economist for Standard and Poor's, Alan Poole, president of the New York Security Analysts, Lucien Hooper, chief analyst for W. W. Hutton, Gilbert Haas, a speaker at a women's investor club meeting who warned that the 1960s were looking much like the 1920s in terms of credit expansion, and Gerald Loeb, author of the bestselling *Battle for Investment Survival.*[345]

Wilma also looked for signs of stock market demand on her own, noting that Western Europeans were buying American securities "for the first time in a long while" in the wake of Kennedy's victory in November 1960. And foreign investors bought "a record chunk of U.S. equities" in the second quarter of 1968, with the Swiss leading the way at a cool billion. Soon after, as a tricky presidential election loomed, she noted that stock prices tended to go up when the outcome of a presidential election was likely, but that they dropped when uncertainty about the election and the direction of the economy loomed.[346]

Analysis of important economic industries also constituted part of Wilma's repertoire. She covered the automobile industry extensively because, as she noted in 1966, "we're still living in an automobile economy with one out of every seven persons said to be employed by the auto industry or an industry dependent on the auto industry." She did not give advice like buy Ford or sell GM, but she did warn listeners about American Motors Corporation (AMC). How can you tell that an automobile manufacturer is in trouble? Go to its annual meeting and count how many of its stockholders drove its cars. When Wilma did that at the AMC meeting in 1967, she found that of the 114 cars in the lot, only 42 were built by American Motors. Plus, the company had a $20 million lien on its inventories and receivables and a $95 million debt coming due in just a few months. "And you think you have troubles," Wilma quipped.[347]

In the mid-1950s, Wilma presciently warned Detroit about the threat posed by small, foreign-owned cars and in the late 1950s she warned Big Steel about foreign competitors. "Plants bombed out in Germany and England during World War II," she reminded them, "have been replaced (with American aid) by plants that are more modern than many of our mills." By the 1970s, foreign cars (including from Japan) and foreign steel began overrunning the U.S. domestic market. The age of the solid gold Cadillac had ended.[348]

Wilma also correctly predicted that the newspaper industry would continue to consolidate. The number of dailies published in New York City, she reminded readers, had been thirteen in the 1920s, when she got her start as a journalist, but by the 1960s it was just four after the demise of the *World Journal Tribune*. By then, 44 percent of U.S. newspapers were under the control of about thirty chains. Only four percent of the 1,200 largest cities in the U.S. had competing newspapers by 1967.[349]

$ $ $

To further establish her authority as a forecaster, Wilma frequently made broader economic, political, and social predictions. While she missed the rise of public unions, she clearly foresaw the weakening of private sector unions. In 1957, for example, she predicted that unions would be more stringently regulated in the future. Three years later, she reported that "unions after twenty years of steady growth lost a half million members between 1956 and '58" because of the difficulty of "organizing white collar workers," the fastest growing segment of the workforce.[350]

When a study linked cigarette smoking to cancer and heart disease, Wilma predicted, correctly, that consumption would continue to shift towards filtered cigarettes and menthols and that big tobacco companies would finally start to diversify into less harmful products, a process that culminated in the merger of R. J. Reynolds Tobacco Company with Nabisco (the old National Biscuit Company) in 1985.[351]

Wilma also predicted that the computer industry, America's newest billion-dollar industry in 1960, would experience bumps because of "some disenchantment with automation . . . until more of the bugs are worked out . . . and more people learn how to use" computers effectively. She was right about that, as economists explained the relative dearth of productivity growth by referencing the time it took to hire workers proficient in work-saving computer programs and protocols. As recently as the 1990s, many offices still duplicated work records, one set digital and another analog (paper). Yet long before then the computer industry had become, much like the auto industry, important in and of itself, just as Wilma suggested. "We're in a computer age," she announced in 1967, noting that "the growth rate of computer sales to industrial nations is said to be almost three times as fast as the annual rate of automobile sales."[352]

We were also in a space age, so Wilma warned listeners that America should be worried about how to claim property rights in celestial objects. If the nation did not establish its rights in space, she warned, it would lose its edge and no longer be the richest country in the world. Her comments were read before the House of Representatives by Abraham J. Multer (D-NY) and made the *Congressional Record*.[353]

Some of Wilma's predictions still resonate today. She mentioned fuel-celled automobiles in 1966 and stagflation, or "both a recession and inflation at once," in 1967, years before they became *au courant*. The workforce was growing, she admitted, but "there is a shortage of skilled labor, particularly the skills we need for the space and computer age."[354]

Most prescient, perhaps, was Wilma's coverage of "Guaranteed Annual Income" beginning in 1965. "Advocates of this proposal," she correctly explained, "say society would be better off with a guaranteed annual income than spending $X billion a year on welfare." Wealth transfer programs provided no answer to America's social ills, she argued, because they did not get at the root problem, but she covered income guarantees in detail. In 1968, she claimed that "you may be closer to a guaranteed annual income whether you work or not than you may realize." Her basic argument was that it was morally, logically, and politically untenable to spend $185 million on food stamps while spending $55 billion on "landowners to withhold production and raise market prices on certain commodities" while at the same time ten million Americans went hungry. Wilma argued that the negative income tax proposed by economist Milton Friedman could prove less expensive than traditional welfare and had some bipartisan support. She also reported on the "National Dividend Plan" of Senator Thurston Ballard Morton (R-KY), which proposed dividing corporate taxes evenly among all federal *voters*, or about $500 per voter in 1968. Today, Universal Basic Income again sits atop the national policy agenda.[355]

In 1968, Wilma presciently, if prematurely, predicted that U.S. Steel would change its name "to reflect diversification of its products . . . If that happens," she said, "remember you heard it first on *Pocketbook News*." U.S. Steel renamed itself USX almost two decades later, in 1986. (It switched back to United States Steel Corporation in 2001 after it dropped its diversification bid. It did, however, retain X as its NYSE ticker symbol.)[356]

Of course, some of Wilma's prognostications never panned out. In 1959, for example, she predicted that by 1970 "drug companies may be regulated like utility companies" and "some of your Christmas cards may be delivered by rocket mail." But she was still a far cry better at prediction than many others, including journalist John Brooks, who in 1966 thought it "weird" that AT&T believed the "telephonic future" would include "picture phones" and that "light beams will carry messages."[357]

$ $ $

Wilma did not coddle her listeners by explaining the news, even foreign affairs, in detail. She jumped right to the investment implications. When the Suez Canal re-opened in March 1957, she did not tell readers where the canal was located or why it had been closed, but rather got right to the point that its reopening was not going to make home oil or gasoline cheaper in the United States until Europe's inventories, which were dangerously low, had been replenished.[358]

While Wilma often criticized U.S. foreign aid, she believed in keeping promises and doing one's fair share, so she chided U.S. allies that failed to pay their part for U.S. troops stationed abroad or U.N. troops fighting communism in the Congo. Wilma saw globalization occurring before her very eyes and tried to help her listeners to navigate it, though without ever using the word. "The world is now so small," she explained, "that trouble in South Africa can be felt in your pocketbook. It used to be said that when America sneezes Europe catches cold. Now when Africa sneezes, U.S. government officials get a headache." The reason was that 175 U.S. companies owned South African subsidiaries and 60 NYSE-listed corporations operated factories there. Riots in Johannesburg were therefore a big deal, whether investors understood the connection or not. And, of course, the question loomed of whether those U.S. corporations should be in South Africa at all, given its unethical apartheid policies. Like advocates of CSR and ESG funds today, Wilma wondered whether investing in unethical companies was itself unethical.[359]

Wilma also tried to prepare listeners for America's inevitable, but relative, decline in the world economy. "Only in agriculture," she correctly predicted, "is it certain that over a long period we can remain superior to the rest of the world." She noted that many large manufacturing companies were establishing plants in the U.S. South to lower their wage bill but knew that even they would find it difficult to compete against even lower paid foreign workers in Japan and South Korea.[360] The oil embargo of 1967 Wilma shrugged off because Middle Eastern oil was less profitable than oil from elsewhere. Standard Oil of New Jersey, for example, got 42 percent of its oil from the Middle East, but only 25.5 percent of its profits.

$ $ $

Wilma was a Republican by default. She was, as she once told a member of Richard Nixon's law firm, "*born* Republican," undoubtedly a reference to her maternal lineage. Her maternal grandfather worked for Germania Life Insurance Company, a mutual life insurer established by classical liberal Germans who fled oppression in their German homelands during the uprisings of 1848. Opponents of human slavery in all its sundry forms, the "Forty-Eighters," led by Carl Schurz, embraced Lincoln's Republican Party and would not let go until the New Deal.[361]

A Republican Wilma remained because, like many involved in business, she believed the Democrats were "the party of spending—and inflation—which has become a 'dead duck,' so far as buying stock is concerned." With many others, Wilma thought that "easy money" was the "traditional policy" of the Democratic Party, "in contrast to the Republican Party as the party of tight money." By 1966, the Democrats had lost their image as the easy money party because nominal interest rates were higher than they had been since the Civil War. But it soon became apparent the high rates were due to high levels of inflation, not a change in Democrats' priorities.[362]

Wilma criticized all Democratic presidents but particularly Kennedy because he had not followed precedent and appointed a woman to his cabinet. He appointed a woman as Treasurer but that position, unlike Treasury Secretary, was "not a policy setting post." JFK had not even asked a woman to advise him at George-town, where he lived during his stints in Congress, or Palm Beach, the "Winter White House." Then as now, philanderers seldom make strong feminists.[363]

Wilma remained too independent and smart to devolve into a mere party hack. She gave credit when she thought it was due, even to her Democratic rival Sylvia Porter, who at a tax conference in 1965 broke ranks to ask difficult questions about the federal government's budget deficit. All Wilma's views, as she said at the end of each broadcast, were her own, and nobody could doubt otherwise. Her political and policy views peppered her shows because investment decisions, politics, and policies often formed a heady mixture sometimes called 'political economy.'[364]

Wilma clearly saw the importance of government as a purveyor of stability and property rights but at the same time she believed that it had gone too far at times. She criticized Social Security, for example, because its taxes kept going up and of course she believed that individuals could make better investment decisions for themselves. "Did you know on January first," Wilma queried listeners in 1960, that "you started to pay a twenty percent increase in Social Security taxes—the fourth increase in six years?"[365]

For years, Wilma covered the build up to President Johnson's Great Society programs, including Medicare, always paying attention to "Federal Fiscal Health." Any program that bankrupted the country would help no one, except the Soviets of course. But social ills also could not be ignored, lest Americans be radicalized. The root problem in healthcare, she noted, was the scarcity of doctors and other healthcare providers. On average, only one doctor served every 763 Americans and, in some areas, only one doctor served two to three thousand people. Little wonder, then, health care costs rose much faster than most of the other 300 items in the consumer goods "basket" used to compute the Consumer Price Index.[366]

Wilma also questioned the high cost of prescription medications. When asked about the prices of its arthritis drugs, a Schering official blamed "inadequate income rather than excessive prices." In other words, if people earned more money, they would be able to afford their prescriptions. Wilma could not endorse that answer, but she did concede that low-cost companies were just manufacturers that had not paid to develop the drugs they sold. Contemporaries called them "coat tail companies" because they profited from drugs that others paid to develop, and development costs were high, especially when dead ends were considered. "There are also more unproductive researches in the pharmaceutical industry costing millions," Wilma explained, "than dry holes in the oil industry." The new drugs that made it to market were often superseded by even newer concoctions before they paid for themselves. Moreover, doctors preferred brand names because their manufacturers maintained better quality controls. She claimed, however, to be confused about why drug prices were lower abroad, as if she did not understand market segmentation and price discrimination.[367]

"Medicare is likely to fall short of the dreamy expectations of many," she predicted in 1965. "When economics and politics mix," she opined, "its provisions will be fought in Congress down to the last gasp." That said, though, she cheered the fact that financial help for seniors was finally on the way. "With the extension of the social insurance principle to protect those over 65," the 65-year-old woman declared, "we're catching up with other parts of the world, not setting a precedent!"[368]

$ $ $

Wilma once complained that common bread groaned under the load of about 150 different taxes. Little wonder that she rarely saw a tax that she liked, for she understood their potential knock-on effects. Stock transfer taxes imposed by New York, for example, could eventually force traders to do business on regional exchanges instead of on Wall Street. Wilma also realized that higher gasoline taxes would mean more demand for smaller cars and hence more demand for foreign cars.[369]

Wilma did support a tax on foreign travel, proposed in 1968 as a way of stemming the flow of gold to France, but only if it was graduated by being set at half a percent of annual income per day spent abroad. That way, the rich would pay a lot for travel abroad, schoolteachers less, and jobless students not at all.[370]

Wilma was no friend of higher income taxes, bringing out the old whipping boy: how long the average Joe, then a guy who made $4,500 a year working eight hours a day, had to toil each day to pay his taxes. The answer was two hours and twenty-nine minutes, and, most importantly for Wilma, longer than for anything else. "Tax laws," she complained, "have been added like cupolas on a Victorian house." No study of the overall tax system had been completed in half a decade, she lamented in 1959.[371]

Sometimes seemingly minor tax issues, including proposed tax changes for mutual savings banks and life insurers, so stirred her that she begged listeners to take political action to thwart the perceived injustice. That was because Wilma knew that minor changes in tax laws could have huge effects on incentives. Other countries have more modern plants than we do, she complained, because they got bombed during the war but also because they had better tax rules. U.S. businesses needed similar rules pronto to induce them to buy expensive new machinery that would bolster U.S. productivity and hence help increase output in a non-inflationary way, and aid the dollar.[372]

Wilma believed in specific, limited government regulation. She believed that disclosure constituted "the cheapest brake a democracy can put on the untoward exercise of self-interest," a view held by many economists to this day. Regulators needed to force conglomerates to report with more transparency by division, for example, so that stockholders could see which divisions were under or overperforming. "Merger-itis," as she called the conglomerate merger wave of the 1950s, had gone too far but so too had regulators who saw monopoly too often. Not every business advantage should be subject to the Clayton Antitrust Act, lest providers of capital (like Wilma and her friends) not receive sufficient remuneration. "We need more stockholder interest," Wilma told an editor at *American Banker*, "not more government control," paraphrasing the statement at the end of some FOWSAB educational reports.[373]

Wilma did not oppose the government's penchant for creating reams of statistics because the numbers helped investors to make better decisions and hence aided capital market efficiency, especially in an age when corporate earnings reports were becoming increasingly "complex to decipher and to compare company with company." She was livid, therefore, when she heard that the Secretary of Commerce, Frederick H. Mueller, held back 75 official industry forecasts at the behest of businesses in those industries. "Such goings on," she rightly complained, "spell more uncertainties for investors."[374]

The government had become too big for its own good, Wilma believed. When told that Johnson's 1968 $186 billion budget was "austere," she retorted that it was "awesome," and more than thirty presidents had spent in 150 years. Wilma often poked fun at bureaucratic complexity. After trying to explain changes in Social Security benefits, she told listeners that if they had any questions: "Don't write me. Contact your local Social Security Office. *Don't wait for it to contact you.*"[375]

Ultimately, Wilma sought *efficient* government, a la Alexander Hamilton. That induced her to argue that "Congress should either repeal the Investment Act of 1940 to protect [mutual fund] investors or give the SEC money enough to administer it properly." The mistaken belief that the SEC had investors' backs, in other words, constituted the real problem. She applauded the SEC when it finally stopped some of the pump and dump schemes, like that of The

Capital Gains Research Bureau, Inc., which bought shares cheap and then told investors they knew that those shares soon would be bought up by mutual funds. As the share price shot up, the pumpers sold out, leaving investors holding the bag. The scammers also played short games by purporting to possess negative inside information about Chock Full O'Nuts and other companies.[376]

The SEC constituted a sort of police force and court system to Wilma, who was aware that corporations could use accounting techniques to puff up or deflate earnings. Investors needed to learn how to interpret earnings reports, and take the time to read the footnotes, where shenanigans often lurked. Only an independent government agency, like the SEC, could apply enough pressure to corporations to keep them from going too far with accounting charades.

At the same time, Wilma explained that the government should deregulate railroads so they could more effectively compete, not against each other as in days of old, but against new modes of transportation like trucks, airplanes, and inland ships (thanks to completion of the St. Lawrence Seaway and other improvements on the Great Lakes in 1959). Paying farmers not to grow wheat and other foodstuffs was little more than a cruel joke to Wilma.[377]

Wilma's policy commentaries were typically clever and at times stunningly clear. She even supported green efforts, like California's smog controls, if they made fiscal sense. "Smog has damaged crops in California's rural areas," she noted, "not to mention what it does to people." Although proposed anti-pollution devices would cost $60 to $200 per automobile, they would "eventually reduce life and health insurance costs and medical expenses, too."[378]

Wilma understood the tradeoffs between the environment and economic growth. She thought women should be in the vanguard and follow Jackie K. and Lady Bird Johnson in their fight against ugly urban buildings. But Wilma did not want to arrest "progress," like a hydroelectric plant that promised to replace a mile of "man-made river slums" with a park. She also backed a GM building that would mesh well with the Plaza Hotel, so she did not support a proposed boycott of GM goods if the automaker built near the historic hotel.[379]

Wilma also happily employed the coercive power of the state to further her own agendas, including the Equal Rights Amendment (ERA). Her solution for "race riots," now generally termed 'urban uprisings,' was more air conditioning along with better housing, education, and employment opportunities. Details about how to achieve those goals, however, were not forthcoming. Wilma's primary focus was, and would forever be, "economic suffrage."[380]

$ $ $

In international affairs, Wilma skewed dovish for both humanitarian and economic reasons. In 1958, she urged listeners to send her notes and postcards in support of her idea to have the word "peace" put back on U.S. currency. "Everyone wants American dollars," she reasoned, "let's show everyone Americans want Peace." The response was strong and often heartfelt. Margaret Chase Smith, a minister's daughter and a descendant of Civil War-era Treasury Secretary Salmon P. Chase, decided to do something more than just send Wilma a postcard and, as one of Maine's U.S. Senators, she had the power to do so by introducing S3463 in March 1958. Smith had been mentioned for the vice presidency in 1950 but nothing came of it as "the feminist movement" was then "a little flat for the moment," as an editor at *The Saturday Review of Literature* put it. Smith ran for president in 1964 but lost the Democratic Party nomination to LBJ. Wilma tried to donate to her campaign, but Smith returned her check and gently explained that she was running a true grassroots campaign that expended little cash.[381]

Ever the media manipulator, Wilma always stressed letters from children and even made one precocious young writer, Rephah (pronounced REE-fa) Berg of Madera, California, an honorary member of FOWSAB. In the end, though, Wilma's peace money campaign didn't work, although American iconography continued to portray the eagle with an olive branch in its dominant, right claw, and with thirteen arrows prominent but secondary in its left claw.[382]

Although she wanted peace, Wilma was certainly no pacifist, and she understood that disarmament would be bad for the economy in the short run. "Disarmament, like automation," she reminded listeners, "is not an unmixed blessing." But longer term, she was for peace. Wilma thought that "world trade is better than world war" and twice wondered aloud if the Japanese would have attacked Pearl Harbor if they had not lost the lucrative silk market to nylon.[383]

Wilma opposed the Vietnam War because of its adverse effects on the balance of payments, and hence America's gold stockpile, as well as her peaceful disposition. "We can't have what is tantamount to full employment and an undeclared war going on without inflation," she explained. "War is inflationary," she repeatedly reminded listeners. "Vietnam is costing us 700 million dollars a year in foreign exchange," she noted in 1967. By 1968, she believed that the war had turned the nation into an "international hippie." What mattered most in the war was "our dwindling pile of gold and not the draft card burners, not the peace candidates, not the polls." After Johnson announced that he would not seek re-election in 1968, Wilma quoted one anonymous expert as saying that "the European financiers are forcing peace upon us . . . For the first time in American history, our European creditors have forced the resignation of an American President."[384]

Wilma naturally disdained communism and did what she could to discredit the Soviet Union and protect America from the Red Menace. In early 1958, for example, she warned that the U.S.S.R. could disrupt global markets by dumping goods like platinum and aluminum at unfavorable times. Disrupting Latin American economic ties with the U.S., especially oil-rich Venezuela, constituted another key Soviet objective. By allying with China, the U.S.S.R.'s steel capacity had grown greater than that of the U.S. for the first time, she also warned. The main goal of the Soviet "sputniks," she argued, was to force the U.S. to run budget deficits that would cause inflation and put "our capitalistic system on the rocks." The "low standard of Soviet living," she argued, meant little in the face of those strategic challenges. Wilma noted that while the world could see sputniks and luniks (moon orbiters) they could not tell if, or rather to what degree, the Soviets cooked their books. Assessing the claim of Soviet premier Nikita Khrushchev that the seventh five-year plan, adopted by the Soviets in 1959, would win the Cold War remained impossible.[385]

When Khrushchev visited the U.S. in 1959, Wilma noted that communists suffered the perpetual disadvantage of not having price signals. "Gold is mined in Russia the way Sputniks are launched . . . that is, regardless of cost." That made the Soviets less efficient but also potentially more powerful because they could just decide to have more gold and more sputniks. Meanwhile, market forces constrained the U.S. government, draining it of gold and rendering it susceptible to financial crisis, perhaps one as bad as that of early 1933, when the payments system shut down for an entire week. In 1960, Wilma explicitly accused Khrushchev of deliberately playing diplomatic games, abruptly starting and stopping peace talks, to cause macro-economic instability in the West. "What Mr. K. likes best is to upset our economy . . . Cheapening and devaluing our dollar is one of the main Communist objectives."[386]

Wilma followed the movements of Soviet officials in the United States and Soviet diplomatic moves abroad. Jack Strauss, chairman of Macy's, told Wilma that during his January 1959 visit Anastas Mikoyan, the "premier salesman of the Soviet paradise" according to the Hearst newspapers, evinced particular interest in synthetics and plastics. Wilma became apoplectic when she learned that National City Bank had thrown a luncheon in Mikoyan's honor, at Mikoyan's request, because the U.S.S.R. defaulted on a $39 million loan from that very same bank, which at its annual meetings offered "not even a sandwich" to the "'capitalistic comrades' who own the bank." The Soviets never repay their debts, starting with the Czar through Lend Lease, and even expropriated the savings of their own people, Wilma pointed out. Khrushchev's American tour in September 1959, she claimed, aimed mostly to steal U.S. technology and money.[387]

Wilma's dread of Communism induced her to keep a close eye on world affairs. She wondered why the U.S. government allowed Iceland, where it needed bases for strategic air defense, to sell its fish to the U.S.S.R. in exchange for oil. She realized that "stronger allies are above all to be desired" so the U.S. should help Iceland to develop its geothermal and hydroelectric resources rather than let it buy commie oil.[388]

America's sugar policies were another area of interest for Wilma. She knew much about the political economy of sugar, not just its domestic uses, including the fact that pre-Castro most U.S. sugar came from Cuba, "about a third more than from our own domestic beet growers." And she understood that "the principal purpose of our paying higher prices for Cuban sugar is to keep imports from underselling our domestic crop." She also believed that the cost of Cuban sugar production was above the world price, so the U.S. subsidized the Cuban economy as well. After Castro came to power, Wilma discussed the intricacies of U.S. trade sanctions against Cuba and the Soviet Union and pointed out how some companies, like Xerox, worked around restrictions by selling through foreign subsidiaries in Canada, Britain, and so forth.[389]

Wilma also kept a close eye on France, especially its nationalization of major industries. "France has long been the exporter of fashions, both frivolous and profound," she noted. "Nobody knows yet if De Gaulle's economic ideas, whether or not they succeed, may take root in the rest of the free world."[390]

The grasping hand of government Wilma fought wherever she perceived it, even at home. She argued, for example, that the U.S. government should not be able to withhold taxes from wages or dividends without paying interest as that practice she perceived as a "form of confiscation." She also worried that "the economy is changing daily in the direction of the most tightly planned, directed, and controlled economy within our time. Massive central planning was indicated by Kennedy's message to Congress on the development of the nation's natural resources."[391]

Evoking Eisenhower, Wilma warned that Americans should not fall too readily for claims made about the "national interest." Under that "patriotic cloak," she reminded listeners, "what crimes have been committed against humanity from Nazi Germany to Red China." The checks and balances established by the Founding Fathers had to be maintained, even in putative wartime. That was why she opposed Johnson's handling of the 1965 steel strike though she was no fan of unions or their alleged inflationary effects.[392]

Throughout it all, Wilma believed that free market capitalism constituted the best system available because it allowed more people to enjoy more freedom and more tangible stuff too. By 1960, she noted, three quarters of all U.S. families owned at least one automobile, 98 percent owned a refrigerator, nine in ten owned a TV, and 6.5 million air conditioners whirred in American homes every summer. Like many others of her generation, however, she could not construe expenditures on leisure as a good thing. Wilma had little patience for people (or companies) who neglected to save. "They have ignored the advice for free from the great-grand-daddy of the economists—Joseph in the Bible who in fat days stored up for lean. They failed to follow the example of the growth companies by plowing back earnings in the business and paying out stingy dividends." Consequently, Wilma repeated the warning of British economist Barbara Ward that "six times as many Americans attend ballroom dance classes as attend colleges and universities," as well as the warning of *Time Magazine*, that "the national budget for fun and leisure now is almost as big as the budget for national defense."[393]

Try as she might, however, Wilma could not ignore reality. "There seems to be plenty of money afloat," she noted, "when it comes to the Four B's—books, boats, bowling and building private swimming pools." She suggested investing in pet company stocks due to the fast growth in the number of dogs in the U.S. and the amount of spending per dog, especially on poodles, which, like swimming pools, had become status symbols. In 1965, Wilma announced that the goal of the middle class was no longer to keep up with the Joneses, it was to keep up with the Joneses' children because of their large and growing purchasing power. By 1968, American youngsters consumed 55 percent of all soft drinks purchased in the country, 53 percent of all movie tickets, 44 percent of all cameras, 30 percent of all watches, and 23 percent of all cosmetics.[394]

Wilma naturally interpreted current political events through the lens of minority stockholder advocacy. When news broke that New England industrialist Bernard Goldfine had apparently tried to bribe Eisenhower's powerful White House Chief of Staff (and former governor of Vermont) Sherman Adams in 1958 with an oriental rug and an expensive vicuna coat, Wilma reminded listeners that one of Goldfine's companies had failed to issue annual reports for five consecutive years without SEC complaint. Only a suit brought by minority stockholders induced the SEC to enforce the law. The implication was that Goldfine was a bad guy, accustomed to bribing his way around regulations, perhaps with Adams's aid. The scandal soon led to Adams's resignation.[395]

When Republican Nelson Rockefeller handily defeated incumbent Democrat W. Averell Harriman for the governorship of New York in 1958, the biggest election sweep for the Republicans since the New Deal, Wilma was elated. Unlike Rockefeller, Harriman "catered to all types of minorities except one," Wilma explained, "small stockholders." Harriman "showed little interest and no sympathy with corporate democracy," she complained, even though "the tax laws have been making Wall Street more and more dependent on little capitalists to finance big corporations through the sale of stock." One of every five corporate stockholders lived in New York State, a demographic that the Democrats should have found too big to ignore.[396]

Wilma also sought certain structural reforms to increase transparency. She believed, for example, that lawmakers, governors, and presidents ought to disclose their business interests and stockholdings so that "there should be no conflict between the legislator's pocketbook and yours." Yet she did not advocate forcing them to divest all their assets, as sometimes required, because that reduced the supply of capable leaders. "The Government has less trouble in keeping youths in the Armed Forces at the risk of life and limb," she noted, "than some of their grandpappies in Washington at the risk of losing their stock options." Being asked to serve in the Cabinet was morally akin to being drafted, Wilma intoned, so to beg off without a good reason was to be nothing more than a draft dodger, no matter how many millions of stocks one had to divest before being eligible to serve. "If it is considered a patriotic duty and an honor for a young man to fight for his country and lay down his life," she asked, "is it then asking too much of an older man to lay down his paycheck?"[397]

Most U.S. voters, Wilma believed, were not averse to rich candidates, whom they perceived to be "more honest, more independent, and less subject to temptations than poor ones." Like other Americans, Wilma criticized campaign finance laws, noting that candidates had to "keep two appeals in mind" when on the stump, "popular appeal and pocketbook appeal since it takes money to raise money to run." She therefore advocated a public finance scheme so that candidates did not go into office beholden to "election 'Sharks'" or special interest groups.[398]

$ $ $

Six weeks before the 1968 election, Wilma recounted one of the most remarkable periods of economic growth in American history, seven and a half years of prosperity during which time GNP growth averaged 5.3 percent per year, corporate profits (pre- and post-tax) doubled, dividends increased 81 percent and share prices increased 85 percent. Over that same period, wages jumped 72 percent and disposable income increased 32 percent. Ten million new jobs absorbed eight million new workers and decreased unemployment to just 3.5

percent. Only inflation blemished the nation's economic record.[399] The inflation of the 1960s, however, paled compared to that of the 1970s, which would be one of the worst decades in U.S. economic, political, and cultural history, especially if you count bell bottom jeans.

Bracket creep is a well understood injustice from the era, a time when tax protesters "sent in band-aids with their returns to show it hurts . . . a lock of hair to indicate that they've been scalped . . . and a piece of shirt off their backs." As inflation drove up nominal incomes, taxpayers in essentially unchanged material circumstances were forced to pay a higher percentage of their incomes in taxes, as if their real incomes had increased.[400]

The euthanasia of fixed-income investors, who saw their real incomes decline as nominal prices rose, has also been studied by researchers such as Niall Ferguson in his classic *The Cash Nexus*. Less well understood is the fact that the financial death of investors in bonds and stocks was aided and abetted by a tax code that treated nominal payments from coupons and dividends as income even when they sagged far below the rate of inflation and that did not adjust asset prices for inflation when computing capital gains.[401]

Unsurprisingly, Wilma led the popular critique of the nominal tax code. Although best known for jousting with the corporate grandees who had seized control of American big business and turned companies into personal piggybacks to be raided at will, always at the expense of shareholders, when government policies threatened the value of her investments, Wilma turned on the responsible parties in Washington. That included Republican president Richard Nixon, after it became clear that his New Economic Policy price controls included *de facto* ceilings on corporate dividend payments and that he favored Big Labor over small shareowners.[402]

Wilma had working knowledge of the individual tax code and personally felt the pressures caused by rising prices and lagging returns. On March 18, 1977, for example, she complained on air that she "received a $6.00 three-months dividend on twelve shares of International Paper at the same time as a bill for $7.10 for two veal chops!" Wilma understood that "inflation is, in itself, a tax" on money balances and at least twice even called it the "greatest tax of all" that she considered a "cruel tax" or even "the cruelest tax." She argued that any inflation above two percent was "terrible" though "not too terrible" if held below four percent. But other inflation costs lurked, virtually unseen, in the nation's tax code.[403]

As early as January 18, 1970, Wilma warned investors on air that their after-tax yield on bonds was likely less than the rate of inflation. On July 25, 1971, Wilma went on an anti-New York City tirade that included the complaint that the seven percent city sales tax rate when "you get five percent for your money in the savings bank" was "immoral." "It should be illegal," she argued that day, "to have a sales tax higher than the people's basic interest rate on savings on which they have to pay income tax besides." She left off that somewhat non-sensical line of reasoning but on January 23, 1972, she noted that all the gain in personal income in 1971 had been erased by increases in inflation and taxes. That was no good because, as Wilma noted in her broadcast on December 9, 1973, "there is an old axiom that the cost of money has to be twice the cost of living if, after taxes, the lender [i.e., the investor] is to stay ahead of the money game."

And Wilma meant the actual cost of living. The government's own inflation statistics, she believed, had a discernible downward bias. On October 7, 1973, she told listeners that "there is generally suspicion that government statistics have become politicized and cosmeticized. The official index for the rate of inflation seems hardly to match anybody's family budget." Years later, she claimed that she kept a bust of British Prime Minister Benjamin Disraeli on her desk to remind her of the claim, whether it was his or not, that "there are three kinds of lies—white lies, damn lies, and statistics." She also realized that changes in the price level could affect states, regions, and metro areas differently. She knew, for example, that in the early 1970s the cost of living in New York City rose four times faster than the national average.

Wilma understood that risk requires compensation so on January 21, 1973, she challenged her listeners to imagine a ten percent increase in stock prices but then to deduct "the rate of inflation, your taxes, worry and risk. Try that on your pocket calculator and see what you have left." A week later she complained that Exxon's common stock yielded only 4.7 percent "while bank interest is five to six percent," a very bad bargain indeed given the risk involved. "Stockholders are not an eleemosynary institution," she reminded corporate executives and policymakers. "We invest our savings to add to our earnings or as a pension," not as a charitable donation.[404]

To her listeners, Wilma also explained that rising stock prices might reflect nothing but fake profits generated by antiquated or even improper accounting methods. The latter stemmed from the ability of managers to manipulate financial outcomes. "Earnings," she warned listeners on January 18, 1970, "are what management and the accountants want them to be." The former was due to using inventory accounting techniques like FIFO, or "first in, first out," instead of LIFO, or "last in, first out." FIFO, she explained, "is likely to beef up profits and make earnings look better than they really are." Wilma even went before the Financial Accounting Standards Board (FASB) to argue for what she called "price level accounting" in the name of transparency and full disclosure. As she explained to listeners on July 11, 1975, "if a dividend hasn't been raised, say, since 1971, it has been *cut*, since the dollar has lost about twenty-four percent in purchasing power since then!" She lauded the Indiana Telephone Company for stating its earnings in constant dollars, using the GNP deflator, one of only a handful of companies to do so.[405]

All those considerations led Wilma to advocate a tax credit based on a realistically computed Consumer Price Index. She never made the details clear but obviously she believed Americans should be compensated for the lost purchasing power of the dollar and inflation-adjusted capital losses. She argued on March 5, 1973 that "nineteen percent devaluation of your dollar within fourteen months means that some, possibly many of you will be paying capital gains taxes on what are capital losses, not to mention the universal tax of inflation on your income, for which there are no tax credits." And on August 12 of that year: "Women investors are beginning to ask what good is eight percent and even nine percent interest on your money on which you have to pay taxes when the price of food is going up twenty percent?" And on April 24, 1974: "Many of us are paying taxes on non-existent profits and income." And so forth, on and on and on, culminating on March 10, 1978, when she reiterated her call for an inflation tax credit and argued that "it is outrageous to have to pay income taxes on five percent interest when the rate of inflation is eight and nine percent, not to mention double digit!"[406]

To provide an income tax credit for actual inflation and to calculate capital gains on a real basis would reduce the government's incentive to cause inflation in the first place, so Wilma's proposal was a political non-starter. But, of course, the woman of a million words had plenty else to say about taxes, which were too numerous, and often worked at cross purposes. Taxes on tobacco products, for example, were imposed while the federal government heavily subsidized tobacco growers. Wilma also reminded listeners that taxes, once implemented, almost always trended upward, like a teaser interest rate. "Remember how low the income and social security taxes started?" she asked on February 6, 1972, in response to calls for a European-style Value Added Tax of "just" 2.5 percent.[407]

America's tax codes, Wilma argued, aided margin speculators while discouraging savings and promoting a "borrow and spend" mentality. "So long as interest rates are less than the inflation rate and the interest [paid on debts] can be deducted from taxes," she noted on February 2, 1980, "people will borrow and spend." Or, a month later, "there is little incentive to save under our tax structure."[408]

The most insidious taxes of all were those that threatened corporate democracy, Wilma's antidote to Soviet communism and European-style state capitalism. "The whole capitalistic dogma falls apart," Wilma argued on April 24, 1974, if investors were not able to earn decent risk-adjusted returns after taxes and inflation. By 1980, corporate democracy had been reduced to a mere shell of its former self. During the 1970s, individual investors began to pour out of the securities markets for several reasons. Trading commissions increased before the May Day 1975 brokerage deregulation, hurting the smallest investors the most. Real returns were poor: the annualized nominal growth rate of the Dow Jones Industrial Average between January 1, 1970 and December 31, 1979 was a mere 0.47 percent. Moreover, dividends dropped from 75 to 40 percent of corporate earnings. The continued double taxation of dividends and other anti-small investor tax policies also contributed to the exodus.[409]

On September 3, 1972, contemplating a victory by Democratic presidential candidate George McGovern, Wilma noted that a "McGovernment" would not end the double taxation of dividends and would likely impose the capital gains tax on inherited stock, prompting one irate listener to wonder "why do they hate children in this country?" Wilma also noted that the 100 percent deductibility of short-term stock market losses, compared to the 50 percent allowed on longer term investments, "encourages speculation" and "discourages investment" while it fattened brokerage commissions.[410]

Wilma became hopeful in August 1973 when the Senate began "studying tax changes to spur more people to invest in common stocks," again in July 1975 when Treasury Secretary William E. Simon made some noises about tax reform, and in the summer of 1976 when double taxation was again discussed in high policy circles. But nothing came of any of those attempts because, as Wilma noted, "the moral aspect of double taxation appeared to bother no one."[411]

Wilma hated the fact that so many little investors, who once took pride in owning a few shares of many different stocks like herself, were now fleeing the market. "Inflation with a couple of stock market crashes in the seventies," Wilma explained to listeners on December 11, 1979, "killed investors' appetite for stocks. The shift has been from long term investment into short term speculation." Traditional, buy-and-hold value investors switched from direct ownership of shares to low-cost mutual funds, most of which refused to intercede in matters of corporate governance.

Throughout the oil embargoes, stock market gyrations, and stagflation of the 1970s, Wilma continued to guide the average investor, free of charge, ten minutes a week, almost every week, year in and out, until in early 1980 age rendered her continuation not impossible but inconvenient. Although Wilma finally hung up her radio mic, much to the sadness of many listeners who had faithfully tuned into her show for years, and some for decades, she continued to battle corporate big shots by showing up at big shareholder meetings armed with a list of tough questions and demands. She seemed a young eighty, but the loss of her husband Joe and the stress of the shareholder meeting circuit were taking a toll. Few years were left to her and her nonprofit.

9

GOODBYE GADFLIES

We have to remind the world that women can
think and think fearlessly.[412]
—Wilma Soss

SEPTEMBER 26, 1973. NEW YORK CITY.

Like many fellow shareholders assembled for the annual meeting of Great Western United Company, Wilma arrived feeling frustrated. She knew that Great Western, a small conglomerate headquartered in Colorado, was in financial trouble. That worried her, but something else wasn't sitting quite right. That something had to do with a cause near and dear to her heart, the scarcity of women on corporate boards. Ever since 1947, when she went on the attack against U.S. Steel, Wilma and FOWSAB had been admonishing management about their boards. But today, Wilma faced an odd predicament. Great Western *was* indeed appointing a woman to its board, but a woman Wilma didn't see as particularly well-qualified.

Wilma firmly believed in vetting women director nominees just as rigorously as male candidates, and that belief guided her actions. That Great Western was experiencing financial trouble was even more reason why it needed a strong board, competent and invested in the company's future.

Ann D. Love was not the best choice, Wilma feared. Love owned no stock in the company and that alone was enough to draw Wilma's ire. Wilma *always* wanted board members to have skin in the game; it was one of her core principles. Moreover, Love's qualifications remained unclear to Wilma. The proxy statement referred simply to "Ann D. Love, housewife," which Wilma found appallingly inadequate disclosure. As Wilma well knew, Love was married to Republican John Love, who had served Colorado as its governor from 1963 to 1973. Wilma wondered why this woman, of all possible people, had been nominated to fill this board seat, and why she'd want to take it, given the company's poor financial condition. Standing at the mic in the auditorium, Wilma observed, "It's a mysterious thing. Here is a prestigious woman, wife of an ex-governor of Colorado who has picked this Colorado company that hasn't paid a dividend in two or three years, that is heavily in debt. It's a mystery as to why she would choose to be on this board, of a company in this situation."[413]

Wilma demanded to know what would make Love a good candidate to take on this board role. Rattled, Love tried to defend herself, timidly asserting that she indeed was competent to assess the company's balance sheets. Coming to Love's aid and trying to shut down Wilma's line of questioning, the chairman told Wilma that no "deals" were struck in appointing Love to the board. Love also told Wilma that while it was true that she owned no stock in the company, she hoped to rectify that soon.[414]

Whether or not all this placated Wilma, she had made her point and had aired her discomfort. "Thank you, Mrs. Love," Wilma said. "You know I am not my sister's keeper. She's asked for it; we'll vote for her." By "we," she was referring to the owners of the proxies she was holding in her hand, which apparently represented a slew of Colorado women.[415]

As Wilma most likely realized, Love's appointment to the board was by then probably a *fait accompli*. In this case, like many others, FOWSAB couldn't muster enough proxies to make a difference. While at first glance it might seem like Wilma voted for Love just because Love was a woman, it was common for Wilma to acquiesce after putting up a fuss when she knew that it was a losing fight. In this case, Wilma and FOWSAB were in an awkward situation, not wanting to be seen as eschewing a woman board candidate. In the early 1970s, Wilma fully realized—and often lamented—that the progress of getting more women on boards was not going as quickly as she'd like. In fact, a mere thirteen percent of 1,350 large U.S. corporations had even one female director. The number would have been even lower without FOWSAB's influence.[416]

While troubled by those statistics, Wilma at the same time sensed a different sort of problem brewing, the problem of inexperienced or plain unqualified women sometimes being appointed to some boards. Some of the "first" women on boards were, for example, relatives of chairmen or civic leaders rather than individuals with business experience. Traditionally, board directors had been prominent senior executives or significant entrepreneurs before assuming board roles. One could argue that given the dearth of women in executive positions, a serious pipeline problem existed. But Wilma insisted that many qualified candidates were being overlooked. Also, Wilma well knew that among male directors, it was common to serve on multiple

boards. Why weren't the best women being tapped by many corporations to serve on their boards? Not that the best men were always
chosen, either.

A short time after the meeting, Wilma complained, "Once we
were glad to break the apartheid line . . . Now it's still apartheid if the
men pick women who don't generally understand what's going on in
business." Surprised by the turn things had taken, she was none too
pleased when inexperienced women were chosen who could be used
as puppets.[417]

Somehow the message that FOWSAB had put forward over the
years—"more *qualified* women on boards"—seemed to have gotten
reduced to "more women on boards," and that was a world of difference. Was Wilma herself to blame? For decades, Wilma had at least
seemed a big proponent of something akin to quotas. On numerous
occasions, she had said, for example, that women deserved to be on
boards in relation to their proportion in the shareholder ranks. In
Wilma's eyes, if half of a company's shareholders were women, half
of the board deserved to be women. Perhaps Wilma was exagger-
ating to make a point that women deserved equal opportunity for
board positions. But maybe the line of reasoning she offered had
been a tactical mistake, inadvertently encouraging more of a focus
on the *number* of women on a board rather than their qualifications.
In truth, Wilma didn't want just any woman on a board—even if
any woman could theoretically provide a "woman's" point of view.
Maybe that line of reasoning about a "woman's" point of view, too,
was flawed.

Perhaps Wilma should not have been worried in the case of Great
Western United. Ann Love might have been the right person for the
job. Notably, after gaining experience on the board, Love went on to
serve from 1978 to 1985 on the Rocky Mountain PBS Governing

Board, and she chaired that board from 1982 to 1985. She was also a trustee for the Thorne Ecological Institute in Boulder.[418]

Nevertheless, in questioning Love's nomination, Wilma was ahead of her time in worrying about something that the SEC would begin to clamp down upon decades later: the trend towards companies choosing celebrity directors who enjoyed name recognition, but not necessarily deep knowledge of the company or industry.[419]

$ $ $

Ask tough questions is exactly what Wilma did a few years later, in 1978, when she interrogated the board of the First Women's Bank of New York. One might think that Wilma, as a passionate advocate of "economic suffrage," would have been a huge champion for the First Women's Bank, which had been formed in 1975 to serve women exclusively and boasted a board roughly half comprised by women. The idea was that women purportedly needed a bank devoted to them, given the challenges they faced at other banks.[420]

By 1978, however, Wilma was one of First Women's Bank's harshest critics. Her qualm this time wasn't board members' qualifications, it was the bank's troubling financial performance. Starting out shakily with a thin capital base, the bank had made some bad loans early on, and had incurred considerable expenses. While the bank under the leadership of President Lynn Salvage finally eked out a small profit in 1979 due to better lending practices and cost-cutting measures, the institution was still financially unstable. In fact, its auditor, Deloitte, inserted into its opinion the prior year a disclaimer questioning the bank's ability to remain a going concern. One of the fifty in attendance at the annual meeting suggested switching auditors, as if that somehow would solve the problem. Wilma was on fire at the meeting, directing probing questions at management, like why one director had resigned. She also complained that the bank's president, "Miss Salvage," owned only a measly ten shares of the bank's stock. Sarah Kovner, acting chairman of the board, tried to wrest control back of the meeting. "I will take one more question and that will be the end." Wilma replied in the same recalcitrant way she would have reacted to any male chairman who tried to shut her down: "Don't you tell me what the end is." Ultimately, the bank's leaders seemed to ignore Wilma's points, which executives had always done at their own peril. The First Women's Bank of New York survived, but never was a resounding financial success, predominantly due to an inconvenient truth: women, at least by the 1970s, didn't really need a woman's bank. In the late 1980s, First Women's Bank seemed to recognize that it wasn't doing anything particularly differently for women than any other bank, and the institution changed its name to First New York Bank for Business.[421]

By that time, women increasingly were being nominated to corporate boards. While in the 1970s, only thirteen percent of 1,350 large U.S. corporations had at least one female director, by 1985, that percentage had increased to 41 percent. While that statistic at first glance might seem impressive, it is less impressive to consider the breakdown by total number of board positions. As late as the 1980s, women held a little more than three percent of Fortune 1000 directorships. As a female management consultant lamented, "It's still a token situation. If a company gets one woman on the board, they don't feel like they have to get more." Wilma, now in her eighties, took some solace in the fact that more qualified women were making inroads getting into board rooms across the country. She still vigorously attended shareholder meetings, making her voice heard on many issues. In September 1986, at the New York Times Company annual meeting, Wilma badgered chairman of the board, publisher Arthur Ochs Sulzberger, for answers. She was a journalist through and through, even in her late years—Columbia's Journalism School must have been proud. Little did anyone know, though, that this would be one of her last appearances.[422]

$ $ $

Just a few weeks after taking on Sulzberger at *The New York Times*, Wilma passed away from cardiac arrest at her home in Manhattan. Contacted for a comment, Sulzberger praised his former antagonist, stating that Wilma, for all their differences of opinion, "represented the small shareholders with dignity, pride and courtesy." He continued, "Sometimes we may have grown a mite impatient with her long lists of questions, but she never provoked dismay or anger. I think her voice will be missed, and we will miss her personally."[423]

No close family remained to mourn her passing—her husband Joe had died years earlier. Her long-standing allies, John and Lewis Gilbert, themselves slowing down, undoubtedly missed her greatly, as did others on the shareholder activist circuit. Many who saw her as a heroine for small investors grieved the loss of this smart, funny, larger-than-life woman, whether or not they knew her personally. As *The New York Times* wrote, Wilma Soss was "one of the country's best known and most colorful corporate gadflies."[424]

Despite Sulzberger's kind words, CEOs and boards of directors across the country must have been torn at her passing, with at least some feeling relief that their fearless nemesis, tiny in stature but large in power, no longer would threaten their status quo. Wilma Porter Weissman Soss had spent decades of her life struggling against corporate privilege and "those cosy [sic] little forms of paternalism that private enterprise hasn't yet quite the courage to do away with," as she once phrased it.[425]

While her death garnered attention from *The New York Times*, *The Wall Street Journal*, and other media outlets, many would too soon forget the contributions of this remarkable woman—a passionate shareholder activist and a staunch proponent of opportunity in the workplace, including in the board room. They would largely forget, too, the organization she founded.

$ $ $

The long suffering FOWSAB died alongside Wilma. By the early 1970s Wilma and FOWSAB's officers were quite geriatric. At one point Treasurer Adele Faloon could not dial the rotary dial telephone on snowy days, even if she drank port before breakfast. Faloon replaced the long-serving Helen Plavin, who had resigned due to poor health. A decade later, Wilma and Faloon commiserated with each other after Faloon suffered a stroke and Wilma went down with an unnamed malady.[426]

FOWSAB itself grew old and tired. Crowds at FOWSAB meetings had once measured in the hundreds but by the early 1970s they were quaint gatherings, many held at the beautiful Lotos Club, of a few dozen people. Even the guests tended to be oldies but goodies, like Lewis Gilbert, instead of fresh faces.[427]

Years of running deficits ate into FOWSAB's bank balance, which dipped below $5,000 by the end of 1975, prompting it to stop accepting new members. It slashed expenses, including giving up its office in 1973, but by 1980 members wondered "will this be Federation's last year?" Membership dues dropped to $1,551 in 1981, when the organization bolstered its sagging bank balance only by selling its shares in Philadelphia Reading for just over $2,000.[428]

FOWSAB clung to life with a little help from the Gilberts, who donated $200 in 1982 as the organization again considered liquidation. The trustees decided to hold on so long as FOWSAB had enough money in the bank to "effectuate the goals for which it was incorporated." FOWSAB still held its "Three Money Matinees" in the last quarter of 1983, led by Ralph Acompora of Kidder Peabody, Patricia D. Prapas of Portfolio Dynamics, and Muriel Siebert, the first female member of the NYSE. But once Wilma was gone, the Gilberts and other friends saw no need to keep the nonprofit going.[429]

Ultimately, FOWSAB fell victim to the times. A younger generation did not take over leadership, or even membership, because in the 1970s individual investors found themselves decimated for the second time in half a century. The Great Inflation essentially euthanized hordes of individual bondholders and shareholders. Eventually, many value investors returned, but primarily through the vehicle of mutual funds, not individual stocks, which became a playground for day traders and other types of speculators who used new discount brokerages, like that of Muriel Siebert & Co. and Joe Ricketts' Ameritrade, to keep transaction costs down. FOWSAB's demise, however, should not be taken as its failure. It claimed significant partial credit for governance reforms and corporate actions, just as the solo-flying Evelyn Y. Davis would claim success as well.[430]

$ $ $

A year after Wilma's passing, in 1987, Davis's tombstone—a super large one of course—was erected at Rock Creek Cemetery. Oddly, though, Davis still was very much alive. The decades premature erection of her tombstone seemed to be another one of those inexplicable behaviors she often exhibited. Upon reflection, though, it was not so strange, given what she had endured in her youth. Like many other Holocaust survivors, she was, in life, preoccupied with the coming of death.[431]

Davis wanted to script exactly what would be written on her headstone and to ensure it was done correctly. She explained, "It's like, you buy a wife a dress for $600, and it may be exquisite and in good taste, but it's not her taste. Rather than leave the [tombstone] design to my estate, I do it myself. That way I get what I want."[432]

For her epitaph, Davis wrote: "Power is greater than love, and I didn't get where I am by standing in line and being shy." "Power is greater than love" was the exact opposite lesson that fellow Theresienstadt survivor Frankl took from his own sufferings. Frankl, whose love for his wife Tillie helped get him through his camp ordeal, contended that "*The salvation of man is through love and in love.*" In contrast, even as she aged, Davis seemed to still take away from living through the Holocaust the paramount need to be famous, and prove your own worth by your accomplishments and those of your network. But even the most stellar of accomplishments wouldn't enable her to cheat death forever.[433]

On her headstone, she also noted that she had served as a "defender of shareholder rights at many stockholder meetings" and that she had been editor and publisher of *Highlights and Lowlights*. Proud of her parents and brother, she made sure to note them, too. She also listed all her ex-husbands, even taking care to have chiseled into the marble her fourth ex-husband, whom she wedded in 1994 and divorced a few months later.

She relished having her headstone exactly the way she wanted it. "Every now and again, I'll ask the stonecutter to carve in a new detail," she once explained. Perhaps the most important detail, though, was something not so noticeable on the marble, as it was carved in small print on the bottom corner, and included just the initials "W.S."[434]

Evidently, Davis never forgot Wilma Soss, her mentor and beloved friend on the gadfly adventure.

$ $ $

Although Wilma also concocted some fuss about herself, she nevertheless made real contributions to the world. "Over the years," one of her chroniclers grudgingly admitted, "she has caused a scattering of reforms." Parsing out her individual contribution, however, remains fraught because almost every position she took was backed by the Gilbert brothers and FOWSAB. Moreover, the arc of her successful reforms was not always steadily upward: she and her cadre often made incursions, like getting certain women named to boards, but sometimes there were backward steps as well. The real world, after all, is not a fairy tale like *The Solid Gold Cadillac* where the good girl always wins, and everybody lives happily ever after. The real world is a competitive space, where every thrust is parried, and every inch of ground gained can be lost.[435]

Wilma's role, then, is best understood as that of an Ajax-like warrior in a centuries long battle between shareholders and management for control of corporations. Early on, shareholders were ascendant, but they lost ground over the second half of the nineteenth and first half of the twentieth centuries. Instead of returning most profits to shareowners in the form of dividends, managers plowed them back into the business with alacrity. By 1951, managers reinvested 60 percent of profits, up from thirty percent in the 1920s, essentially doubling their power over shareholders' property. Little wonder that the editors of *Fortune* called shareholders "a kind of contingent bondholder rather than a part owner" and management gurus like Peter Drucker advocated stripping shareholders of all voting and other rights so that managers could rule their corporate dominions without interference from pesky gadflies.[436]

Wilma formed an integral part of the mid-century counterattack against managerial ascendance. One major victory, the SEC's declaration that "a corporation is run for the benefit of its shareholders and not that of its management" had already been won by Lewis Gilbert just as Wilma entered the scene in 1947. But many more battles remained to be fought until the corporate gadfly movement gave way to the leveraged buyout craze of the 1980s, which disciplined managers via stock prices and a market for corporate control. Management retaliated with poison pills and other governance tactics that effectively ended hostile takeover bids. More recently, however, some hedge and pension funds and other institutional investors have leveraged regulatory changes, many inspired by the rise of socially responsible investing, and used their enormous portfolios to pressure management into implementation of more investor-friendly dividend and other policies. Some entrenched board members have had to give up their seats. Some activist fund managers have even managed to take control of troubled corporations, much like shareowner activist Gerald Armstrong once did.[437]

That said, swarms of flies have been known to drive creatures much larger than themselves absolutely batty and force them to change their behavior, at least temporarily. And that is exactly what Wilma and other postwar gadflies did.

Wilma, FOWSAB, and gadfly allies like Evelyn Davis achieved much, including:

- the successful nomination of numerous qualified female board directors;

- the general adoption of rotating annual meetings in accessible places;

- inducing RCA and other corporations to hold televised shareholder meetings;

- teaching corporate leaders they couldn't treat women as second class citizens without cost;

- eliminating "Miss or Mrs." from stock certificates;

- defeating a bill that would have ended mandatory cumulative voting for stockholders in national banks;

- inducing the NYSE to make proxy solicitation a requirement for listed companies;

- coaxing Exxon to increase the number of outside directors from zero to twenty;

- persuading AT&T to spin off Western Electric;

- cajoling AT&T, Chase Manhattan, Citicorp, Chase, DuPont, Exxon, GM, IBM, J.P. Morgan, Manufacturers Hanover, Mobil, RCA, Sperry, and Xerox to adopt the secret ballot;

- helping to open Harvard Business School to women.[438]

FOWSAB also spurred the creation of other groups dedicated to organizing stockholders to take up causes of their own, if not under the mantle of women's and investor rights. Corporate governance scholar Richard Marens credits FOWSAB for influencing the creation of the ICCR (Interfaith Council on Corporate Responsibility) and the gadflies for inspiring Robert Monks of the Council of Institutional Investors.[439]

Nevertheless, greater board representation, broader financial literacy, and wider adoption of the secret ballot still have a long way to go, and double taxation of dividends remains ensconced in the tax code. Wilma's words continue to ring true. As she liked to say, women and all small investors needed to "wake up . . . speak up . . . and help us keep up!" in the name of security and freedom, because "there is no freedom without economic freedom, there is no security without economic security."[440]

Perhaps most importantly, the gadflies induced directors and executives to concede that shareholders were their bosses, which eventually changed the whole tenor of shareholder relations. They also convinced some important investors, like Benjamin Graham, to publicly argue for a new "Wall Street rule": "If you don't like the management sell your stock, provided you can get a fair price. If you can't, do something about the situation."[441]

Thanks to Wilma and friends, annual meetings became more accessible. Before the gadflies swarmed, shareholder meetings were often held in cramped quarters, in places, jokingly referred to as Sqeedunkus and Hohokus by B. C. Forbes, that seemed purposely out-of-the-way. For years, AT&T did not even print the address of its annual meeting place on its proxy statements. "U.S. Steel's reply" to Wilma's suggestion that Hoboken was not the best place to hold its annual meetings was "that they meant to keep right on meeting in

Hoboken because they'd always met in Hoboken. Imagine!" Wilma exclaimed to a reporter. Many companies, though, proved much more amenable and soon were switching their meetings to Manhattan or other big cities where their stockholders were concentrated, and into larger venues.[442]

By the early 1960s, "any number of companies [had] agreed to rotate their meetings to various parts of the country for the convenience of stockholders." That meant that more meetings were held in major cities instead of in Wilmington, Delaware or "some out-of-the-way railway station" in New Jersey. But it also meant that fewer meetings were held in or around Manhattan, which of course made it more costly for Wilma, the Gilbert brothers, and other New York City-based gadflies to attend. FOWSAB's biggest single expense was getting Wilma to meetings "now being held in all parts of the country." Moreover, some corporations decided to swamp the gadflies with other stockholders by making meetings more accessible and even by providing meals and gifts to those in attendance. Such tactics greatly increased attendance. In 1961, more than 20,000 shareholders attended AT&T's annual meeting.[443]

Also driving up attendance was the fact that stockholder meetings had become more interesting and informative and less staid affairs. Before the gadflies came along, one shareholder told a reporter for *The New Yorker*, "they used to be cut-and-dried affairs, lasting maybe half an hour—read last year's minutes, elect a package block of directors, commend the officers on the statesmanlike way they doubled their salaries during the year, and that was that."[444]

Meetings also became more democratic and courteous over time thanks to the gadflies. Gone were the days when directors would laugh at stockholders, treat them sarcastically, or ignore their questions and recess for lunch without a second thought. Wilma once introduced

Lewis Gilbert as "the man who used to be invited 'out in the alley' at stockholder meetings, now is invited 'out to lunch'." Anything that made it easier for Wilma and other professional stockholders to speak, however, also made it easier for non-professionals to take up the microphone as well, and their contributions, according to reporter John Brooks, tended to "run strongly to ill-informed or tame questions and windy encomiums of management."[445]

"Are tycoons getting soft? . . . Tycoons *are* getting soft," was the verdict of an anonymous reporter for *The New Yorker* in 1956. By 1949, many of those old softies—including American Airlines, GE, General Foods, GM, National Biscuit (Nabisco), Standard Oil, Union Carbide, United Airlines, and U.S. Steel—were issuing post-meeting reports so that those who missed the meeting could find out what took place. Of course, some corporations conveniently left out damning details and even, in at least one case, "*all the criticism that was made at the Annual Meeting*," which ran directly counter to FOWSAB's position that good post-meeting reports should present "an impartial account of stockholders' comments, management's statements and answers to stockholders' questions."[446]

The gadflies, but especially Wilma, also managed to end the almost complete male monopoly on corporate directorships. By 1951, they had gotten board seats for four women, Mary Burnett Horton in Sheffield Farms, Mrs. Madeleine Edison Sloane in Western Union, Miss Alice E. Crawford in the Corn Exchange Bank, and Mrs. Mildred McAfee Horton in NBC.[447] By 1954, Wilma boasted that women were being named to boards left and right and immediately followed that up with the complaint that "*First* woman shouldn't be news anymore. *Which* woman should be the news."[448]

By 1963, additional women owed their board seats to Wilma. By 1974, 65 out of 800 companies surveyed by the American Society of Corporate Secretaries had a woman on the board. "Soss was ahead of her time" when it came to female representation on corporate boards according to corporate law professor Harwell Wells. By often demanding that management start by naming one qualified woman to their board, Wilma, however, inadvertently may well have aided and abetted tokenism in the board room. In 2005, two out of every five corporations in the Fortune 500 had one, and only one, female director.[449]

Since Wilma's passing, increasing numbers of women have obtained graduate degrees in business and law. Yet, due in part to a so-called "leaky pipe," they have not made commensurate inroads on corporate boards and executive teams. Each year, for a variety of reasons, some women leave their professions towards the height of their careers, just as they start to have enough experience to be considered for top positions.[450]

Wilma tried to persuade business leaders and policymakers that women should not be simply *allowed* to ascend the corporate ladder but *aided* in the ascent because their presence enhances corporate economic performance. That argument, however, has not gained much traction, perhaps because Wilma was never able to prove this beyond reasonable doubt. Recent studies into this have been mixed. Regarding the gender quota system imposed on boards in Norway, the results thus far suggest that increasing the share of female directors neither helps nor hurts corporate performance. Studies of nations that merely have recommended increased board diversity, like Australia, also show that having female board members neither helps nor hurts company performance by much, and in sum appears to be a wash. Such studies suggest, that perhaps after all, the most important word in Wilma's demand was *qualified*.[451]

Wilma also pushed for cumulative voting, which allowed share-holders to concentrate all their votes on a single board candidate rather than having to spread them over an entire slate. It was not a kooky idea at all. In the mid-1960s, cumulative voting was mandatory for corporations chartered in some twenty states and used by about 400 companies listed on the New York Stock Exchange. Nevertheless, many large corporations like GE fought its implementation by arguing it might have a "divisive and disruptive effect," which was an odd contention given that most directorial elections were "rubber stamp" affairs, with what one wag called "a certain Russian ring—ninety-nine percent or more of the votes cast in favor."[452] Although Wilma pushed for cumulative voting and some gains were made, by the mid-1990s the cause had atrophied to the point that a legal scholar published an article in *Columbia Law Review* that advocated reintroducing cumulative voting in corporations to replace the dying market for corporate control. He mentioned the Gilberts, but not Wilma.

The mode of voting was also important to Wilma and her gadflies. Indeed, Wilma once said she hoped that the secret ballot would be "part of my legacy to the American people." Despite gaining little traction at first, the gadflies continued to push for the secret ballot into the 1970s and in 1977 won over a major company, AT&T, in a proposal formally put forth by Wilma, who told a reporter that if her husband outlived her, "whatever I have goes for the secret ballot." By 1979, she was pressing hard for the secret ballot at Exxon, DuPont, RCA, IBM, Citicorp, Gemera, and Standard Oil of California and convinced most of them to reform.[453]

Secret voting in corporate elections did not, however, catch on and arguably for good reason—shareholders want to know who is supporting whom, or what, during proxy battles, much the same way that voters want to know how their elected officials vote in the legislature, if only to ensure that proxy holders voted as promised.[454]

Wilma and the gadflies also opposed the stagger system in which only a few directors came up for election each year, preferring instead the annual election of the entire board. The latter made takeovers easier and faster. Staggered or "classified" boards remain common and, unsurprisingly, have been shown econometrically to entrench management and reduce company value.[455]

Wilma and her colleagues argued that directors ought to have a material incentive to do a good job, which meant that they should own a lot of stock in the companies they directed. Early resolutions usually called for at least 100 shares. She often lambasted directors who were happy to receive meeting fees but not invest them in company stock. Companies have responded by giving directors stock, which is not exactly what Wilma had in mind. Executives also had to be remunerated correctly if they were to do their best. If they were paid too little, they would slink off to higher paid work. But if they were paid too much, or not according to their performance, they would linger like leeches. Many early proxy resolutions called for executives to limit their pay to $25,000 (or some other relatively low figure) if earnings slipped or dividends had to be reduced. Of course, great managers could fail, and poor ones do a decent job, due solely to external circumstances, like the overall state of the economy or the cost of capital. Nevertheless, in meetings, Wilma often slyly inquired "whether there is anything in the company's bylaws to prevent her from introducing a little resolution to put a ceiling on the recalcitrant executives' salaries, stock bonuses, and non-contributory pensions." She also pointed out that "if a $200,000 chairman can't master running an annual meeting . . . what he needs is a cut in salary."[456]

The gadflies made little headway here, even though many female stockholders (and some male ones) wondered how "any man" could be worth $100,000 plus a year. Prior to the 1970s, only sixteen percent of the CEOs of America's largest corporations received performance-based compensation. That number increased to almost half in the 1990s. But the devil was in the details, as usual. Unsurprisingly, many CEOs manipulated whatever financials they needed to "earn" big bonuses and in many companies no gadflies or independent auditors possessed sufficient power to stop them. So executive remuneration continued to spiral ever upward. "Say-on-Pay," part of the Dodd-Frank reforms passed after the Panic of 2008, only affected executive compensation in ten percent of cases, like that of JPMorgan Chase's CEO Jamie Dimon in 2022. Shareholders usually dutifully approve executive pay packages, though perhaps they shouldn't.[457]

Lord only knows what costumes Wilma would have worn in the wake of the accounting scandals at Enron, Xerox, and elsewhere, or to protest the subprime mortgage debacle. Truth be told, she saw it all coming. Not the details, of course, as she was not psychic. But the broad outlines were clear. Auditors, she knew, were worthless if not independent. Auditors should be selected by shareholders, not directors, and certainly not by executives, and they should be qualified, not mere celebrities. But corporate bigwigs would not even consent to disclose the fees they paid to their auditors when the gadflies pushed for it.[458]

$ $ $

In the 1950s, institutional investors accounted for about six percent of corporate ownership. By 2009, they accounted for almost 75 percent. Had some institutional investors not stepped up, shareholder activism would be all but dead. Starting in the latter half of the 1980s, though, shareholder proposals backed by major institutional investors became much more common, and significantly more potent than they had been in the hands of the gadflies and social justice warriors. Few proposals passed but they received about a third of the votes on average and hence brought considerable pressure on management. In 1992, changes in SEC proxy solicitation rules made it easier for institutional and other large stockholders to communicate with each other. As the power of the new institutional corporate activists grew, managers increasingly agreed to meet with them directly to "jawbone" about issues of interest throughout the year and not just during the traditional annual meeting season in the spring.[459]

Legal restrictions on holders of large blocks of stock still prevent most institutional investors from exerting control. Managers remain ensconced in power, except when attacked in takeover situations. Their decisions, however, are conditioned by the knowledge that institutions with more clout and economic power than Wilma could muster are watching, and ready to act if necessary. That indirect influence explains why researchers cannot show statistically that institutional corporate activism enhances firm performance. Moreover, if the "wolf packs" grow too powerful, corporate bigwigs will likely find ways to induce the government to reduce their effectiveness.[460]

Another major problem lurks in the agency costs that arise between institutional investors and the individuals who invest via them. We may well see individual investors trying to cajole their mutual and pension funds into action. Unless, that is, publicly traded corporations simply go the way of the dinosaur. The number of listed firms peaked in 1997 and has since fallen by half. Today, fewer publicly traded corporations operate than when Wilma died, even though the economy is much larger in inflation-adjusted terms. The government is not nationalizing them, as Wilma feared, but many large businesses are opting to stay, or go, private.[461]

In the end, then, Wilma's greatest contribution to America was intangible—her cheerful confidence that society's greatest challenges could at least be ameliorated, if not perfectly solved. For Wilma "the tide indeed is turning," even when others saw only a stagnant pool. She even hoped to turn the more radical types "from revolution to evolution. Admittedly," she characteristically continued, "this is a long shot [but] that is our optimistic hope." Executives still rule corporate America too often for their own benefit, rather than in the interests of the hundreds of millions of shareholders, men and women, foreign and domestic, young and old, institutional and retail, who, as Wilma so clearly understood, ultimately own the corporations that those execs operate.[462]

But the corporate governance revolution grows louder by the year, perhaps awaiting a new Wilma-like corporate activist to galvanize investors and lead the charge for even more substantial change.

EPILOGUE:

FORTUNE FAVORS
THE BRAVE

This story is so much bigger than me . . . I support these
retail investors, their ability to make a statement.

—Keith Gill, aka "Roaring Kitty," January 2021.[463]

Left for dead, small investors have roared back into relevance. While institutions like hedge funds, pension funds, insurance companies and mutual funds account for roughly 90 percent of stock trades in the United States, recent events highlight that the ten percent of volume generated by individual, retail investors can pack quite a punch when it all moves the same way. Decades ago, Wilma and her gadflies envisioned the enormous power small investors could wield, if they could just act as one. Yet for many reasons, FOWSAB couldn't muster a strong enough media platform to motivate retail investors to act *en masse* in real time. FOWSAB—along with the Gilbert brothers and other shareholder activists—enjoyed periodic victories, but even Wilma was frustrated that they couldn't do more.

During the heart of the Covid pandemic, however, the world got a glimpse of the revolutionary power of small investors, as the so-called "Reddit Rebellion" swept the United States and sent what had been a relatively unloved company, GameStop, "to the moon."[464]

$ $ $

In 2021, from his basement in a working-class Boston suburb, Keith Gill—an Everyman sort of figure—led a diverse group of small investors on the Reddit discussion forum WallStreetBets to promote GameStop stock, which he thought to be seriously undervalued. Convinced by Gill, a loosely organized band of traders managed what many professional investors assumed to be impossible—retail investors "squeezing the shorts," in this case, prominent hedge funds betting against GameStop's shares. Together, these ordinary investors, many of them new to the stock market with recently opened accounts on apps like Robinhood, drove GameStop up from a few bucks a share to hundreds of dollars, some making fortunes for themselves and causing hedge funds to lose billions.[465]

It's the classic David vs. Goliath story Wilma would have loved. Gill's advice to hold the stock with "diamond hands" would have sounded funny, but not unfamiliar. It's unlikely Wilma would have gotten swept up in the mania, but she certainly would have owned a share or two to weigh in at the annual meeting. Though she saw the stock market as a generator of wealth, her opinion of the GameStop saga would have focused less on "gains" and more on the principle—the relevance of the individual investor—that Reddit traders brought back into vogue. Little guys matter, and the poorest of the gadflies would have agreed.

It is difficult to imagine Wilma not being thrilled with the fact that ordinary shareholders found the gumption to speak out and coordinate their efforts.[466] She was a fierce advocate for free speech—particularly for those who felt forgotten. She likely would have applauded Elon Musk's bid for Twitter as a corporate promise to uphold freedom of expression for all in the Internet's public square.[467] Though she would not get to see the technologies that shape our lives today—the Internet, social media, and new asset classes, like crypto-currencies—she'd know full well the opportunities they represent for all Americans who believe in the system of free enterprise."

There's an old Latin saying, often heard on Wall Street, that "fortune favors the brave."[468] Wilma believed in making brave moves herself and encouraged others, women in particular, to take calcu-lated risks—to be fearless in their careers, bold (but not speculative) in their investing, and unabashed about speaking their minds. She believed in being fearless, well before the bronze *Fearless Girl* statue appeared in the spring of 2017 on lower Broadway, staring down Arturo Di Modica's iconic *Charging Bull*. We cannot help but see Wilma's ghost behind *Fearless Girl*, who now stands tall before the New York Stock Exchange. Tiny but resolved, Wilma would spend the second half of her long life staring down charging bulls in corpo-rations nationwide—and never gave an inch.

Fortune favors the brave; and whether it's Keith Gill, Evelyn Davis, *Fearless Girl*, or Elon Musk, all who make their voices heard—who stand resolute for a better financial tomorrow—are on firmer ground today thanks to the Queen of the Corporate Gadflies, Wilma Soss.

ENDNOTES

CHAPTER ONE: Here To Stay

1   Wilma Soss, "Business Women Are Here to Stay," *Forbes* (15 Dec. 1945), 18-19.

2   B.C. Forbes, *Men Who Are Making America* (New York: B.C. Forbes Publishing Co, 1917, 1926), v, vi, vii; B.C. Forbes, *Keys to Success: Personal Efficiency* (New York: B.C. Forbes Publishing Co., 1918), 3; https://libquotes.com/b-c-forbes/quote/lbc4v6o. Accessed 3 May 2022.

3   Moira Forbes, "Welcome to ForbesWoman," *Forbes* (1 Apr. 2009). https://www.forbes.com/2009/04/01/magazine-web-professional-women-leadership-publication.html?sh=17a06eeb38f4. Accessed 20 May 2022.

4   "Share Owner Better than Stock Holder," *Forbes* (1 Dec. 1950), 12-13.

5   On some of the scams in the pre-SEC era, see Clifton Woolridge, *The Grafters of America: Who They Are and How They Work* (Chicago: Monarch Books, 1906).

6   Soss, "Business Women," 18-19.

7   Kenneth Lipartito, "When Women Were Switches: Technology, Work, and Gender in the Telephone Industry, 1890-1920," *American Historical Review* 99, 4 (1994): 1,075-1111.

8   Soss, "Business Women," 18.

9   Soss added, "Therefore it is good public relations to prepare for the day when the woman majority stockholders are going to become articulate." Soss, "Business Women," 18.

10   She added, "Unless you have begun to recognize that your business has a woman's angle, you have yet to modernize your public relations in keeping with the findings of to-day and management's responsibilities in anticipation of tomorrow." Soss, "Business Women," 19.

11   FOWSAB, "Stockholders Calendar," 1964, Box 10, Wilma Soss Papers (WSP), American Heritage Center, Laramie, Wyoming."; A. Wilfred May, "Can Investors Be Unionized? Their Joan-of-Arc Says 'No'," *Commercial and Financial Chronicle* (30 Jun. 1949), 4. Lewis Gilbert was called "The Conscience of American Big Business." Frank D. Emerson and Franklin C. Latcham, *Shareholder Democracy: A Broader Outlook for Corporations* (Cleveland: Press of Western Reserve University, 1954), 113; Richard Gehman, "Guardian Angel of Shareholders," *Cosmopolitan* (Apr. 1963), 64.

CHAPTER TWO: Woman of Steel

12   Soss to U.S. Steel board, 1947, Wilma Soss Papers (WSP), American Heritage Center, Laramie, Wyoming.

13   George Lipsitz, *Class and Culture in Cold War America: 'A Rainbow at Midnight'* (South Hadley: J.F. Bergin Publishers, 1982), 233-234; *Monthly Labor Review* (Mar. 1947), 411.

14   The company was Lindstrom Tool and Toy Company. See Lipsitz, *Class and Culture*, 233-234; "Bridgeport Bans Jobs for Women; One-Third of Labor Force in War, They Now Appeal to WLB in Boston," *New York Times* (20 Sep. 1945), 18.

15   "More Girls on Job at Stock Exchange: 150-Year Tradition Now Thoroughly Smashed, but 'Business as Usual' Wins…," *New York Times* (13 Jul. 1943), 18.

16   Arturo and Janeann Gonzalez, "Where No Woman Reaches the Summit: Thousands of females work in Wall Street but few attain executive status and none has scaled the peak," *New York Times* (17 Aug 1959), SM 34. Also see Sheri J. Caplan, *Petticoats and Pinstripes: Portraits of Women in Wall Street's History* (Santa Barbara: Praeger, 2013).

17   Lewis Kimmel, *Share Ownership in the United States*, (Washington D.C., 1952). This is the Brookings Report, commissioned by the NYSE. A copy resides in the New York Stock Exchange Archive (NYSEA). See also Marshall E. Blume, Jean Crockett, and Irwin Friend, "Stockownership in the United States: Characteristics and Trends," *Survey of Current Business* 54, 11 (1974): 16-40.

18   Richard Marens, "Inventing Corporate Governance: The Mid-Century Emergence of Shareholder Activism," *Journal of Business and Management* 8, 4 (2002): 368.

19   WSP. For more on the long shadow cast by the Great Crash, see Janice M. Traflet, *A Nation of Small Shareholders: Marketing Wall Street After World War II* (Baltimore: Johns Hopkins University Press, 2013).

20   See Benjamin Graham and David Dodd, *Security Analysis* (New York: McGraw Hill, 1934).

21   Winston Churchill, The Sinews of Peace ("Iron Curtain") Speech, Westminster College, Fulton, Missouri, 5 Mar. 1946. https://winstonchurchill.org/resources/speeches/1946-1963-elder-statesman/the-sinews-of-peace/. Accessed 5 May 2022.

22   Marens, "Inventing Corporate Governance," 375; Pocketbook News (PN), 28 May 1972, Box 9, Wilma Soss, "Role of Stockholders," *New York Times* (30 Jun. 1952); Soss, "FOWSAB," n.d., Box 10, WSP; Lauren Talner, *The Origins of Shareholder Activism* (New York: Investor Responsibility Research Center, 1983), 2; Jackson Martindell, *The Scientific Appraisal of Management: A Study of the Business Practices*

of Well-Managed Companies (New York: Harper & Brothers, 1950), vii, 268; Frank D. Emerson and Franklin C. Latcham, *Shareholder Democracy: A Broader Outlook for Corporations* (Cleveland: Press of Western Reserve University, 1954), 171 n.164.

23   Talner, *Origins*, 1; "Rocky and Lewis Sequel to 'Adlai and Wilma'," *Commercial and Financial Chronicle* (28 Jul. 1960), 5; Marens, "Inventing Corporate Governance," 370-71, 378; Wilma Soss, "The Solid Gold Chevrolet," *Commercial and Financial Chronicle* (21 Apr. 1955), 24.

24   Kenneth Warren, *Big Steel: The First Century of the United States Steel Corporation, 1901-2001* (Pittsburgh: University of Pittsburgh Press, 2001).

25   Wilma qtd. in "Pressure Group," *The New Yorker* (25 Jun. 1949), 15.

26   Adolph Berle and Gardiner Means, *The Modern Corporation and Private Property* (New York: McMillan, 1932), 355.

27   When she made insufficient headway, Wilma concluded that "the men of this country aren't what they used to be, and that it was up to the women to take over." Andy Logan, "Hoboken Must Go!," *The New Yorker* (17 Mar. 1951), 44; Marvin Murphy, "How to Use the Public Relations of an Advertising Agency," in *Your Public Relations: The Standard Public Relations Handbook,* Glenn Griswold and Denny Griswold, eds. (New York: Funk & Wagnalls, 1948), 98-109.

28   Wilma alluded to being "tied up with the New York subway account" in an early 1947 letter, indicating that Budd was only one of the accounts that she juggled. Soss to Mrs. Elizabeth L. Klinger, 6 Feb. 1947, Box 14, WSP; "Pressure Group," *The New Yorker* (25 Jun. 1949), 15; Soss to Fowler McCormick, 17 Sep. 1947, Soss to Mabel Glass, 4 Nov. 1947, Box 7, Folder 3, McCormick/International Harvester Papers, Wisconsin Historical Society (WHS), Madison, Wisconsin; Logan, "Hoboken Must Go!," 42; Roderick M. Grant to Soss, 11 Nov. 1946, Soss to Patrick O'Sheel, 21 Dec. 1946, "The Tooling Up Period," n.d., Soss to Jessica Daves, 30 Dec. 1946; Soss to Elizabeth Francis, 25 Mar. 1947, Soss to Ailene Talmey, 16 May 1947, Elizabeth L. Klinger to Soss, 24 Feb. 1947 and undated manuscript notes accompanying it, James Stewart-Gordon to Charlotte Wilkinson, 3 Dec. 1946; John J. Sughrue to Soss, 18 Dec. 1946, S. T. Neidlinger to Charlotte Wilkinson, 12 Dec. 1946, Bryna Ivens to Soss, 2 Jan. 1947, Soss to Countess Grace de Munn, 24 Apr. 1947, Soss to Miss Farrell, 3 Jan. 1947, O. E. Schoeffler to Soss, 7 Apr. 1947, Simmons-Boardman Publishing Corporation to Mr. Woodworth, 15 May 1947, Box 14, WSP. Another big achievement for Wilma was a slightly earlier article in *Popular Science Monthly* called "Stitching Steel Into Streamliners." See Perry Githens to Soss, 3 Mar. 1947, Box 14, WSP.

29   Soss to Dale Cox, Soss to Fowler McCormick, 8 Jan. 1947, Soss to Fowler McCormick, 17 Sep. 1947, Box 7, Folder 3, International Harvester Company, "Common and Preferred Stock, Distribution of Stock According to Types of Stockholders, October 31, 1950," Box 7, Folder 4, Soss to Fowler McCormick, 17 Oct.

1947, Soss to Mabel Glass, 4 Nov. 1947, Box 7, Folder 3, McCormick/International Harvester Papers, WHS; Emerson and Latcham, *Shareholder Democracy*, 105.

30   Dale Cox to Soss, 11 Nov. 1947, Soss to Dale Cox, 19 Nov. 1947, Box 7, Folder 3, McCormick/International Harvester Papers, WHS; Leo Fontaine to Soss, 15 Feb. 1949, Box 14, WSP.

31   Soss, "Five Years of Progress," Harvard Law School (27 Feb. 1961), Box 15, WSP; Logan, "Hoboken Must Go!," 34-35, 51; "Pressure Group," *The New Yorker* (25 Jun. 1949), 16; Soss to Mary Morris, 20 Apr. 1949, Box 14, WSP.

32   Qtd. in Traflet, *Nation*, 60.

33   For a more critical assessment of the "democratic capitalism" rhetoric, see Art Preis, "'Myth of 'People's Capitalism,'" *International Socialist Review* no. 1 to 23, 1 (Winter 1962): 3-9; Aaron Brenner, "The Myth of the Shareholder Nation," *New Labor Forum* no. 2 to 13, 2 (Summer 2004): 20-35.

34   On the NYSE's public relations work, see Traflet, *Nation*. See also Julia Ott, *When Main Street Met Wall Street: The Quest for an Investors' Democracy* (Cambridge, MA: Harvard University Press, 2011); Rob Aitken, "'A Direct Personal Stake': Cultural Economy, Mass Investment, and the New York Stock Exchange," *Review of International Political Economy* 12, 2 (2005): 334-66.

35   For an overview, see Glenn Griswold and Denny Griswold, eds. *Your Public Relations: The Standard Public Relations Handbook* (New York: Funk & Wagnalls, 1948). On AT&T's "Investment democracy" advertisements in the early 1900s, see Roland Marchand, *Advertising the American Dream: Making Way for Modernity* (Berkeley: University of California Press, 1985), esp. 74-82. See also Pamela Walker Laird, *Advertising Progress: American Business and the Rise of Consumer Marketing* (Baltimore: Johns Hopkins University Press, 1998); Jackson Lears, *Fables of Abundance: A Cultural History of Advertising in America* (New York: Basic Books, 1994); Richard S. Tedlow, *Keeping the Corporate Image: Public Relations and Business, 1900-1950* (Greenwich: JAI Press, 1979); David Nye *Image Worlds: Corporate Identities at General Electric, 1890-1930* (Cambridge, MA: MIT Press, 1985).

36   On Sinatra being booed at the Union Club, see Kitty Kelley, *His Way: The Unauthorized Biography of Frank Sinatra* (New York: Bantam Books, 2015), 557.

37   Wilma recounted frequently her performance at that U.S. Steel meeting on May 5, 1947. See, for example, "Pressure Group," *The New Yorker* (25 Jun. 1949), 15; Logan, "Hoboken Must Go!," 35-36.

38   Qtd. in "Pressure Group," *The New Yorker* (25 Jun. 1949), 15. "Woman Want More Say in Business," *Kiplinger Magazine* (May 1949), 31.

39   "Woman Want More Say," 31.

40   Logan, "Hoboken Must Go!," 35.

41   Logan, "Hoboken Must Go!," 36.

42   Logan, "Hoboken Must Go!," 35.

43   Qtd. in Logan, "Hoboken Must Go," 35; Soss to Merle Crowell, 3 Jun. 1949, Box 14, WSP.

44   Gonzalez, "Where No Woman Reaches the Summit," SM 34.

45   Qtd. in "Pressure Group," *The New Yorker*, 15.

46   "For Love," *The New Yorker* (24 Apr. 1954), 26.

47   Logan, "Hoboken Must Go!," 45-46, 50; Penelope McMillan, "Wilma Soss Revisited," *New York News Magazine* (13 Jan. 1974), 6; Membership List, n.d., Box 10, WSP; John Brooks, "Stockholder Season," *The New Yorker* (8 Oct. 1966), 177, 184; Marens, "Inventing Corporate Governance," 366, 376; Richard Gehman, "Guardian Angel of Shareholders," *Cosmopolitan* (Apr. 1963), 66.

48   Grace Kingsley, "Woman Heads Film Company," *Los Angeles Times* (20 Aug. 1919), II4; Susan Ingalls Lewis, *Unexceptional Women: Female Proprietors in Mid-Nineteenth Century Albany, New York, 1830-1885* (Columbus: Ohio State University Press, 2009). Kingsley in 1919 reported that Curtis "has personally interviewed the powers of Wall Street, and finally got certain of them not only to believe that after all, a woman might head a motion picture company, but to furnish her with practical aid."

49   Kingsley, "Woman Heads Film Company," II4; "Cathrine Curtis Prefers to Drive: Undertakes Long Trip to Movie Location and Expects to Make Speed," *Los Angeles Times* (14 Sep. 1919), V17.

50   Objectives quoted in "Women Investors of Nation Organize: New Group Plans to Serve as Agency for a United Front in Financial World," *New York Times* (4 May 1935), 19. Italics added for emphasis. Also see "Women Investors in America, Inc., Is Formed to Preserve Rights Guaranteed by Constitution," *Wall Street Journal* (14 May 1935), ; "Women Investors in America," *Wall Street Journal* (13 Mar. 1937), 3.

51   "Organizing Women Investors," *The Washington Post* (26 May 1935), B6. On Women Investors' effort to educate women on financial matters, see, for example, "Congress on Finance is Called for Women," *New York Times* (31 May 1936), N7. "Women Investors in America," *Wall Street Journal* (19 Apr. 1937), 3.

52   Kari Frederickson, "Cathrine Curtis and Conservative Isolationist Women, 1939-1941," *The Historian* 58, 4 (1996), 825-39; "Fiscal Ignorance Is Scored: Miss Cathrine Curtis Assails Men for Failing to Aid in Money Matters," *New York Times* (16 Oct. 1935), 23.

53   Frederickson, "Cathrine Curtis," 825-39.

54   As quoted in Marens, "Inventing Corporate Governance," 368. See also Lewis D. Gilbert, *Dividends and Democracy* (Larchmont, New York: American Research Council, 1956); Lewis Gilbert, "Small Stockholders Need to Organize," *Kiplinger Magazine: The Changing Times* (Apr. 1939), 3-4; John Bainbridge, "The Talking Stockholder -- I," *The New Yorker* (11 Dec. 1948); John Bainbridge, "The Talking Stockholder -- II," *The New Yorker* (18 Dec. 1948).

55   WSP.

56   Douglas Martin, "John J. Gilbert Is Dead at 88; Gadfly at Corporate Meetings," *New York Times* (17 Jul. 2002), C16.

57   Leonard Sloane, "Lewis Gilbert, 86, Advocate of Shareholder Rights," *New York Times* (8 Dec. 1993).

58   Qtd. in J.A. Livingston, *The American Stockholder* (Philadelphia: J.B. Lippincott, 1958), 96-97; P. Sargant Florence, *The Logic of British and American Industry* (New York: Taylor & Francis, 2013), 186; Lewis D. Gilbert, *Dividends and Democracy* (Larchmont, New York: American Research Council, 1956).

59   Gilbert, *Dividends and Democracy*; Livingston, *The American Stockholder*, 96-99.

60   Bainbridge, "The Talking Stockholder -- I,"; Bainbridge, "The Talking Stockholder – II."

61   "Stockholder Foes Defied by Schwab: Minority Hecklers at Meeting of Bethlehem Steel Routed in Attack on Leader," *New York Times* (13 Apr. 1938), 33; "Senate Committee Hears 2 Investors: L. Coshland and L. Gilbert," *New York Times* (14 May 1937). See also Arundel Cotter, *The Story of Bethlehem Steel* (New York: Moody Magazine and Book Company, 1916); Mark Reutter, *Making Steel: Sparrows Point and the Rise and Ruin of American Industrial Might* (University of Illinois Press, 2004), 286.

62   https://ephemeralnewyork.wordpress.com/2015/12/07/the-most-spectacular-mansion-on-riverside-drive/. Accessed 4 May 2022.

63   "Stockholder Foes Defied by Schwab," 33. Reutter, *Making Steel*, 286-87.

64   "Stockholder Foes Defied by Schwab," 33. Christopher Gray, "The Late Great Charles Schwab Mansion," *New York Times* (8 Jul. 2010).

65   Lewis, *Dividends and Democracy*; "Stockholders Hit Schwab's Pay of $250,000 Yearly," *Winona Republican-Herald* (10 Apr. 1935).

66   Marilyn Bender, *At the Top: Behind the Scenes with the Men and Women Who Run America's Corporate Giants* (Garden City: Doubleday & Co., 1975); Sheldon E.

Bernstein and Henry G. Fischer, "The Regulation of the Solicitation of Proxies: Some Reflections on Corporate Democracy," *University of Chicago Law Review* 7 (1940): 226-49.

67   Marens, "Inventing Corporate Governance," 370; John Brooks, "Stockholder Season," *The New Yorker* (8 Oct. 1966), 159.

68   Bernstein and Fischer, "Regulation of the Solicitation of Proxies," 229. Between 1948 and 1951, 97.7% of stockholder resolutions failed. About a third or so, though, garnered more than eight percent support, which was remarkable in an age when management reserved the prerogative, vigorously opposed by the gadflies, of voting unmarked proxies. Soss, "FOWSAB," n.d., Irene Rutherford O'Crowley, "Statement in Favor of the Secret Ballot," n.d., "Stockholder Proposal No. 2 (Disclosure of Auditor's Fees)," 1982, Box 10, WSP. On management's tactic of voting unmarked proxies, see Soss, "Five Years of Progress," Harvard Law School (27 Feb. 1961), Box 15, WSP. Discussing the propensity of institutional investors to cower in the corner, see Marens, "Inventing Corporate Governance," 377; Emerson and Latcham, *Shareholder Democracy*, 112-13.

CHAPTER THREE: Pinnacle of Power

69   Qtd. in Eric Pace, "Mary Roebling, 89, First Woman to Head Major U.S. Bank, Dies," *New York Times* (27 Oct. 1994).

70   "Women Want More Say in Business, and a New Federation Works to Help Them Get It," *Changing Times: The Kiplinger Magazine*, 3, 5 (May 1949): 31; Andy Logan, "Hoboken Must Go!," *The New Yorker* (17 Mar. 1951), 36. Notably, in 1949, Pecora became FOWSAB's first male speaker. Soss, "Five Years of Progress," Harvard Law School (27 Feb. 1961), Box 15, Soss to Clinton B. Axford, 21, 23 Mar. 1949, Soss to City News Bureau of Associated Press, 7 Apr. 1949, Box 14, Wilma Soss Papers (WSP), American Heritage Center, Laramie, Wyoming.

71   The phrase "corporate democracy" became increasingly popular in the mid twentieth century. Lewis Gilbert claimed, probably incorrectly, that he first said it, but he certainly did spread it.

72   On Rohde's life, see http://biography.yourdictionary.com/ruth-bryan-owen-rohde#GwDUpmwqekofrHop.99. Accessed 5 May 2022. "Mrs. Rohde Chosen by Women's Group," *New York Times* (28 Oct. 1948), 48. According to the *Times*, other officers were Mary G. Roebling (treasurer), Eleanor Bayuk Green (secretary), Mrs. Horstense Odium, former chairman of the board of Bonqit Teller (trustee). Originally, FOWSAB was only open to women. The organization's purpose, the newspaper reported, was "economic enlightenment for woman ... to enable women to exercise their economic franchise more intelligently and effectively in a country where women own 70 per cent of the privately held wealth."

73   Carmen Godwin and Fernanda Perrone, "Woman in a Man's World: The Career of Mary G. Roebling," *The Rutgers Scholar* 1 (1999). Roebling's papers are at Rutgers University, New Brunswick, New Jersey. Her second husband was the grandson of the architect who built the Brooklyn Bridge.

74   http://biography.yourdictionary.com/ruth-bryan-owen. Accessed 5 May 2022. "Mrs. Rohde Chosen by Women's Group," 48. Godwin and Perrone, "Woman in a Man's World: The Career of Mary G. Roebling." J. A. Livingston, "U.S. Steel Festival at Hoboken Is Source of Sauce for the Soss," *Evening Bulletin* (5 May 1949), 125-26. He continued, "Her background is that of publicity agent, and she functions in that capacity as president of FOWSAB."

75   Hutton devised the idea of changing the name "stockholder" to "shareowner," as he contended it carried more positive connotations for capitalism. Agreeing, B.C. Forbes, founder and editor of *Forbes Magazine*, decided that all of his magazines henceforth would only use the term "shareowner." "'Share Owner' Better Than 'Stock-holder,'" *Forbes* (1 Dec. 1950), 12, 13.

76   Penelope McMillan, "Wilma Soss Revisited," *New York News Magazine* (13 Jan. 1974), 7; Richard Marens, "Inventing Corporate Governance: The Mid-Century Emergence of Shareholder Activism," *Journal of Business and Management* 8, 4 (2002): 378; Wilma Soss, "FOWSAB," n.d., Box 10, WSP; Keith A. Libbey, "Mrs. Soss Speaks to Bull & Bear," *Harvard Law Record* 32, 4 (2 Mar. 1961), FOWSAB, "Second Annual Meeting," Box 15, WSP; Birdie Safion to Members from 1975-76, Soss to Harry J. Gray, 12 May 1981, Box 10, WSP; Soss to Merle Crowell, 3 Jun. 1949, Box 14, WSP; Soss to Fowler McCormick, 17 Sep. 1947, 23 Dec. 1949, Box 7, Folder 3, McCormick/International Harvester Papers, Wisconsin Historical Society (WHS), Madison, Wisc. Logan, "Hoboken Must Go!," 46; FOWSAB, "1964 Ratings of Annual Meetings: Some Halos Slipped, Some New Halos," 1964, Box 10, WSP.

77   Barbara Fischer memorandum, "Federation of Women Shareholders in American Business," 1947, Box 14, WSP; FOWSAB, "Second Annual Meeting," Box 15, WSP; "Pressure Group," *The New Yorker* (25 Jun. 1949), 16.

78   "Women Want More Say," 31.

79   Wilma Soss, "Women as Stockholders," Symposium on the Status of Women in America, Bryant College Centennial, 1963, Box 15, WSP; Frank D. Emerson and Franklin C. Latcham, *Shareholder Democracy: A Broader Outlook for Corporations* (Cleveland: Press of Western Reserve University, 1954), 104; Pocketbook News (PN), 20 Apr. 1959, Box 8, WSP; Soss, "Women as Stockholders," Symposium on the Status of Women in America, Bryant College Centennial, 1963, Box 15, WSP.

80   "Women Want More Say," 31-32.

81   Soss to Clinton B. Axford, 21, 23 Mar. 1949, Box 14, WSP; Marens, "Inventing Corporate Governance," 371; Logan, "Hoboken Must Go!," 35; "Women Want More

Say," 32. Wilma's 6 million female stockholders number we now know was significantly (and probably unintentionally) inflated, as there were at the time fewer than 6 million total shareowners total in the United States. But she was roughly correct about the proportion of female to male investors.

82   Harry Reichenbach and David Freedman, *Phantom Fame: The Anatomy of Ballyhoo* (New York: Simon and Schuster, 1931), 9; FOWSAB, "Women and Wealth: What Every Stockholder Should Know About the Post Meeting Report," n.d., 7, Box 10, WSP.

83   Nancy Woloch, "Feminist Movement," in *The Reader's Companion to American History*, Eric Foner and John A. Garraty, eds. (Boston: Houghton Mifflin Company, 1991), 391; Nancy F. Cott, *The Grounding of Modern Feminism* (New Haven: Yale University Press, 1987); Ellen Carol DuBois, *Feminism and Suffrage: The Emergence of an Independent Women's Movement in America* (Ithaca: Cornell University Press, 1978). Elizabeth Cady Stanton, "Declaration of Sentiments," Seneca Falls, qtd. in "Declaration of Sentiments," *Modern History Sourcebook* https://sourcebooks.fordham.edu/mod/senecafalls.asp. Accessed 5 May 2022. Noted abolitionist Frederick Douglass, who had escaped slavery, was vocal at the Seneca Falls convention and helped sway many to sign the document.

84   Barbara Fischer memorandum, "Federation of Women Shareholders in American Business," 1947, Box 14, WSP.

85   Soss, "FOWSAB," n.d., FOWSAB, "Women Shareholders in 26 States Vote 3 Shares of Big Steel Stock: Refuse Instructed or Coerced Vote, Give Reasons for Voting Against the Tide," FOWSAB, "You and Your Dollars," 1951-1952, "How to Make Your Money Talk," n.d., FOWSAB, "You and Your 1954 Proxy," 1954, FOWSAB, "Your Proxies Are Needed for 1965-66," 1965, FOWSAB, "Calendar of Stockholder Meetings," 1970, Adele Faloon to FOWSAB members, n.d., Box 10, WSP.

86   Soss, "Position Paper of the Federation of Women Shareholders in American Business, Inc.," 16 Nov. 1970, Box 10, WSP.

87   "Women Want More Say," 32.

88   Logan, "Hoboken Must Go!," 36.

89   Livingston, "U.S. Steel Festival."

90   Logan, "Hoboken Must Go!," 36; Mary Morris to Soss, 6 May 1949; Soss to Mary Morris, 6, 10 May 1949, Box 14, WSP; https://en.wikipedia.org/wiki/We_the_People_(U.S._TV_series). Accessed 5 May 2022.

91   Qtd in Logan, "Hoboken Must Go!," 36.

92   According to Logan, the stockholder calling Soss "Mrs. Apple Soss" was J. Newcomb Blackman. Logan, "Hoboken Must Go!," 34, 36.

93   Logan, "Hoboken Must Go!," 36.

94   Soss, "Five Years of Progress," Harvard Law School (27 Feb. 1961), Box 15, WSP.

95   "Women of Steel Give the Top Brass a Hard Time," *Life* (1 Mar. 1950), 46.

96   Logan, "Hoboken Must Go!," 34-35; "For Love," *The New Yorker* (24 Apr. 1954), 26.

97   "Women of Steel," 46.

98   "Women of Steel," 46.

99   Qtd. in "Women of Steel," 46.

100   "Women of Steel," 46.

101   Qtd. in J.A. Livingston, *The American Stockholder* (Philadelphia: J.B. Lippincott, 1958), 126. Also see Livingston, "U.S. Steel Festival," 124-126.

102   Livingston, *American Stockholder*, 127.

103   Logan, "Hoboken Must Go!," 47; "Truck Kills Widow, 74," *New York Times* (4 Apr. 1953); FOWSAB, "Second Annual Meeting," Box 15, WSP; Chairman of Membership to ?, n.d., Rosa Condello, Membership Application, 5 Dec. 1972, Box 10, WSP; Soss to Dorothy Dunbar Bromley, 1 May 1947, Soss to Virginia Blood, 26 May 1948, Soss to Sylvia [?], 24 May 1948, Soss to Stella [?], 25 May 1948, Soss to Iphigene Sulzberger, 26 May 1948, Soss to Lee Cornell, 24 May 1948, Soss to Marie Denicore, 28 Dec. 1948, Box 14, WSP.

104   FOWSAB, "Second Annual Meeting," Box 15, WSP; Logan, "Hoboken Must Go!," 45; Soss to Clinton B. Axford, 21, 23 Mar. 1949, Chairman of Administration to Verna Small, 17 Dec. 1952, Soss to City News Bureau of Associated Press, 7 Apr. 1949, Soss to Mr. Durkin, 7 Apr. 1949, "Press List Telephoned by Mrs. Soss," 16 Oct. 1952, Soss to Ama Barker, 22 Oct. 1952; Secretary-Treasurer to City Editor, *Brooklyn Eagle*, 16 Oct. 1952, "Poor Little Rich Girl vs. Enfranchised Lady Shareholder," and its addendum, n.d., "Women of Achievement," Geoffrey T. Hellman to Soss, 11 May 1949, Ruth Adams to Soss, 17 May 1949, Carla Adelt Sykes to Soss, 17 Nov. 1948, Joan Carter to Soss, 27 Apr. 1949, Jeanne Lowe to Soss, 11 Mar. 1949, Richard Ziesing, Jr. to Soss, 25 Apr. 1949, Box 14, WSP.

105   FOWSAB, "You and Your Dollars," 1951-1952, Box 10, WSP; Soss to Fowler McCormick, 23 Dec. 1949, 6 Jan. 1950, Fowler McCormick to Soss, 4 Jan. 1950, Box 7, Folder 3, WHS; Logan, "Hoboken Must Go!," 34, 45; "Pressure Group," *The New Yorker* (25 Jun. 1949), 16; Soss to Gurney Williams, 13 Jan. 1949, Box 14, WSP.

106   FOWSAB, "Second Annual Meeting," Box 15, WSP; Livingston, "U.S. Steel Festival"; FOWSAB to Faith McNulty, 2 Mar. 1949, Box 14, WSP.

107 Richard Gehman, "Guardian Angel of Shareholders," *Cosmopolitan* (Apr. 1963), 64; Logan, "Hoboken Must Go!," 45-46; Harwell Wells, "A Long View of Shareholder Power: From the Antebellum Corporation to the Twenty-First Century," *Florida Law Review* 67, 3 (2016): 1,080; Marens, "Inventing Corporate Governance," 375-76; FOWSAB, "Second Annual Meeting," FOWSAB circular, "Bearing Up in a Bear Market," 5 Jun. 1962, Box 15, WSP; Elsa M. Paul to Members, 1952, Helen Plavin to Members, ? 1972, Box 10, WSP.

108 Ms. E. C. Lyon (California) to Soss, 14 Mar. 1979; Jarmela Speta (Illinois) to FOWSAB, 27 Mar. 1979; Kelton Roberts (Vermont) to FOWSAB, 19 Mar. 1981; Joan L. Miller (Philadelphia) to Joan Safion, 22 Sep. 1981, Robert R. Citron to Soss, 19 Jul. 1961; Patricia P. Widmer/Mrs. Albert R. Widmer, Jr. to Soss, 9 Nov. 1965, Box 10, WSP; Mrs. L. R. Benninghoff to Soss, 18 Jul. 1966, Willard P. Brown to Soss, 5 Sep. 1973, Box 3, WSP.

109 Elsa M. Paul to Members, 1952, Box 10, WSP; Gehman, "Guardian Angel," 64.

110 Soss to Fowler McCormick, 23 Mar. 1951 Box 7, Folder 3, WHS; Soss to New York Stock Exchange, 31 Mar. 1975, FOWSAB, "April Stockholders Calendar," 1965, FOWSAB, "Calendar of Stockholder Meetings," 1970, Box 10, WSP.

111 FOWSAB circular, "Bearing Up in a Bear Market," 5 Jun. 1962, A. W. Zelomek, "A Changing America and the Stock Market," n.d., Box 15, WSP; FOWSAB, "First Open Meeting This Season," 16 Oct. 1967, "Monthly Members Meeting," 17 Oct. 1966, FOWSAB, "The Stock Market – *Understand It Yourself*," 1954, FOWSAB, "Four Wednesday Money Matinees," 1958, FOWSAB, "Here Are Your Workshops for Spring 1953," 1953, Box 10, WSP.

112 FOWSAB Press Release, n.d.; Soss to Wilfred May, 12 Nov. 1952, "Women 'Holders Plan Lectures," 6 Nov. 1952, New York *World-Telegram and Sun*, Box 14, WSP; FOWSAB, "How to Invest in 1954," "Eleventh Annual Woman Investor's Clinic," 1968, FOWSAB, "FOWSAB Summer Chronicle," 1956, Box 10, WSP; FOWSAB Press Release, 20 Nov. 1962, Box 15, WSP; FOWSAB, Invitation to Annual Woman Investor's Clinic," 9 Nov. 1965, Box 10, WSP.

113 Soss to the Editors of *Living for Young Homemakers*, n.d., Box 14, WSP; FOWSAB, "Annual Woman Investors Clinic," 16 Nov. 1970, Box 10, WSP; Nancy Fraser, "Queen of the Corporate Gadflies," *Life* (18 Mar. 1966), 123; Adele Faloon to Soss, n.d., Evelyn M. Kovacs to FOWSAB, 29 Jun. 1980, ? to Arthur Bowers, 18 May 1974, Box 10, WSP.

114 Gehman, "Guardian Angel," 67; FOWSAB, "You and Your 1954 Proxy," 1954, FOWSAB, "Your Proxies Are Needed for 1965-66," 1965, Box 10, WSP; FOWSAB, "Second Annual Meeting," Box 15, WSP; FOWSAB, "You and Your 1954 Proxy," Box 10, WSP.

115   Logan, "Hoboken Must Go!," 35; Adele Gutman Nathan to Soss, 17 Apr. 1966, Box 10, WSP.

116   Logan, "Hoboken Must Go!," 34; FOWSAB, "April Stockholders Calendar," 1965, Bertha Small, "Notice to Members," 25 May 1966, FOWSAB, "April Stockholders Calendar," 19??, Box 10, WSP; Fraser, "Queen of the Corporate Gadflies," 116.

117   AT&T, "Certificate of Exemption," n.d., National City Bank, "Substitute W 6 and W 7," n.d., Form 1024, n.d., "Notice to Vendors," n.d., FOWSAB to Member and Friends, n.d., FOWSAB, "You and Your Dollars," 1951-1952, Box 10, WSP; FOWSAB, "Second Annual Meeting," Box 15, WSP; "FOWSAB Stocks Held," 1973, Louis L. Pettit to FOWSAB, 24 Sep. 1973, Soss, "FOWSAB's Portfolio," ? 1980, Box 10, WSP.

CHAPTER FOUR: Proxy Fights and Solid Gold

118   Lorraine Hopkins, "She's the Scourge of Board Chairmen," *Providence Sunday Journal* (24 Nov. 1963).

119   "500,000 Own Stock of GM," *Los Angeles Times* (21 Nov. 1954), C1. While a pittance today, 494,632 GM shareowners was a huge number at the time, also relative to most other publicly trading corporations. AT&T in the 1950s beat GM, though, in being the first U.S. corporation to have more than 1 million shareowners. On the NYSE's postwar public relations campaign, see Janice Traflet, *A Nation of Small Shareholders: Marketing Wall Street After World War II* (Baltimore: Johns Hopkins, 2013).

120   "50,000,000th GM Auto Will Be Gold Plated," *Los Angeles Times* (21 Nov. 1954), C1. As the *LA Times* related, the gold-plating task was not an easy one, and Chevrolet's "styling engineers" had to make sure that the color gold was exactly right.

121   "The Solid Gold Cadillac," screenplay by Abe Borrows, based on the play by George S. Kaufman and Howard Teichmann, and produced by Fred Kohlmar for Columbia Film; Anne Teek, "Too Old," *The Washington Post Herald* (14 Nov. 1954), SS2.

122   On Soss being the inspiration for the play and movie, see an untitled article in *Directors and Boards* (Fall 1978), 8, Box 4, Clippings, Wilma Soss Papers (WSP), American Heritage Center, Laramie, Wyoming.

123   Interestingly, the playwrights didn't put Partridge into the CEO role. In real life, not one woman was CEO of any Fortune 500 company in the country, so this would have constituted an even more dramatic plot twist.

124   Frank D. Emerson and Franklin C. Latcham, *Shareholder Democracy: A Broader Outlook for Corporations* (Cleveland: Press of Western Reserve University, 1954),

51-70; Carroll R. Wetzel, "Conduct of a Stockholders' Meeting," *The Business Lawyer* 22, 2 (1967): 303. "The Solid Gold Cadillac," screenplay, 64-65.

125   Kaufman and Teichmann, "Solid Gold Cadillac"; Bosley Crowther, "Screen: Judy Holliday Takes Financiers for Ride," *New York Times* (25 Oct. 1956), 40.

126   Crowther, "Screen," 40; J.P. Shanley, "Josephine Hull Returns to Play: Actress Makes a Surprise Appearance," *New York Times* (16 Aug. 1954), 13. "Josephine Hull, Actress, Dead; Stage Career Spanned 50 Years," *New York Times* (13 Mar. 1957), 31.

127   Thomas M. Pryor, "Columbia to Film 'Gold Cadillac,'" *New York Times* (22 Nov. 1954), 29.

128   Holliday was born in 1923, and died young, at age 41, in 1965. "Judy Holliday, Winner of Oscar, Dies of Cancer," *Los Angeles Times* (8 Jun. 1965). In her *obituary, it was noted that* "she had lent her name and made contributions to leftist causes." Holliday later reportedly said, "I have awakened to a realization that I have been irresponsible and slightly—more than slightly---stupid. When I was solicited [by leftist organizations], I always said: 'Oh, isn't that too bad. Sure, use my name."

129   Crowther, "Screen," 40.

130   Milton Esterow, "Trailing a 'Solid Gold Cadillac': Film Crew Shoots Real Backgrounds Locally," *New York Times* (6 Nov. 1955), x5.

131   Soss, "FOWSAB," n.d., Box 10, WSP. On Sloan's golf comment, also see Andy Logan, "Hoboken Must Go!," *The New Yorker* (17 Mar. 1951), 46.

132   Mrs. E. H. Berendsohn to Clara Weissman, 22 Sep. 1943, Box 3, WSP; Paul Denis, "Wilma Soss: A Woman Should Have Money of Her Own," *Radio Voice of the Month* (Jan. 1970); "Soss, Wilma (Porter)," *Current Biography*; Mary Prime, "Women in the News," *United States Press Radio*, n.d., Box 3, WSP. Evans Corp., *Evans Dual Purpose Streamlined Auto-Railers* (1936); Evans Corp., *Off the Rails Without a Stop* (193?).

133   Clair Wilcox, *Public Policies Toward Business* (Homewood, Ill.: Richard D. Irwin, 1960), 644-65; Pocketbook News (PN), 7 Mar., 18 Oct. 1970, 11 Nov., 23 Dec. 1973, Box 9, WSP. Most famously, perhaps, Soss announced in 1974 that "the east is plagued with an ancient railroad system that delivers coal as efficiently as shoveling snow with a spoon." PN, 23 Mar. 1974, Box 9, WSP.

134   PN, 12 Mar. 1972, Box 9, WSP.

135   PN, 24 May 1970, Box 9, WSP; Joseph Borkin, *Robert R. Young, the Populist of Wall Street* (New York: Harper & Row, 1969), 20; Wilcox, *Public Policies*, 663.

136   Borkin, *Robert R. Young*.

137   Leverett S. Lyon, *Education for Business* (Chicago: University of Chicago Press, 1922), ix, 322.

138   Borkin, *Robert R. Young*, 1. For more on Young's battles, see also Jeff Gramm, *Dear Chairman: Boardroom Battles and the Rise of Shareholder Activism* (New York: HarperBusiness, 2016).

139   Qtd. in Borkin, *Robert R. Young*, 10-11, 1; "Felicitous Occasion," *The New Yorker* (6 Jun. 1956), 27.

140   Matthew Josephson, *The Robber Barons* (New York: Harcourt, Brace & World, Inc., 1962), 187.

141   Borkin, *Robert R. Young*, 44-55.

142   Borkin, *Robert R. Young*, 56-69.

143   Borkin, *Robert R. Young*, 70-93, quote from 88-89.

144   Borkin, *Robert R. Young*, 94-131.

145   Borkin, *Robert R. Young*, 132-45.

146   Borkin, *Robert R. Young*, 162, 167, 170.

147   Borkin, *Robert R. Young*, 146-57.

148   Borkin, *Robert R. Young*, 158-74.

149   "Mrs. Soss Plans Action," *New York Times* (27 Feb. 1954); Soss to William E. Morley of the SEC, ? Aug. 1986, Box 3, WSP; "S.E.C. to Study Plan for Secret Ballot at Central Meetings, Idea of Mrs. Soss," *New York Times* (24 Mar. 1954); "Rivals in Central Vie for News, Too," *New York Times* (26 Mar. 1954).

150   "Changes Opposed for Proxy Rules," *New York Times* (17 Dec. 1953).

151   Borkin, *Robert R. Young*, 175-88.

152   Borkin, *Robert R. Young*, 188-204; Meyer Berger, "About New York: Embattled Stockholders of Central to Share Special Albany Train for Wednesday Vote," *New York Times* (24 May 1954); Meyer Berger, "Sound, Fury Mark Central Meeting," *New York Times* (27 May 1954).

153   Berger, "Sound"; Robert E. Bedingfield, "Central Vote In; Meeting Recessed," *New York Times* (27 May 1954).

154   Borkin, *Robert R. Young*, 205-9.

155 Benjamin Graham, "Foreword," in Emerson and Latcham, *Shareholder Democracy*, v.

156 "Financial and Business Sidelights: 'Small' Central Meeting," *New York Times* (24 May 1955); Robert E. Bedingfield, "Central Meeting Strong for Young," *New York Times* (27 May 1955); FOWSAB to Members, ? Jul. 1955, Box 10, WSP.

157 "Felicitous Occasion," *The New Yorker* (6 Jun. 1956), 26; Lorraine Hopkins, "She's the Scourge"; Richard Gehman, "Guardian Angel of Shareholders," *Cosmopolitan* (Apr. 1963), 65.

158 Borkin, *Robert R. Young*, 211-26.

159 PN, 3 Feb. 1958, 7 Dec. 1959, 25 Sep. 1960, Box 8, WSP.

160 Gehman, "Guardian Angel of Shareholders," 65; Hopkins, "She's the Scourge"; PN, 7 Mar., 24 May 1970, 25 May 1974, Box 9, WSP; Penelope McMillan, "Wilma Soss Revisited," *New York News Magazine* (13 Jan. 1974), 7, 39.

161 Nancy Fraser, "Queen of the Corporate Gadflies," *Life* (18 Mar. 1966), 115-16, 119-20, 123; Wetzel, "Conduct," 305; "'Investments' Subject of 1-hr. TV Program," *Commercial and Financial Chronicle* (5 Mar. 1959), 27; PN, Memo from Wilma Soss, n.d., Box 10, WSP.

162 Wilma Soss, "Women as Stockholders," Symposium on the Status of Women in America, Bryant College Centennial, 1963, Box 15, WSP.

163 Frances H. Wilmoth of the Parkersburg (West Va.) Woman's Club to Soss, 19 May 1962, Box 10, WSP; "Municipal Bondwomen to Hold Spring Meeting," *Commercial and Financial Chronicle* (19 May 1949), 29; George F. Shaskan, Jr., "Investment Planning for Women," *Commercial and Financial Chronicle* (16 Mar. 1950), 4; Charles H. Russell to Soss, 12, 19 Nov. 1963, Gertrude Meth Hochberg to Soss, 20 Nov. 1963, Box 15, WSP; Hopkins, "She's the Scourge"; Beverly Susskind to Soss, 1 Nov. 1971, Box 10, WSP; "Wilma Soss" bio blurb, *The Status of Women in America Symposium*, 18 Nov. 1963, Box 15, WSP; Keith A. Libbey, "Mrs. Soss Speaks to Bull & Bear," *Harvard Law Record* 32, 4 (2 Mar. 1961); Soss, "Five Years of Progress," Harvard Law School (27 Feb. 1961), Box 15, WSP; Jennifer L. Carter, "The Rise and Rise of the Specialty Journals at Harvard Law School," *NELLCO Legal Scholarship Repository* (8 Jan. 2007), 7; Joanne Knoch, "Wilma Gets Message Over Sans Megaphone," *Chicago Daily Tribune* (18 Sep. 1956); John Brooks, "Stockholder Season," *The New Yorker* (8 Oct. 1966), 164; G. Keith Funston to Soss, 18 Dec. 1963, Box 10, WSP.

164 Dorothy Armbruster to Soss, 5 Nov. 1962, Box 3, Bertha Small, "Notice to Members," ? 1966, Box 10, WSP. On the eventual falling out between Wilma and Kelekian, see "Sidelights: Assistant Gadfly Leaves Queen," *New York Times* (5 May 1966), 70; "Sidelights: Chapter II: Reply by Mrs. Soss," *New York Times* (6 May 1966), 70.

CHAPTER FIVE: Camelot Come and Gone

165 At the time, Camelot was a popular Broadway play by Lerner and Loewe. In an interview with *Life*, Jacqueline Kennedy invoked the lyrics shortly after her husband was assassinated, recalling how much JFK loved that line. See Theodore H. White, "An Epilogue," *Life*, 6 Dec. 1963, https://www.jfklibrary.org/asset-viewer/archives/THWPP/059/THWPP-059-009. Accessed 8 May 2022.

166 Tom Wicker, "Weather Limits Crowds at Fetes," *New York Times* (20 Jan. 1961), 1, 14. See also Anthony Lewis, "Presidential Diary: Kennedy's Day is Long, Exhilarating and Occasionally Tedious," *New York Times* (21 Jan. 1961) 1.

167 Lewis, "Presidential Diary," 1.

168 PN, 11 September 1960. Images 5208ff. On Wilma's radio show, see Robert E. Wright "Pioneer Financial News: National Broadcast Journalist Wilma Soss, NBC Radio, 1954-1980," *Journalism History*, 44:3 (2018): 138-49. Pocketbook News (PN), 11 Sep. 1960, Box 8, Wilma Soss Papers (WSP), American Heritage Center, Laramie, Wyoming.

169 PN, 28 Dec. 1959, Box 8, WSP. SNCC was founded in the spring of 1960. Freedom rides ran from 4 May to 10 Oct. 1961.

170 For more on the Commission, see Folder Title: Commission on the status of Women, Papers of John F. Kennedy, Presidential Papers, President's Office Files, Departments and Agencies, "Statement by the President on the Establishment of the President's Commission on the Status of Women," Office of the White House Press Secretary, Commission on the Status of Women, https://www.jfklibrary.org/asset-viewer/archives/JFKPOF/093/JFKPOF-093-004. Accessed 9 May 2022.

171 Perhaps Wilma didn't fall prey to the lure of McCarthyism in part because she had so many friends in the theatre world, some of whom were not nearly as capitalist as she was. PN, 11 Jun. 1972, 16 Jul. 1976, Box 9, WSP.

172 Dr. Martin Luther King, at a NAACP rally on 1 Jan. 1957 proclaimed, "I have come to see more and more that one of the most decisive steps that the Negro can take is that little walk to the voting booth. That is an important step. We've got to gain the ballot, and through that gain, political power." King qtd. in https://www.naacp.org/dr-martin-luther-king-jr-mw/. Accessed 9 May 2022. King was born in 1929—the same year as Evelyn Davis.

173 Logan, "Hoboken Must Go!," 50; Nancy Fraser, "Queen of the Corporate Gadflies," *Life* (18 Mar. 1966), 120; Gehman, "Guardian Angel of Shareholders," 66.

174 Carroll R. Wetzel, "Conduct of a Stockholders' Meeting," *The Business Lawyer* 22, 2 (1967): 303-5; Gehman, "Guardian Angel of Shareholders," 65. As *Cosmopolitan* reported, Wilma had "donned so many costumes that financial writers now review them, as though they were theater critics."

175   Brooks, "Stockholder Season," 164; Marylin Bender, *At the Top: Behind the Scenes with the Men and Women Who Run America's Corporate Giants* (Garden City, N.Y.: Doubleday & Co., 1975), 404; Logan, "Hoboken Must Go!," 48.

176   Penelope McMillan, "Wilma Soss Revisited," *New York News Magazine* (13 Jan. 1974), 38; Wilma Soss to FOWSAB Members, Jul. 1955, Box 10, WSP; Wetzel, "Conduct," 306; Gehman, "Guardian Angel," 66; Lorraine Hopkins, "She's the Scourge of Board Chairmen," *Providence Sunday Journal* (24 Nov. 1963).

177   Gehman, "Guardian Angel," 64.

178   Brooks, "Stockholder Season," 159; Logan, "Hoboken Must Go!," 48; Gehman, "Guardian Angel," 65-66.

179   Gehman, "Guardian Angel," 64. Gehman attributes the five women directors (unnamed) as wins for Wilma—though it is unclear whether it was just Wilma claiming this. In interviews (including the 1963 *Cosmo* one), Wilma remained cagey about FOWSAB's membership rosters, refusing to give concrete information about the number of members.

180   In the 1965 Comsat meeting, Wilma was carried out bodily by Pinkerton guards. It would not be the last time.

181   Aileen Mehle, "Money and the Presidency," 42-49, Ayn Rand, "The Money Making Personality," 37-41, Bob Hope, "Moscow Wants My Money!" 12, Richard Gehman, "Guardian Angel of Shareholders," 64-67, Don and Gael Forst, "Income Tax Loopholes," 74 in *Cosmopolitan* (Apr. 1963). Inside cover: "It used to be said that money was a hindrance to men seeking the President, but John F. Kennedy and his charming wife have singlehandedly made money fashionable—in the political way."

182   Sadly, Gehman died young, a decade after writing the piece on Soss. "Richard Gehman, Author, 50, Dead," *New York Times* (14 May 1972). Gehman, "Guardian Angel," 64-67.

183   Gehman, "Guardian Angel," 64. He continued, "Upon first encounter, Mrs. Soss strikes a stranger as an appealingly feminine little woman who wears off-the-face sunburst hats and transparent-plastic harlequin glasses. She seems about as determined and rigid as, say, Spring Byington. Strangers soon find out they are mistaken."

184   PN, 18 May 1959, Box 8, WSP.

185   Wilma Soss, "Five Years of Progress," Harvard Law School (27 Feb. 1961), Box 15, WSP. A. Wilfred May, "Can Investors Be Unionized? Their Joan-of-Arc Says 'No'," *Commercial and Financial Chronicle* (30 Jun. 1949), 4.

186   Gehman, "Guardian Angel," 67; McMillan, "Wilma Soss Revisited," 7.

187 Cowan speech delivered on 16 Sep. 1959 to the Pittsburgh Advertising Club, qtd. in Thomas Fisher at CBS, Letter to Honorable Maky Jane Manning, Secretary, FCC, 18 Sep. 1958, in *Investigation of Television Quiz Shows: Hearings before a Subcommittee of the Committee on Interstate and Foreign Commerce*, House of Representatives, Eighty-Sixth Congress, first session. 6-10 Oct., 12 Oct., 1959, Full text available at https://archive.org/stream/investigationoft01unit/investigationoft01unit_djvu.txt. Accessed 9 May 2022. See also the obituaries of two prominent figures from the 21 scandal, Charles Van Doren and Albert Freeman: David Marino Nachison, "Charles Van Doren, Central Figure in 1950s Quiz Show Scandal Dies at 93," *Washington Post* (10 Apr. 2010); "Albert Freeman, Producer of Rigged 1950s Quiz Show, Dies at 95," *New York Times* (22 Apr. 2017). See also https://en.wikipedia.org/wiki/The_$64,000_Question. Accessed 9 May 2022.

188 Qtd. in "Hearings before a Subcommittee."

189 Qtd. in "Hearings before a Subcommittee."

190 On the price-fixing scandal, also see "Government: The Price-Fixing Case," *Time* (5 May 1961).

191 Bernard D. Nossiter, "Cheering Stockholders Back GE Management: Stockholders Not Angry," *Washington Post, Times Herald* (27 Apr. 1961), A7. Gehman, "Guardian Angel," 64.

192 Soss qtd. in Gehman, "Guardian Angel," 64. By the autumn of 1959, it had become obvious that the price fixing deceptions were even more massive than originally thought, necessitating an expansion of the grand jury investigation. See William H. Andrews, "The Great Price Conspiracy," *Indiana Law Journal* Vol. 39, Issue 1 (Fall 1963), 172. In 1956, Kefauver ran for Vice President of the United States. The Stevenson/Kefauver ticket lost, however, to Eisenhower/Nixon. See https://www.senate.gov/artandhistory/history/common/investigations/Kefauver.htm. Accessed 9 May 2022.

193 Andrews, "Great Price Conspiracy," 172.

194 Ganey qtd. in "The Great Price Conspiracy," 195.

195 Whittinghill qtd. in Andrews, "The Great Price Conspiracy," fn. 12.

196 Cullen qtd. in Andrews, "The Great Price Conspiracy."

197 Nossiter, "Cheering Stockholders," A7, estimated the crowd at "2,750 ladies and gentlemen."

198 Nossiter described Soss as "a perennial battler for shareholder democracy," Nossiter, "Cheering Stockholders," A7.

199 Cordiner qtd. in Nossiter, "Cheering Stockholders," A7.

200   Soss, "Five Years of Progress," Harvard Law School (27 Feb. 1961), Box 15, FOWSAB, "FOWSAB Summer Chronicle," 1956, Irene Rutherford O'Crowley, "Statement in Favor of the Secret Ballot," n.d., Box 10, FOWSAB Annual Meeting Notes, n.d., Box 15, Soss to FOWSAB Members, Jul. 1955; Soss to Tom, 16 Apr. 1979, Box 10, WSP. H. J. Maidenberg, "A.T. & T. to Allow Secret Proxy Vote," *New York Times* (21 Apr. 1977), 82; Keith A. Libbey, "Mrs. Soss Speaks to Bull & Bear," *Harvard Law Record* 32, 4 (1961); "Felicitous Occasion," *The New Yorker* (6 Jun. 1956), 27.

201   PN, 24 May 1954, Box 8, WSP.

202   Robert C. Toth, "Crowd Cheers as Two Tossed Out by Comsat," *Los Angeles Times* (12 May 1965), B10, B11. See also Larry Weekley, "Two Stockholders Ejected at Stormy Comsat Meeting: Protest Follows," *Washington Post* (12 May 1965), A1.

203   See https://en.wikipedia.org/wiki/Pinkerton (detective agency). Accessed 9 May 2022. Seven Pinkerton agents also died in the 1892 Homestead Strike. Toth, "Crowd Cheers," B10.

204   Weekley, "Two Stockholders," A1; Wilma qtd. in Toth, "Crowd Cheers," B11.

205   Gilbert and Wilma qtd. in Weekley, "Two Stockholders," A1.

206   Wilma qtd. in Weekley, "Two Stockholders," A1.

207   Weekley, "Two Stockholders," A1. One proposal endeavored to impose age limits on board members.

208   Fraser, "Queen," 123; McMillan, "Wilma Soss Revisited," 7.

209   Whether or not this was the true reason for Kelekian's resignation can be debated. Wilma felt Kelekian was just using this as an excuse.

210   Kelekian qtd. in Weekley, "Two Stockholders," A1; PN, 19 May 1968, Box 8, WSP.

211   The lighted cigar is mentioned and Evelyn Davis qtd. in Weekley, "Two Stockholders," A1.

CHAPTER SIX: Queen of the Corporate Jungle

212   On Davis' tombstone inscription, very prematurely drawn up by Davis, see Amy Feldman, "Fighting the Fat Cats for Decades, Evelyn Davis Has Grilled Business Bigwigs in Outrageous Fashion," *New York Daily News* (24 May 1998), http://www.nydailynews.com/archives/news/fighting-fat-cats-decades-evelyn-davis-grilled-biz-bigwigs-outrageous-fashion-article-1.790296. Accessed 10 May 2022.

213 Peter Carlson, "The Stock Character," *The Washington Post* (20 Apr. 2003). Martin Knudsen, Walter Froh and Jim Patterson were other of her divorcees. Much later in her life, Evelyn confided to a reporter that the Holocaust "had an effect on my marriages…You feel enclosed. You feel you don't have freedom. Anyone who has been in those camps -- it's difficult to lead a normal life." She said something similar in Leslie Bennetts, "The C.E.O.'s Worst Nightmare," *Vanity Fair* (2 Jul. 2002).

214 On *Solid Gold Cadillac*, see https://www.imdb.com/title/tt0049777/characters/nm0122675. Accessed 10 May 2022. Traflet phone interview with Jim Patterson, Jul. 2018 (Traflet-Patterson Interview). See also Jim Patterson, "60th Anniversary Thoughts on The Solid Gold Cadillac and Evelyn Y. Queen of the Corporate Jungle Davis," *LinkedIn* (22 Apr. 2016), https://www.linkedin.com/pulse/60th-anniversary-thoughts-solid-gold-cadillac-eve-lyn-y-patterson. Accessed 10 May 2022.

215 Carter F. Henderson and Albert C. Lasher, *20 Million Careless Capitalists* (Garden City: Doubleday & Company, Inc., 1967), 234; Amy Feldman, "Fighting the Fat Cats for Decades, Evelyn Davis has Grilled Business Bigwigs in Outrageous Fashion," *New York Daily News* (24 May 1998); Jerome, "Evelyn Y. Davis."

216 "Unstoppable" is the description American Express official Stephen Norman gave Davis in a *Vanity Fair* interview. According to Norman, Evelyn was "full of mischief—infuriating, outrageous, and unstoppable." He added, "Without any staff or legal establishment helping her, she has resolutely survived four decades of corporate opposition. You've got to be obsessive and single-minded to do that. . . . She can be cruel, vulgar, hurtful, and self-aggrandizing, but she is unbowed, and I respect her for that." Bennetts, "The C.E.O.'s Worst Nightmare." The 120 number is from Courtland Milloy, "Entrusting Her Epitaph to No One," *Washington Post* (31 Dec. 1995). For background on Evelyn's life, see SEC.gov, "Biography of Evelyn Y. Davis," https://www.sec.gov/spotlight/proxyprocess/bio052507/eydavis.pdf. Accessed 10 May 2022.

217 "Crackpots or Crusaders? Defending the Rights of Minority Shareholders" is a chapter title about the gadflies in Henderson and Lasher, *20 Million Careless Capitalists*, 234.

218 On Evelyn being a hellraiser, see Richard Jerome, "Evelyn Y. Davis," *People.com*, 20 May 1996, http://people.com/archive/evelyn-y-davis-vol-45-no-20/. Accessed 24 May 2022. Henderson and Lasher, *20 Million Careless Capitalists*, 234. On the Own Your Share campaign, see Janice Traflet, *A Nation of Small Shareowners: Marketing Wall Street After World War II* (Baltimore: Johns Hopkins, 2013), esp. 68-87.

219 Jerome, "Evelyn Y. Davis."

220 Milton Friedman, "The Social Responsibility of Business is to Increase Its Profits," *New York Times Magazine* (13 Sep. 1970).

221   For Evelyn's suspicions regarding corporations' choice of charities, we are indebted to conversation with ex-husband Jim Patterson. Traflet-Patterson Interview; Feldman, "Fighting the Fat Cats."

222   For background on the YMCA—including the role of the Associated Press publishing arm with regard to Dale Carnegie, see "Our History: A Brief History of the YMCA Movement," https://www.hopkinscountyymca.com/index.php/news/get-involved/230-our-history-a-brief-history-of-the-ymca-movement. Accessed 10 May 2022. Reportedly, Buffett's Carnegie certificate of completion is the only diploma he has in his office, revealing the importance he placed on that class.

223   Jerome, "Evelyn Y. Davis"; Feldman, "Fighting the Fat Cats."

224   Jerome, "Evelyn Y. Davis."

225   AP File Photo, "Evelyn Davis in HotPants," Comsat Meeting, (11 May 1971); "HotPants, Or 'Knockout-Shorts,' Worn by Sexy, Proud Women," *Jet* (25 Mar. 1971); Carlson, "The Stock Character."

226   Patterson, "60th Anniversary Thoughts." Interestingly, at around the same time, Muriel Siebert, the first woman to hold a seat at the NYSE, was doing something very similar with reporters, urging them to cover her beauty, too.

227   Henderson and Lasher, *20 Million Careless Capitalists,* 235.

228   Henderson and Lasher, *20 Million Careless Capitalists,* 235.

229   Henderson and Lasher, *20 Million Careless Capitalists,* 235, 238.

230   Carlson, "The Stock Character."

231   Henderson and Lasher, *20 Million Careless Capitalists,* 238.

232   Jerome, "Evelyn Y. Davis." The "by the balls" comment was directed to Citicorp's John Reed. See Carlson, "The Stock Character." Gilbert qtd. in Jerome. John was 82 at the time of this quote. In 1996, corporate governance expert Nell Minow echoed John Gilbert's assessment of Evelyn. While acknowledging that "Many of her proposals are good ones," Minow went on to say, "But her behavior makes even her useful initiatives easy to dismiss. It's embarrassing to me as a shareholder activist to have her out there."

233   Carlson, "The Stock Character."

234   Jim Patterson, "Opinion: Evelyn Davis, the 'Vamp of Wall Street,' Was Pioneer of Women's Rights," *Montgomery Advertiser* (14 Sep. 2017).

235   Jerome, "Evelyn Y. Davis"; Patterson, "Opinion."

236   Richard Gehman, "Guardian Angel of Shareholders," *Cosmopolitan* (Apr. 1963), 66; "Convicted U.N. Prostitute to Face Penalty," *Chicago Tribune* (Jun. 1963).

237   Paul Tharp, "Bulls Eye: Old Hangups," *New York Post* (4 Apr. 2004)

238   Tharp, "Bulls Eye."

239   Traflet-Patterson Interview; Feldman, "Fighting the Fat Cats."

240   On Davis' playing up the notoriety from her prostitution arrest, see Patterson, "Opinion."

241   For a description of the Highlights and Lowlights publication, see SEC.gov, "Biography." Jerome, "Evelyn Y. Davis." Jerome notes, "Don't look for H and L down at the 7-Eleven: It's disseminated only to corporate presidents and CEOs, at $480 per subscription."

242   Carlson, "The Stock Character."

243   Jerome, "Evelyn Y. Davis."

244   Jerome, "Evelyn Y. Davis."

245   "IBM Shows Canada an American Meeting, Mrs. Soss and All," *Wall Street Journal* (27 Apr. 1971), 33.

246   "IBM Shows Canada."

247   Henderson and Lasher, *20 Million Careless Capitalists*.

248   Davis later recalled that she had tried first to buy a Chrysler, but Chairman Lee Iacocca didn't agree to deliver it fast enough. Donald Peterson at Ford was faster on the uptake. After this episode in the early 1980s, she would go on to demand afterwards that every new car she bought was delivered to her. Jerome, "Evelyn Y. Davis."; Milloy, "Entrusting Her Epitaph to No One." Eventually, three CEOs, one from each of the Big Three auto manufacturers, wound up delivering a car at some point to Davis. Bennetts, "CEO's Nightmare."

249   Notably, there is no mention of her Holocaust experience on her SEC profile. SEC.gov, "Biography."

250   Jerome, "Evelyn Y. Davis"; Feldman, "Fighting the Fat Cats"; Viktor E. Frankl, *Man's Search for Meaning* (Boston: Beacon Press, 2006), 6, 155. Frankl's book, which went on to sell millions of copies around the world, debuted in German in 1946.

251   Patterson, "Opinion."

252   SEC.gov, "Biography"; Jerome, "Evelyn Y. Davis."

253   As scholar Anna Hajkova notes, "these were the *Jewish crème de la crème* of Dutch society." Anna Hajkova, "'Poor devils' of the camps: Dutch Jews in Theresienstadt, 1943-1945", (2015), 86, https://warwick.ac.uk/fac/arts/history/people/

staff_index/hajkova/hajkova_poor_devils_yvs_2015.pdf. Accessed 24 May 2022. https://en.wikipedia.org/wiki/The_Saved. Accessed 10 May 2022. See also https://www.tracesofwar.com/sights/484/Castle-De-Schaffelaar.htm. Accessed 10 May 2022. In 1996, a documentary entitled "The Saved" debuted that detailed the experiences of those sent to Barneveld Castle.

254 *Paul Cohen and Oeke Hoogendijk, directors, "The Saved," Icarus Films Documentary (May 2008);* Hajkova, "'Poor Devils'"; Anna Hajkova, "Prisoner Society in the Terezin Ghetto, 1941-1945," (Ph.D. Diss., University of Toronto, 2013); Steven Frank, "How I Survived the Holocaust - and Why I Tell My Story," *The Jewish Chronicle,* https://www.thejc.com/news/news-features/steven-frank-how-i-survived-the-holocaust-and-why-i-tell-my-story-1.479151. Accessed 10 May 2022.

255 Frank, "How I Survived."

256 Steven Frank was the son of a highly regarded Jewish lawyer in Amsterdam, Leonard Frank. Leonard, a member of the Dutch resistance, heroically helped many fellow Jews escape, eschewing the opportunity himself to do so. Betrayed, he was captured and tortured before dying in the gas chambers in Auschwitz. But through the intercession of non-Jewish friends, his family got placed onto the protected list and were sent to Barneveld castle. Frank, "How I Survived."

257 Some Holocaust scholars call Theresienstadt a concentration camp, others, a ghetto. See Hajkova, "Prisoner Society in the Terezin Ghetto." For more on Theresienstadt, see "Transit Camps," Holocaust Memorial Trust, https://www.hmd.org.uk/learn-about-the-holocaust-and-genocides/the-holocaust/the-camps/transit-camps/. Accessed 10 May 2022. This article describes conditions at Theresienstadt as "incredibly harsh," and also mentioned the hoax perpetuated by the Nazis as they cleaned up the camp prior to the 23 Jul. 1944 visit of the Red Cross. See also Wikipedia, "Theresienstadt Ghetto," https://en.wikipedia.org/wiki/Theresienstadt_Ghetto. Accessed 10 May 2022.

258 Hajkova, "'Poor Devils'", 85. On Frankl's pre-WWII career, see Winslade in Afterword to Frankl, *Man's Search*, 157.

259 "Definition of 'mica', *Collins Dictionary,* https://www.collinsdictionary.com/us/dictionary/english/mica. Accessed 10 May 2022. Arthur Bevan, "War Minerals – Mica," *The Scientific Monthly* 60, 5 (May 1945): 393-95; Carlson, "Stock Character."

260 Frankl, *Man's Search*, 76, 82; Herbert Bower, "The Concentration Camp Syndrome," *Australian & New Zealand Journal of Psychiatry* 28, 3 (1994): 391-97, 395.

261 Feldman, "Fighting the Fat Cats."

262 Traflet-Patterson Interview; Feldman, "Fighting the Fat Cats."

263 Frankl, *Man's Search*, 20. Also see Frankl, *Man's Search*, 88, 91-92, 157.

264   SEC.gov, "Biography"; Traflet-Patterson Interview.

CHAPTER SEVEN: Progress, Protest and Inflation

265   Emily Langer, "Muriel Siebert, First Woman to Join the New York Stock Exchange Dies at 84," *Washington Post* (27 Aug. 2013). Accessed 10 May 2022. See also Muriel Siebert with Aimee Lee Ball, *Changing the Rules: Adventures of a Wall Street Maverick* (New York: The Free Press, 2002).

266   Siebert, *Changing the Rules*, 31. Many didn't know Siebert was Jewish, and sometimes accidentally made anti-Semitic remarks in front of her. Occasionally, she'd later send them a note to correct them and call them out: "Roses are red, violets are bluish, in case you didn't know it, I'm Jewish." Siebert qtd. in Langer, "Muriel Siebert."

267   For more on Funston's thoughts, see Arturo and Janeann Gonzalez, "Where No Woman Reaches the Summit: Thousands of females work in Wall Street but few attain executive status and none has scaled the peak", *New York Times* (17 Aug. 1959) SM 34.   "NOW," *Wikipedia*, https://en.wikipedia.org/wiki/National_Organization_for_Women. Accessed 10 May 2022.

268   Allen Fisher, "Women's Rights and the Civil Rights Act of 1964," National Archives, https://www.archives.gov/women/1964-civil-rights-act. Accessed 10 May 2022. Mulcahey qtd. in Siebert, *Changing the Rules*, 31.

269   On AMEX's admission of these two women, see Siebert, *Changing the Rules*, 31. Sheri Caplan devotes a chapter to Mary Roebling (Ch. 9) which precedes chapters on Julia Montgomery (Ch. 10) and Muriel Siebert (Ch. 11). The order is revealing. See Sheri J. Caplan, *Petticoats and Pinstripes: Portraits of Women in Wall Street's History* (Santa Barbara: Praeger, 2013), esp. 105-144.

270   On the LSE's rebuff of the "petticoat invasion," see Siebert, *Changing the Rules*, 31 and Caplan, *Petticoats*, 138. Caplan notes the rumor of Florence Stephens trying to buy a seat on the NYSE in 1927.

271   "Muriel Siebert Dies at 84: First Woman on NYSE," *Los Angeles Times* (25 Aug. 2013); Gloria Feldt, "Start Your Own Game: Muriel 'Mickie' Siebert—Leadership Lessons for Women from Wall Street," 4 Sep. 2013, https://gloriafeldt. com/2013/09/04/start-game-muriel-mickie-siebert-leadership-lessons-women-wall-street/. Accessed 10 May 2022. "Invasion" was a word the press used a lot in the late 1960s and early 1970s for any woman breaking boundaries on Wall Street. Also of note: Wilma did not leave a record of how she felt about Siebert's membership, but based on all her other writings, it would be inconceivable that she would not have supported Siebert's bid to break the gender barrier at the NYSE. Siebert, *Changing the Rules*, 37.

272   Gloria Feldt, "Start Your Own Game: Muriel 'Mickie' Siebert—Leadership Lessons for Women from Wall Street," 4 Sep. 2013, https://gloriafeldt.com/2013/09/04/start-

game-muriel-mickie-siebert-leadership-lessons-women-wall-street/. Accessed 10 May 2022.

273 "Demonstration at Chase Manhattan Bank," 19 Mar. 1965, African Activist Archive, http://africanactivist.msu.edu/image.php?objectid=32-131-179. Accessed 10 May 2022.

274 Kembrew McLeod, *Pranksters Making Mischief in the Modern World* (New York: NYU Press, 2014), 137-40, 142.

275 A very good discussion of the Hoffman episode, including the installation of the bullet-proof glass three months later, is provided in James Ledbetter, "The Day the NYSE Went Yippie," *CNN Money* (23 Aug. 2007), https://money.cnn.com/2007/07/17/news/funny/abbie_hoffman/. Accessed 10 May 2022. The incident is also mentioned in Siebert, *Changing the Rules*, 2. Matthew Kassel, "Once Popular NYSE Has No Plan to Reopen to the Public," *Wall Street Journal* (7 Aug. 2016).

276 Abbie Hoffman throwing dollars on the Exchange floor incident is lore on Wall Street. See Lorraine Boissoneault, "How the New York Stock Exchange Gave Abbie Hoffman His Start in Guerrilla Theater," *Smithsonian Magazine* (24 Aug. 2017), https://www.smithsonianmag.com/history/how-new-york-stock-exchange-gave-abbie-hoffman-his-start-guerrilla-theater-180964612/. Accessed 10 May 2022. This article also mentions the Chase sit-in in 1965.

277 "Muriel Siebert Dies"; Siebert, *Changing the Rules*, 2.

278 Reportedly, there were 16,592 U.S. killed in Vietnam in 1968 versus 27,915 North Vietnamese killed. For more on the Tet offensive, see Kenneth T. Walsh, "50 Years Later, the Tet Offensive in Vietnam Still Resonates," *US News and World Report* (29 Jan. 2018).

279 The My Lai massacre occurred on 16 Mar. 1968, but the American public would not find out about it until Nov. 1969. See "My Lai Massacre," *Wikipedia*, https://en.wikipedia.org/wiki/My_Lai_Massacre. Accessed 10 May 2022.

280 For a gripping account of those years, see Amity Shlaes, *Great Society: A New History* (New York: HarperCollins, 2019).

281 Pocketbook News (PN), 5 May 1958, 8 Oct. 1966, 28 Apr., 8 Sep. 1968, Box 8, Wilma Soss Papers (WSP), American Heritage Center, Laramie, Wyoming. Stock turnover was roughly 20 percent in 1967, which apparently was a typical year. "A lot of stocks are kept in safe deposit boxes," Soss explained, "and never come to market."

282 "Mutiny at a Great University," *Life* (10 May 1968), 35-43.

283 "The Inside View from the Ghetto-Ringed Campus," *Life* (10 May 1968), 44-49. On 4 May 1970, at a demonstration at Kent State protesting Nixon's decision to enlarge the scope of the Vietnam conflict by authorizing incursions into Cambodia,

frightened Ohio National Guardsmen killed four unarmed protestors, two of them women. Nine others were wounded.

284   By maintaining an anti-Vietnam War stance during his campaign, Nixon ironically may have lengthened the Vietnam War by interfering behind the scenes with peace talks. See, for instance, Colin Schurtz, "Nixon Prolonged Vietnam War for Political Gains, and Johnson Knew About it, Newly Unclassified Tapes Suggest," *Smithsonian Magazine* (18 Mar. 2013), https://www.smithsonianmag.com/smart-news/nixon-prolonged-vietnam-war-for-political-gainand-johnson-knew-about-it-newly-unclassified-tapes-suggest-3595441/. Accessed 10 May 2022.

285   PN, 12 Mar. 1961, ? Aug. 1957, Box 8, WSP.

286   PN, 7 Jan. 1968, Box 8, WSP.

287   PN, 13, 20 Nov. 1960, Box 8, WSP.

288   Shlaes, *Great Society*.

289   PN, 29 Nov. 1964, 17 Mar., 21 Jul. 1968, Box 8, WSP.

290   PN, 26 Nov. 1967, Box 8, WSP.

291   PN, 31 Mar. 1968, Box 8, WSP.

292   PN, 17, 31 Mar. 1968, 12 Jan. 1959, Box 8, WSP.

293   PN, 3 Dec. 1967, 13 Aug. 1966, Box 8, WSP.

294   PN, 7, 14 Feb. 1965, Box 8, WSP.

295   PN, 1 Oct. 1966, Box 8, WSP.

296   Kevin Granville, "A President at War with the Fed Chief, 5 Decades Before Trump," *New York Times* (13 Jun. 2017); PN, 18 Aug. 1968, Box 8, WSP.

297   PN, 2 Sep., 1 Oct. 1968, Box 8, WSP.

298   PN, 10 Jan. 1965, 13, 27 Apr. 1959, Box 8, WSP.

299   PN, ? Jan. 1960, 27 Jul., 4 May 1959, Box 8, WSP.

300   PN, 3 Oct. 1965, Box 8, WSP.

301   PN, 15 Oct., 12 Nov. 1967, 18 Jan. 1969, Box 8, WSP.

302   PN, 7 Apr. 1957, Box 8, WSP.

303   PN, 1 May 1960, 22 Jul. 1962, 11 Sep. 1960, Box 8, WSP.

304   PN, 10 Apr., 19 Jun. 1966, 10 Dec. 1967, Box 8, WSP.

305   PN, 3 Nov. 1958, Box 8, WSP. For the distinction between debt optimists and pessimists, see Richard Salsman, *The Political Economy of Public Debt: Three Centuries of Theory and Evidence* (New York: Edward Elgar, 2017). PN, 3 Jan. 1965, Box 8, WSP.

306   PN, 22 Jan. 1961, 13 Aug. 1966, 22 Jul. 1962, 7 May 1967, Box 8, WSP.

307   PN, 21 Feb. 1965, 13 Jun. 1965, 3 Apr. 1960, 31 Mar. 1968, Box 8, WSP.

308   PN, 14 Jul. 1968, 12 Nov. 1967, 13 Oct. 1968, Box 8, WSP.

309   PN, 12 Jan. 1959, 9 Dec. 1962, 26 Nov. 1967, 13 Oct., 17 Nov. 1968, Box 8, WSP.

310   PN, 24 Dec. 1967, Box 8, WSP.

CHAPTER EIGHT: Pop Economist

311   Richard Gehman, "Guardian Angel of Shareholders," *Cosmopolitan* (Apr. 1963), 64-65.

312   Andy Logan, "Hoboken Must Go!," *The New Yorker* (17 Mar. 1951), 34; Patricia P. Widmer to Wilma Sass [sic], 9 Nov. 1965; Rosa Condello to Soss, 12 Apr. 1972, Box 10, Wilma Soss Papers (WSP), American Heritage Center, Laramie, Wyoming.

313   Logan, "Hoboken Must Go!," 38; Gehman, "Guardian Angel, 66; Richard Marens, "Inventing Corporate Governance: The Mid-Century Emergence of Share-holder Activism," *Journal of Business and Management* 8, 4 (2002), 381; A. W. Zelomek, "A Changing America and the Stock Market," n.d., Box 15, WSP. Martindell died of cancer in 1990 at age 89. See his obituaries in the *New York Times* (9 Mar. 1990), Fort Lauderdale *SunSentinel* (10 Mar. 1990), *Los Angeles Times* (12 Mar. 1990).

314   Particularly cringeworthy are a series of soap puns about Procter and Gamble president Neil H. McElroy when he was up to replace Charlie Wilson as Eisenhower's Secretary of Defense. Pocketbook News (PN), 11 Aug. 1957, Box 8, WSP. Denise Norton to Soss, 29 Apr. 1962, Professional Correspondence Folders, Box 3, WSP; PN, 12 May 1957, Box 8, WSP.

315   PN, 3 Aug. 1957, 13 Apr., 14 Dec. 1959, Box 8, WSP.

316   PN, 8 Jun. 1959, 8 Apr. 1962, 23 Oct. 1966, Oct. 1968, Box 8, WSP.

317   PN, 25 Mar. 1961, 14 Jul. 1968, Box 8, WSP.

318   PN, 19 Jan. 1959, 23 Nov. 1959, 7 Mar. 1965, Box 8, WSP.

319   PN, 12 Mar., 24 Dec. 1967, Box 8, WSP.

320 PN, 7 Mar. 1965, Box 8, WSP.

321 PN, 22 Oct., 3 Dec., 17 Dec. 1967, 12 May, 15, 29 Dec. 1968, Box 8, WSP.

322 PN, 5 Feb. 1961, 26 May 1968, Box 8, WSP.

323 PN, 30 Mar. 1959, ? Jan. 1960, Box 8, WSP.

324 Barbara Fischer memorandum, "Federation of Women Shareholders in American Business," 1947, Box 14, WSP; PN, 7, 15 Feb. 1960, Box 8, WSP.

325 PN, 24 Apr. 1960, 29 Dec. 1958, Box 8, WSP.

326 PN, 16 Apr. 1967, Box 8, WSP.

327 PN, 22, 29 Oct. 1967, Box 8, WSP.

328 PN, 16 Dec. 1957, Box 8, WSP; Wilma Soss, "The Soviet Threat to the Diamond Market," *Commercial and Financial Chronicle* (9 Jan. 1958); PN, 5 Nov. 1967, Box 8, WSP.

329 PN, 3 Mar. 1957, 17 Dec. 1967, Box 8, WSP.

330 PN, 4 May 1959, 2 Apr. 1961, 5 May 1958, Box 8, WSP.

331 PN, 30 Mar., 26 Feb. 1959, Box 8, WSP.

332 PN, 4 May 1959, 23 Sep. 1968, Box 8, WSP; Edward Chancellor, *Capital Returns: Investing Through the Capital Cycle* (New York: Palgrave, 2015).

333 PN, 3 Aug. 1959, Box 8, WSP; Carmen Reinhart and Kenneth Rogoff, *This Time Is Different: Eight Centuries of Financial Folly* (Princeton: Princeton University Press, 2009); PN, 9 Apr. 1961, 4 May, 3 Aug. 1959, 26 Jul. 1968, Box 8, WSP.

334 PN, 12 May 1958, Box 8, WSP; Wilma Soss, "Women as Stockholders," Symposium on the Status of Women in America, Bryant College Centennial, 1963, Box 15, WSP.

335 PN, 24 Mar. 1958, Box 8, WSP.

336 PN, 21 Apr. 1958, Box 8, WSP.

337 PN, 10 Apr. 1960, 15 Sep. 1962, Box 8, WSP.

338 PN, 15 Feb. 1960, 18 Aug. 1968, Box 8, WSP; Wilma Soss, "Women as Stockholders," Symposium on the Status of Women in America, Bryant College Centennial, 1963, Box 15, WSP. Notably, Wilma at first was not an advocate of indexing when Jack Bogle pioneered the first index fund in 1975, believing instead that retail investors

could, and should, put together their own, highly tailored portfolios of hand-picked individual stocks.

339 PN, 3 Nov. 1958, 1 Dec. 1958, Box 8, WSP.

340 PN, 8 Dec. 1958, Box 8, WSP.

341 PN, 28 Apr. 1957, 1 Jun. 1959, Box 8, WSP.

342 Gehman, "Guardian Angel," 66; PN, 2 Jun. 1958, 4 May 1959, 7 Feb. 1960, Box 8, WSP; Simon Constable and Robert E. Wright, *The Wall Street Journal Guide to the 50 Economic Indicators That Really Matter: From Big Macs to "Zombie Banks," the Indicators Smart Investors Watch to Beat the Market* (New York: HarperCollins, 2011); Jackson Martindell, *The Scientific Appraisal of Management: A Study of the Business Practices of Well-Managed Companies* (New York: Harper & Brothers, 1950), 74.

343 PN, 29 Jul. 1962, 16 Jun. 1958, Box 8, WSP.

344 PN, 2 Apr. 1961, 19 Dec. 1966, Box 8, WSP.

345 PN, 13 Mar. 1960, 28 Feb. 1965, 24 Mar. 1968, Box 8, WSP.

346 PN, 13 Nov. 1960, 2 Sep. 1968, 20 Oct., 14 Jul. 1968, Box 8, WSP.

347 PN, 24 Nov. 1966, 5 Feb. 1967, Box 8, WSP.

348 PN, 15 Dec. 1968, 20 Jul. 1959, Box 8, WSP.

349 PN, 22 Oct., 7 May 1967, Box 8, WSP.

350 PN, 12 Apr. 1957, 7 Feb. 1960, Box 8, WSP.

351 PN, 1, 28 Apr. 1957, Box 8, WSP.

352 PN, 1 Jan. 1961, 5 Mar. 1967, Box 8, WSP.

353 PN, 9 Dec. 1957, Box 8, WSP; "Abraham Multer, Ex-Congressman," *New York Times* (7 Nov. 1986)' Wilma Soss' PN, Monday Feature on NBC Radio's Nightline, 22 Jan. 1958, *Congressional Record*, Box 9, WSP.

354 PN, 1 Oct. 1966, 5 Mar. 1967, 3 Jan. 1965, Box 8, WSP.

355 PN, 22 Aug. 1965, 5, 19 May 1968, Box 8, WSP. For more on recent basic guaranteed income or universal basic income proposals, see Robert E. Wright and Aleksandra Przegalińska, *Debating Universal Basic Income: Pros, Cons, and Alternatives* (New York: Cambridge University Press, forthcoming).

356 PN, 18 Aug. 1968, Box 8, WSP.

357   PN, 28 Dec. 1959, Box 8, WSP; John Brooks, "Stockholder Season," *The New Yorker* (8 Oct. 1966), 166.

358   PN, 10 Mar. 1957, Box 8, WSP.

359   PN, 27 Nov., 3 Apr. 1960, Box 8, WSP.

360   PN, 1 Jan. 1961, 26 Jul. 1964, Box 8, WSP.

361   PN, 6 Oct. 1968, Box 8, WSP. For more on Germania, see Anita Rapone, *The Guardian Life Insurance Company, 1860-1920: A History of a German-American Enterprise* (New York: New York University Press, 1987) and Robert E. Wright and George D. Smith, *Mutually Beneficial: The Guardian and Life Insurance in America* (New York: New York University Press 2004).

362   PN, 15 May 1960, 18 Sep. 1965, 13 Nov. 1966, 13 Oct. 1968, 18 Jan. 1969, Box 8, WSP.

363   PN, 25 Dec. 1960, Box 8, WSP.

364   PN, 9 Apr. 1965, Box 8, WSP.

365   PN, 3 Aug. 1957, 4 Jan. 1960, Box 8, WSP.

366   PN, 17 Apr. 1960, Box 8, WSP.

367   PN, 14 Dec. 1959, 24 Nov. 1966, Box 8, WSP.

368   PN, 28 Mar., 22 Aug. 1965, Box 8, WSP.

369   PN, 22 Jul. 1962, 6 Mar. 1966, 26 Jan. 1959, Box 8, WSP.

370   PN, 14 Jan. 1968, Box 8, WSP.

371   PN, 2 Feb. 1959, Box 8, WSP.

372   PN, 26 Feb. 1959, 25 Mar. 1961, Box 8, WSP.

373   Anat R. Admati, "A Skeptical View of Financialized Corporate Governance," *Journal of Economic Perspectives* 31, 3 (2017): 139; PN, 16 Apr. 1957, Box 8, WSP; Soss to Clinton B. Axford, 21, 23 Mar. 1949, Box 14, WSP; FOWSAB, "Women and Wealth: What Every Stockholder Should Know About the Post Meeting Report," n.d., Box 10, WSP.

374   PN, 19 Jan. 1968, 1 Jan. 1961, Box 8, WSP.

375   PN, 13 Feb. 1968, 8 Jan. 1961, Box 8, WSP.

376 Harvey Flaumenhaft, *The Effective Republic: Administration and Constitution in the Thought of Alexander Hamilton* (Durham: Duke University Press, 1992); PN, 13 Apr. 1959, 27 Nov. 1960, Box 8, WSP.

377 PN, 18 Jan. 1969, 12 Jan. 1959, 22 Jul. 1962, Box 8, WSP.

378 PN, ? Nov. 1957, 10 Apr. 1960, Box 8, WSP.

379 PN, 24 Jan. 1965, Box 8, WSP.

380 PN, Box 8, WSP.

381 PN, 26 Jul. 1964, 24 Feb. 1958, Box 8, "Peace on Our Dollars" Petition, n.d., Box 3, Julia A. Mark to Soss, 19 Mar. 1958, George Byerly to Soss, 21 Feb. 1958, Professional Correspondence Folders, Box 3, PN, 24 Mar. 1958, Box 8, Harrison Smith, 16 Jun. 1950, Margaret Chase Smith to Soss, 23 Apr. 1964; Soss to Esther Petersen, 8 Jul. 1964, Box 10, WSP.

382 Rephah Berg to Soss, 5 Mar. 1958, Professional Correspondence Folders, Box 3, WSP. Janice Traflet / Robert Wright Email Correspondence with Rephah Berg, 7, 10 Jul. 2017.

383 PN, 9 Apr. 1961, 10 May 1964, 20 Oct. 1968, Box 8, WSP.

384 PN, 30 May 1965, 21 Aug. 1966, 5 Mar. 1967, 24 Mar., 7 Apr. 1968, Box 8, WSP.

385 PN, 17 May 1958, 2 Feb. 1959, Box 8, WSP.

386 PN, 14 Sep. 1959, 22 May 1960, Box 8, WSP.

387 PN, 19 Jan., 21 Sep. 1959, Box 8, WSP.

388 PN, 5 Jan. 1959, Box 8, WSP.

389 PN, 13 Mar. 1960, 10 May 1964, Box 8, WSP.

390 PN, 7 Feb. 1960, Box 8, WSP.

391 PN, 3 Apr. 1960, 12 Mar. 1961, Box 8, WSP.

392 PN, 29 Aug. 1965, Box 8, WSP.

393 PN, ? Jan. 1960, 15 Feb. 1970, in 1968 folder, 4 Jan. 1960, Box 8, WSP.

394 PN, 5 Jun., 15 Feb. 1960, 21 Feb. 1965, 7 Jul. 1968, Box 8, WSP.

395 PN, 30 Jun. 1958, Box 8, WSP.

396 PN, 10 Nov. 1958, Box 8, WSP.

397   PN, 6 Apr. 1959, 14 Jun. 1964, 18 Dec. 1960, Box 8, WSP.

398   PN, 10 Apr. 1960, Box 8, WSP.

399   PN, 29 Sep. 1968, Box 8, WSP.

400   PN, 12 Apr. 1970, Box 9, WSP.

401   PN, 5 Sep. 1973, Box 9, WSP.

402   PN, 10 Oct., 20 Nov. 1971, Box 9, WSP.

403   PN, 24 Dec. 1972, 8 Sep. 1973, 16-17 Mar. 1974. 15-16 Jul. 1974, 25 Mar. 1976?, 25 Jun. 1972, Box 9, WSP.

404   PN, 25 Mar. 1976?, 27 Apr. 1974. 20 Mar. 1971, Box 9, WSP.

405   PN, 7 Jun. 1970, 14 Oct., 25 Nov., 30 Dec. 1973, 7 May 1977, 14 Apr. 1979, 20 Jul. 1974, 24 Apr. 1974, Box 9, WSP.

406   PN, 18 May, 13, 15 Jul., 1 Jun. 1975, 24 Mar., 7 Apr. 1979, Box 9, WSP.

407   PN, 17 Sep., 1972, 13 Jan. 1978, Box 9, WSP.

408   PN, ? Mar. 1980, Box 9, WSP.

409   Adele Faloon to Members, 1973, Box 10, WSP. PN, 1 Feb. 1970, 26 Dec. 1975, 2 Jul. 1976, 15 Feb., 12 Jul. 1970, 7 Nov. 1971, 24 Apr. 1974, 11, 29 Dec. 1979, Box 9, WSP.

410   PN, 17 Sep. 1972, Box 9, WSP.

411   PN, 5 Aug. 1973, 16 Jul., 17 Sep. 1976, 11 Jul. 1975; 22 Jul. 1977, Box 9, WSP.

CHAPTER NINE: Goodbye Gadflies

412   Soss to E. F. Tompkins, 10 Oct. 1949, Box 14, Wilma Soss Papers (WSP), American Heritage Center, Laramie, Wyoming.

413   Penelope McMillan, "Wilma Soss Revisited," *New York Sunday News* (13 Jan. 1974), 39. See also 6-7, 38. In later years (particularly after Wilma died), there would be a trend of troubled companies choosing women as directors and CEOs—in part perhaps because many men didn't want to risk taking on such challenges.

414   McMillan, "Wilma Soss Revisited," 39.

415   McMillan, "Wilma Soss Revisited," 39.

416   On the 13% statistic, see Clare Ansberry, "The Board Game: More Women Are Becoming Directors, But It's Still a Token Situation," *Wall Street Journal* (24 Mar. 1986), 89.

417   McMillan, "Wilma Soss Revisited," 39.

418   See http://www.rmpbs.org/volunteer/sam/womens-history/. Accessed 15 Nov. 2019; Gloria H. Decker, ed. *Conservation Directory* (Washington, DC: National Wildlife Federation, 1976), 75-76.

419   Caleb Newquist, "SEC Rule Would Crack Down on Celebrity Board Members," *Going Concern* (1 Jul. 2009), https://goingconcern.com/sec-rule-would-crack-down-on-celebrity-board-members/. Accessed 10 May 2022. Steven Davidoff Solomon, "Handicapping IAC's Investment in Chelsea Clinton," *New York Times* (4 Oct. 2011). When Chelsea Clinton, the daughter of former President Bill Clinton and former Secretary of State Hillary Clinton, became a board member for IAC Interactive in 2011 at the relatively young age of 31 years old, even *The New York Times* questioned the pick. Clinton was smart and could make a great director, said the *Times* reporter, but at the same time, it was hard to fathom, beyond the celebrity factor, why she was nominated over a pool full of other intelligent, talented people, some boasting a lot more experience.

420   For additional context, see Robert E. Wright, *Financial Exclusion: How Competition Can Fix a Broken System* (Great Barrington, Mass.: American Institute for Economic Research, 2019), 213-74.

421   Deborah Rankin, "Policies Defended at Women's Bank," *New York Times* (22 Dec. 1978), D1, D7. Also, "First Women's Bank Changes Name to Reflect Changing Times," *AP News* (24 Apr. 1989), https://apnews.com/9d805874ac8e8e3ebef26127c5b2e1e5. Accessed 11 May 2022.

422   Michael Norman, "Wilma Porter Soss, 86, A Gadfly At Stock Meetings of Companies," *New York Times* (16 Oct. 1986), B20.

423   Sulzberger qtd. in Norman, "Wilma," B20.

424   John Gilbert lived to be 88, dying in 2002. Lewis Gilbert died in 1993. Norman, "Wilma," B20.

425   C. Wright Mills, *The Power Elite* (New York: Oxford University Press, 1956); Wilma Soss, "The Solid Gold Chevrolet," *Commercial and Financial Chronicle* (21 Apr. 1955), 24.

426   Adele Faloon to Soss, 3 Jan. ?, Helen Plavin to FOWSAB, 16 Oct. 1972, Soss to Helen Plavin, 5, 30 Oct. 1972, Soss to Olive Bendix, 6 Nov. 1972, Helen Plavin to Soss, 5 Dec. 1972; Adele Faloon to Soss, n.d., Adele Faloon to Soss, 27 Jan., 15 Oct. 1982, Box 10, WSP.

427   FOWSAB Meeting, 5 Dec. 1972; 8 Jan. 1973; 14 Jan., 18 Mar., 7 Oct. 1974; 22 Sep., 14 Oct., 10 Nov., 8 Dec. 1975; 12 Jan., 8 Mar., 15 Nov. 1976, Box 10, WSP.

428   FOWSAB, "Statement of Cash Receipts and Disbursements," 31 Dec. 1975, Birdie Safion to Members from 1975-76, Adele Faloon to Members, 1973, Adele Faloon, "It's That Time of Year Again," ? 1975(?) or 1980(?), FOWSAB, "Statement of Cash Receipts and Disbursements," 31 Dec. 1981, Box 10, WSP.

429   Minutes (mss.), 20 Sep. 1982, Birdie Saffion to Shareholders, 18 Oct. 1982, FOWSAB 34th Annual Meeting Minutes (typescript), 20 Sep. 1982, FOWSAB, "Y'all Come Now, by Popular Request," 1983, Box 10, WSP.

430   On the massive defection of millions of small investors from the market in the 1970s, see Barry Ritholtz, "The Death of Equities," *Business Week* (13 Aug. 1979). The reporter quotes a young business executive as saying, "Have you been to an American stockholders' meeting lately? They're all old fogies. The stock market is just not where the action's at."

431   Evelyn bought the plot in 1981; the headstone was erected in 1987. On the tombstone, see Courtland Milloy, "Entrusting Her Epitaph to No One," *Washington Post* (31 Dec. 1995); James Patterson, "Evelyn Y. Davis: Dragging Me Into the Afterlife," *Baltimore Sun* (8 Aug. 2019). Also, on the tombstone, see http://allen-browne.blogspot.com/2011/08/queen-of-corporate-jungle.html. For obituaries after Davis' death, see James R. Hagerty, "Evelyn Y. Davis Would Have Wanted a Bigger Headline on This Obituary," *Wall Street Journal* (9 Nov. 2018); James R. Hagerty, "Shareholder Activist Evelyn Y. Davis, Longtime Scourge of CEOs, Dies at 89," *Wall Street Journal* (5 Nov. 2018).

432   Milloy, "Entrusting Her Epitaph to No One."

433   Evelyn Y. Davis, Gravestone, Washington, DC; Milloy, "Entrusting Her Epitaph to No One." At the time he divined this understanding, Viktor E. Frankl, in a concentration camp struggling to survive, didn't even know if his young wife Tillie was alive or dead. Nevertheless, he mentally conversed with her: "Set me like a seal upon thy heart, love is as strong as death." Tillie perished at Bergen-Belsen. Viktor E. Frankl, *Man's Search for Meaning* (Boston: Beacon Press, 2006, 1959), 37-39.

434   Qtd. in Milloy, "Entrusting Her Epitaph to No One."

435   Nancy Fraser, "Queen of the Corporate Gadflies," *Life* (18 Mar. 1966), 115.

436   For more on the history of corporate governance, see Robert E. Wright, *Corporation Nation* (Philadelphia: University of Pennsylvania Press, 2014). See also Harwell Wells, "A Long View of Shareholder Power: From the Antebellum Corporation to the Twenty-First Century," *Florida Law Review* 67, 3 (2016): 1,033-98, 1,075, who noticed the recent revival of corporate activism. Editors of *Fortune* and Russell W. Davenport, *USA: The Permanent Revolution* (New York: Prentice Hall, 1951), 74-75,

80; Peter Drucker, *The Unseen Revolution: How Pension Fund Socialism Came to America* (New York: Harper & Row, 1976), 339-42.

437   Richard Marens, "Inventing Corporate Governance: The Mid-Century Emergence of Shareholder Activism," *Journal of Business and Management* 8, 4 (2002), 379; Henry G. Manne, "Mergers and the Market for Corporate Control," *Journal of Political Economy* 73, 2 (1965): 110-20; George Baker and George Smith, *The New Financial Capitalists: Kohlberg Kravis Roberts and the Creation of Corporate Value* (New York: Cambridge University Press, 1998); Lauren Talner, *The Origins of Shareholder Activism* (New York: Investor Responsibility Research Center, 1983), 43-49.

438   FOWSAB, "Stockholders Calendar," 1964, FOWSAB, "FOWSAB Summer Chronicle," 1956, Birdie Saffion to Shareholders, "What Has Federation of Women Shareholders Accomplished," 18 Oct. 1982, "American Home Products Secret Ballot Resolution," 1982, "Secret Ballot for Stockholders Have Been Adopted By," 1980?, FOWSAB, "Stockholders Calendar," 196?, Box 10, WSP.

439   Marens, "Inventing Corporate Governance," 366-67, 374, 384.

440   Birdie Saffion to Shareholders, "What Federation Has to Accomplish," 18 Oct. 1982, Box 10, WSP.

441   Andy Logan, "Hoboken Must Go!," *The New Yorker* (17 Mar. 1951), 37; Benjamin Graham, "Foreword," in Frank D. Emerson and Franklin C. Latcham, *Shareholder Democracy: A Broader Outlook for Corporations* (Cleveland: Press of Western Reserve University, 1954), vii.

442   Soss, "Solid Gold Chevrolet," 24; Logan, "Hoboken Must Go!," 34-37; Soss to Robert P. Vanderpoel, 9 May 1949, Box 14, WSP.

443   Richard Gehman, "Guardian Angel of Shareholders," *Cosmopolitan* (Apr. 1963), 67; Davenport, *USA: The Permanent Revolution*, 81; John Brooks, "Stockholder Season," *The New Yorker* (8 Oct. 1966), 160; Wilma Soss, Memorandum, n.d., Box 10, WSP; Wells, "A Long View of Shareholder Power," 1,082.

444   Logan, "Hoboken Must Go!," 35; Gehman, "Guardian Angel," 66.

445   Brooks, "Stockholder Season."

446   Marens, "Inventing Corporate Governance," 377; "Pressure Group," *The New Yorker* (25 Jun. 1949), 15; Talner, *Origins of Shareholder Activism*, 2; FOWSAB to Member and Friends, n.d., Box 10, WSP; Brooks, "Stockholder Season," 161; "Felicitous Occasion," *The New Yorker* (6 Jun. 1956), 27; Robert P. Vanderpoel, "Stockholders Want Post-Meeting Reports," *Chicago Herald-American* (30 Apr. 1949); FOWSAB, "Women and Wealth: What Every Stockholder Should Know About the Post Meeting Report," n.d., 3, Box 10, WSP; Gehman, "Guardian Angel," 66; Bernard Gelles to

Albert Gore, 10 Jul. 1962, FOWSAB, "Women and Wealth: What Every Stockholder Should Know About the Post Meeting Report," n.d., 5, Box 10, WSP.

447   Logan, "Hoboken Must Go!," 48.

448   "For Love," *The New Yorker* (24 Apr. 1954), 26.

449   Gehman, "Guardian Angel," 67; McMillan, "Wilma Soss Revisited," 7; Wells, "A Long View of Shareholder Power," 1,080; Joan Macleod Heminway and Sarah White, "Branson, No Seat at the Table: How Corporate Governance and Law Keep Women Out of the Boardroom," *Pace Law Review* 29, 2 (2009): 257.

450   Douglas M. Branson, *No Seat at the Table: How Corporate Governance and Law Keep Women Out of the Boardroom* (New York: NYU Press, 2007).

451   Leo Fontaine to Soss, 15 Feb. 1949, Box 14, WSP; Heminway and White, "Branson, No Seat at the Table," 249-91; "Ten Years on from Norway's Quota for Women on Corporate Boards," *The Economist* (17 Feb. 2018); Larelle Chapple and Jacquelyn H. Humphrey, "Does Board Gender Diversity Have a Financial Impact? Evidence Using Stock Portfolio Performance," *Journal of Business Ethics* (2014): 709-23.

452   Brooks, "Stockholder Season," 176; Wilma Soss, "Role of Stockholders," *New York Times* (30 Jun. 1952); Brooks, "Stockholder Season," 159.

453   Jeffrey N. Gordon, "Institutions as Relational Investors: A New Look at Cumulative Voting," *Columbia Law Review* 94, 1 (1994): 124-92; "For Love," 26; McMillan, "Wilma Soss Revisited," 7; Lorraine Hopkins, "She's the Scourge of Board Chairmen," *Providence Sunday Journal* (24 Nov. 1963); Marens, "Inventing Corporate Governance," 377; AT&T, "Notice of 1977 Annual Meeting and Proxy Statement," 1 Mar. 1977, Box 10, "Directors & Boards," (Fall 1978), 18, "Scene" framed picture, verso, Box 1, WSP; Soss, "Solid Gold Chevrolet," 24; Soss to Tom ?, 16 Apr. 1979, Box 10, WSP.

454   Allison R. Hayward, "Bentham & Ballots: Tradeoffs Between Secrecy and Accountability in How We Vote," *Journal of Law & Politics* 26 (Fall 2010): 39-78.

455   Talner, *Origins of Shareholder Activism*, 3; Olubunmi Faleye, "Classified Boards, Firm Value, and Managerial Entrenchment," *Journal of Financial Economics* 83, 2 (2007): 501-29.

456   Brooks, "Stockholder Season," 176; Emerson and Latcham, *Shareholder Democracy*, 105-6; McMillan, "Wilma Soss Revisited," 39; Jackson Martindell, *The Scientific Appraisal of Management: A Study of the Business Practices of Well-Managed Companies* (New York: Harper & Brothers, 1950), 2, 71; Logan, "Hoboken Must Go!," 34; Wilma Soss, "Five Years of Progress," Harvard Law School (27 Feb. 1961), Box 15, WSP.

457   Mathurin Dondo to Soss, 14 Apr. 1966, Box 10, WSP; Anat R. Admati, "A Skeptical View of Financialized Corporate Governance," *Journal of Economic Perspectives* 31, 3 (2017): 133; Wells, "A Long View of Shareholder Power," 1,096-97.

458   Gehman, "Guardian Angel of Shareholders," 66; "Stockholder Proposal No. 2 (Disclosure of Auditor's Fees)," 1982, Box 10, WSP.

459   Admati, "A Skeptical View of Financialized Corporate Governance," 134; Wells, "A Long View of Shareholder Power," 1,093.

460   Wells, "A Long View of Shareholder Power," 1,095-96; Luigi Zingales, "Towards a Political Theory of the Firm," *Journal of Economic Perspectives* 31, 3 (2017): 122-29.

461   Lucian A. Bebchuk, Alma Cohen, and Scott Hirst, "The Agency Problems of Institutional Investors," *Journal of Economic Perspectives* 31, 3 (2017): 89-112; Kathleen M. Kahle and Rene M. Stulz, "Is the US Public Corporation in Trouble?" *Journal of Economic Perspectives* 31, 3 (2017): 67-88.

EPILOGUE: Fortune Favors the Brave

462   Soss to Mary Morris, 20 Apr. 1949, Box 14, Wilma Soss, "Position Paper of the Federation of Women Shareholders in American Business, Inc.," 16 Nov. 1970, Box 10, WSP.

463   Gill qtd. in Julia-Ambra-Verlaine and Gunjan Banerji, "Keith Gill Drove the GameStop Reddit Mania. He Talked to the Journal," *Wall Street Journal* (29 Jan. 2021).

464   Thyagaraju Adinarayan, "Retail Traders Account 10% US Stock Trading Volume-Morgan Stanley," *Reuters* (30 Jun. 2021), https://www.reuters.com/business/retail-traders-account-10-us-stock-trading-volume-morgan-stanley-2021-06-30/. Accessed 15 May 2022.

465   "What the GameStop Frenzy Reveals About America's Stock Market," *Economist* (30 Jan. 2021). For conflicting accounts of the GameStop saga, see Ben Mezrich, *The AntiSocial Network: The GameStop Short Squeeze and the Ragtag Group of Amateur Traders That Brought Wall Street to its Knees* (New York: Hachette Books, 2021); Spencer Jakab, *The Revolution That Wasn't: GameStop, Reddit, and the Fleecing of Small Investors* (New York: Portfolio/Penguin, 2022).

466   Wilma might have been struck by another feature of the saga—that so many of the aggressive day traders of GameStop were men. As some behavioral economists noted, men, typically to their detriment, tend to trade more frequently than women, who tend to invest less money in the market but are more likely to buy and hold. See Brad M. Barber and Terrance Odeon, "Boys will be Boys: Gender, Overconfidence, and Common Stock Investment," (SSRN, Nov. 1998), https://ssrn.com/abstract=139415. Accessed 19 May 2022.

467 Dan Milmo, "How 'Free Speech Absolutist' Elon Musk Would Transform Twitter," *The Guardian* (14 Apr. 2022), https://www.theguardian.com/technology/2022/apr/14/how-free-speech-absolutist-elon-musk-would-transform-twitter. Accessed 10 May 2022.

468 Crypto.com Commercial, "Fortune Favours the Brave," (Sep. 2021), https://www.youtube.com/watch?v=9hBC5TVdYT8. Accessed 10 May 2022. Also see "Crypto.com teams up with Matt Damon and Wally Pfister," https://crypto.com › fftb; "Fortune Favours the Brave," https://www.adsoftheworld.com/campaigns/fortune-favours-the-brave; Kevin Helms, "Matt Damon Stars in Global Crypto Ad 'Fortune Favours the Brave' to Air in 20 Countries," *bitcoin.com* (28 Oct. 2021), https://news.bitcoin.com/matt-damon-stars-global-crypto-ad-fortune-favours-the-brave-air-in-20-countries/. Accessed 10 May 2022.

INDEX